KILLER FANDOM

KILLER FANDOM

Fan Studies and the Celebrity Serial Killer

Judith May Fathallah

media
studies.
press

Killer Fandom

Judith May Fathallah

Published by:
mediastudies.press
414 W. Broad St.
Bethlehem, PA 18018, USA

Copy-editing: Emily Alexander

Cover image: drow_easy

Landing page: mediastudies.press/killer-fandom

mediastudies.press acknowledges with gratitude the support of Lancaster University Library (Pilot University OA Fund 2023-2024 - Books)

Media Manifold series - issn (*online*) 2832-6202 | issn (*print*) 2832-6199

isbn 978-1-951399-36-8 (*print*) | isbn 978-1-951399-23-8 (*pdf*)

isbn 978-1-951399-25-2 (*epub*) | isbn 978-1-951399-24-5 (*html*)

doi 10.32376/3f8575cb.c2702120

Edition 1 published in November 2023

Contents

List of Figures

List of Tables

Introduction

"Their declarations of lust and love wouldn't seem out of place on a message board for the newest chart-topping boy band of the month," the stern and worried article at feminist site *Bitch Media* opens. "But these devoted fans are not beguiled by harmonized pop songs or synchronized dance moves: They're obsessed with serial killers" (Willoughby 2017). The piece is titled "Killer Crush: Inside Tumblr's Serial Killer Fandom Problem." This interestingly ambiguous piece of phrasing could grammatically render the fandom, its object, or both as the posited "problem." Of course, it wasn't so long ago that fandom itself was, unambiguously, the "problem." Many of us in the field of fan studies still remember our obsession with media and textual objects being a teenage secret, our guilty awareness that it wasn't quite "normal" to be so "obsessed" with a fictional text. Or a series. Or a band. Or all of the above. The first wave of fan studies was more-or-less devoted to undoing this stigmatization, to demonstrating that media fandom was a social, productive, creative, life-enriching, and positive experience (Jenkins 1992; Bacon-Smith 1992). Later work, of course, has been more nuanced, inspecting fandom's relationship with capitalism and with conservative ideologies, its reinforcement of classed, racial, and gendered hegemonies, as well as its progressive and creative aspects (Leppänen 2009; Scott 2011; Fathallah 2017; Pande 2018).

The field of fan studies is now well-established. The study of true crime, as a genre and a mode of digital media, is likewise a flourishing field. Yet the obvious—if difficult—conjunction of these themes in the popular phenomenon of serial killer fandom remains strikingly underexplored. In some ways, this is surprising: Fandom of serial killers is older than the term "serial killer," and has actually been one of the most publicly visible forms of fandom historically, from Victorian hawkers selling bottled dirt from murder-sites as souvenirs to media moralizing over the contemporary sexualization of Richard "The Night Stalker" Ramirez or Ted Bundy. Yet, in other ways, it is expected. Remember that fan studies evolved from a place of pathologization, seeking to reclaim the positions and affinities of fans from the labels of "freak," "obsessive," and "abnormal." Early fan studies scholars can perhaps be excused for their avoidance of so-called "dark fandoms," which a handful of scholars are just beginning to explore (Broll 2020, Jones 2020). But these days, surely, the figure of the media fan is sufficiently mainstreamed and visible—not to mention commercialized—that, for better or worse, one can assume that the category of "fan" as such is a neutral descriptor. What one is a fan of, and in what ways, can of course still produce all kinds of (gendered and raced) stigmatization. But scholars should not avoid the discussion of more confronting fandoms on the grounds that it might reinforce lazy stereotypes that "being a fan" makes one crazy.

In this book, I want to look at contemporary serial killer fandom online, considering the ways in which it is or is not like other forms of fandom, and what fan studies scholars can learn from applying some frames that fan studies has now established. The small body of work on fandom of criminals so far has tended to focus on school shooters, probably because of their problematized connections with youth subcultures and the vast amount of media coverage they generate. Certainly, there is crossover between serial killer fandom and school shooter fandom, in the sense that they share a common stigma, but I wish to open a discussion on serial killer fandom specifically now, because it has a specific mediated history. The relationship of the mainstream media to serial killing and the celebrification of serial killers is quite distinct and deserves specific attention.

Across the coming chapters, I'll be utilizing four of the major frames applied to fan studies generally: fandom as textual poaching, convergence culture, and/or fandom as the discursive construction of its object (Jenkins 1992; Jenkins 2006; Fathallah 2020); fandom as affective community (Baym 2000; Bury 2005); fandom as subculture through the lenses of capital building and gatekeeping (Thornton 1995; Hills 2002; Fathallah 2020); and fandom as digital play (Booth 2015, 2017; Fathallah 2020). This introduction provides an overview of the key work that has been done on true crime and killer fandoms, scattered across a variety of academic fields and in the popular press, noting the absence or intermittent, scattershot use of the theoretical lenses that fan studies has established for media fandom. I then give a brief overview of the fan studies frames I will be applying, though each will also be explicated more fully at the start of the relevant chapter. Chapter 1 presents a historical retrospective of serial killer fandom as it emerged amid Victorian era tourism practices through to the twentieth century discursive construction of the serial killer as celebrity. I will consider what scholars can learn from applying fan studies frames to this pre-digital history. Subsequent chapters (2–5) turn to the digital sphere, especially Tumblr and TikTok, where serial killer fandom flourishes, but also to fanfiction sites and sites for the sale of so-called "murderabilia." In each chapter, I focus on applying one of the established fan studies frames, investigating what, if anything, is unique or distinctive about this most-moralized form of fandom, and what it has in common with more mainstream fandoms. I'll also be concerned with the construction of the serial killer as celebrity in the mainstream media texts that fans utilize, as these intersect and interact with more underground and pathologized texts, each feeding off the other in the creation of a full-fledged "serial killer industry." Indeed, one primary argument of the book, explicated most fully in the final chapter, is that serial killer fandom is *not* particularly unique, nor is it directly opposed to the mainstream construction of serial killers. It might operate "at the edges" of popular discourse—it might even stretch the limits—but just as with any fandom, the material and textual roots of serial killer fandom are already part of the cultural fabric. Fans did not make serial killers into celebrities: We all did.

For the purposes of this research, I will be taking a primarily discursive perspective on the term "fan." By this I mean that I define a serial killer fan as a person who claims to be one, and or/professes love and dedication to a serial killer. Granted, there is a blurred line between "serial killer fandom" and true crime fandom: Many true crime fans express empathy or at the very least pity for serial killers with particularly awful backstories and display the same kind of fannish tendencies to documentation, collection, and focused reading and research that self-professed killer fans do (Barnes 2019). Yet at the same time, true crime aficionados are typically keen to distinguish themselves from serial killer fans, looking down on these fans as the pathologized Bad Other or Bad Fan of the broader true crime community (Daggett 2015, 53; Fathallah 2022). True crime fans state, loudly and often, that they are *not* serial killer fans, much as they might display similar behaviors. There may well be a different study to make here, on the degree to which self-professed true crime fans actually differ from self-professed serial killer fans in their interests and practices, but there is certainly a sufficient number of the latter, and a sufficient number of fanworks praising and celebrating serial killers that, as the first extended academic foray into serial killer fandom, it makes sense to focus this project on these manifestations. Nonetheless, I will now review some of the key work on true crime fandom as part of this introduction, before narrowing down the focus to murder-related fandoms and serial killer fandom specifically, because all of it provides important insights on fan practices for the work to come.

Serial Killing and the Media, Part 1: The Creation of Celebrity Killers

> *Serial killing is predominantly a media event.*
> —Haggerty, "Modern Serial Killers" (2009)

The serial killer is a modern invention (Haggerty 2009). Naturally, there have always been humans who killed a series of other humans over a period of time, but the term "serial killer" was popularized in the 1970s by FBI agent Robert Ressler.[1] This peculiarly modern discursive construct has always existed at the intersection of the media, the judicial system, and public imagination. In a US context, the figure partly served to take the place of the criminal gangs that had operated during Prohibition: an ever-present domestic threat whose existence helped to justify the functions, operations, and continued funding of the FBI (Schmid 2005). The news media have always paid disproportionate attention to serial killings, which make up a miniscule fraction of all crime. This is particularly true when the victims are deemed appropriately sympathetic and the killings sufficiently sensationalist. Police investigators and the murderers themselves have often had a contentious yet productive relationship with the media industries, which have served by turn to assist with, interrupt, compromise, and promote investigations, motivate and encourage murderers, and disseminate public safety information (Gibson 2006).

Kevin Haggerty suggests that the serial killer is a creature (and creation) of modernity, and "the mass media and the attendant rise of a celebrity culture"

[1] It is difficult to claim that any one person coined the term, but it certainly didn't have much currency before the 1970s. The English phrase might be a direct translation of "Serienmörder," which can be reliably dated to 1931.

have been key factors in this creation (2009, 168). There have always been people who kill a number of other people, but the serial killer as a "type" or "kind" of person is a twentieth century invention, in which the mass media play a critical part. Jean Murley explains:

> Serial killing is not new—there are records of such deeds throughout recorded human history—but the phenomenon was named in the 1970s and it was constructed in 1980s true-crime murder narratives [. . .] as a new kind of murder, one that reflected and refracted fears about anonymity, depersonalization, and the consequences of extreme self-interest. (2008, 156)

Haggerty similarly designates the rise of a relatively anonymous society, the marginalization of particular groups and opportunities for victimization, and the notion of society as engineerable (e.g., by mission-orientated killers who target groups they consider undesirable, such as sex workers or the homeless) as socio-cultural resources that co-create the serial killer as a modern phenomenon. Multiple writers have commented on the media construction of the serial killer as celebrity in the modern sense, where celebrity applies to the property of "knownness" rather than virtue or achievement (Schmid 2005; Gibson 2006; Haggerty 2009). Gibson documents the media treatment of twelve cases of serial murder in the US, UK, and France, from the early to late twentieth century. In each case, the media industry, the killer themself, and to a more conflicted degree, law enforcement, collaborate in the creation of the serial killer celebrity. Most serial killers read their press: indeed, they contribute to it, and have done so for a hundred and fifty years. The infamous "Dear Boss" letters attributed to Jack the Ripper may be unverifiable, but nineteenth century American killer H. H. Holmes confessed publicly (and exaggeratedly) to his crimes in both the *New York Times* and the *Philadelphia Inquirer*.

There is, likewise, a huge public appetite for stories about serial killers, from (in roughly more-to-less normalized order) the consumption of mainstream news stories; to reading and collecting crime books; to the collection of murderabilia—souvenirs and artifacts associated with serial killers and their victims. People who perform these widespread and often mainstream practices would usually deny that they are fans of serial killers, but there is no denying that "serial killing [. . .] has become big business within the culture industry" (Jarvis 2007, 327). Again, while I will be focusing on serial killer fans, the reader ought to bear in mind that the material of their fandom is generated by a much broader background of general fascination with serial killers. In their edited volume *Criminals as Heroes in Popular Culture*, Roxie James and Katherine Lane argue that "while we may need heroes, we want criminals" (2020, 3, italics in the original). Rather than serial killers as such, their volume is concerned with "ambiguous figures" who have clearly broken the law and often violently, yet are generally not considered evil (4). Drawing on Paul Kooistra's work, they argue that the criminal hero is understood to be rebelling against some brutally corrupt authority or political regime. They are driven to crime by their injustice of their life and situation; their actions are illegal but justified, at least to a degree, by a morality higher than law (2020, 4). Moreover, James and Lane contend that "we no longer expect our heroes to be picture perfect" but "expect/accept a duality in our heroes" (5).

Typically, serial killer fans do not consider their heroes to be "moral and honorable men," but they *do* often consider them as victims of social injustice and as standing against some authoritarian figure or regime, such as in the case of Aileen Wuornos, a sex worker who was systematically abused by men from an early age. There are echoes here of a cultural tendency identified by Lionel Trilling (1972) in his lectures on sincerity and authenticity: specifically, the location of the authentic in a form of insanity that defies all social restriction in favor of total self-realization. The ultimate origins are Freudian, conflating "authenticity" with some received idea of the id drive. Relatedly, James and Lane cite Wayne J. Douglass on the popular appeal of the psychopathic criminal, who "assert[s] their identity through their violence and disregard for societal strictures," to become "an existentialist hero rebelling against the conformist demands of modern society" (8). British serial killer Ian Brady self-consciously framed himself in this way in his book *Gates of Janus*.

> Why are the mass media and the public so fascinated by serial killers, yet show not the least interest in, and quite frankly, absolute boredom with, far more prolific legalized killers? [. . .] It becomes transparent that the reason why the media and public are so fascinated by serial killers is that these people kill at will, requiring no legislation, without asking for or needing permission, the very concept never entering their mind. (quoted in Gibson 2006, 69)

Via the available discourses of existentialism and anti-authoritarianism, Brady, who is a diagnosed psychopath, constructs himself as an existentialist antihero. Ironically, as Brett Easton Ellis so powerfully showed us, it could equally well be argued that psychopathic serial murder is merely the full expression of the ultra-rational, neoliberal hyper-capitalism that dominates Western societies (cf. Haggerty 2009; Jarvis 2007). In his book *Natural Born Celebrities*, David Schmid has a similar view regarding the celebrification of serial killers, observing that

> the serial killer both outrages and thrills us by his seeming ability to stand outside the law, to make his own law, in a gesture whose ambivalent destructiveness and creativity mirror our ambivalent response to the killer, composed of both fear and attraction. (2005, 24)

Schmid builds on Walter Benjamin's observations that "the figure of the 'great' criminal" has often "aroused the secret admiration of the public" for his "violence confronts the law with the threat of declaring a new law" (24). Though we might consciously condemn their acts, many people are at some level attracted to the existential outsider, who appears to operate outside all established moral and social systems. For Schmid, this is a peculiarly American phenomenon, rooted in frontier mythology and the cult of the individual. He observes that "even the most explicit rejection and condemnation of serial killer celebrity can find itself implicated in (and perhaps even unwittingly encouraging the growth of) that celebrity" (2005, 2). At one extreme, he gives the example of the murderabilia industry, through which one can "now purchase the nail-clippings and hair of some killers, as if they were religious icons," but notes equally that features of supposedly public-service orientated programs like *America's Most Wanted* "pander to the same prurient public interest in crime that the program supposedly condemns" (3).

Public appetite for true crime is apparently insatiable—Schmid called the genre a "phoenix" for its remarkable ability to morph, adapt, and resurge through transformations in social structures and the media industry (175)—and it is impossible to draw clean moralistic lines regarding the uses and gratifications of either its producers or consumers. According to Schmid, the contemporary evolution of the concept of fame has "allow[ed] not only for the existence of criminal celebrities such as the serial killer but also make[s] the serial killer the exemplary modern celebrity" (4). Fame, after all, is now characterized by "visibility rather than achievement" and "it no longer makes sense to distinguish between good and bad forms of fame" (9). Schmid stresses the "multiaccentuality of serial murder": that is, the way that "serial murder can be used to support such a wide variety of ideological agendas," as useful to policy makers and law enforcement as to novelists, sociocultural critics, and filmmakers (6). From the perspective of media studies, one might call the media construction of serial killers a producerly text, which John Fiske defined as a text which contains multiple gaps and potentials onto which diverse groups and individuals project and construct meaning (1989, 104). The shocking and antisocial nature of the acts demands hypotheses and explanation from the psychological to the socioeconomic to the religious. It can even play a comforting, nostalgic role: a domesticated, explicable, understandable threat to contrast against the politicized unknown quantity of the terrorist or radical extremist (Schmid 2005, 27).

Drawing on Leo Braudy (1986), Schmid argues that the modern celebrity is defined more by a performed identity than achievements or actions. He writes that, as the "exemplary modern celebrity," the serial killer is "widely known and famous for being himself"—famous for what he *is*. Granted, what he *is* is defined by series of acts (murders), but in the serial killer "action and identity are fused" (2005, 15). He is himself because he is a serial killer, and he is famous for being himself. This tendency is evident in serial killer fandom, wherein a killer's name evokes in shorthand a whole range of known characteristics. Schmid contends that true crime as a genre serves a primarily conservative function (see also Murley 2008 and Browder 2006). Typically, popular true crime narratives depict serial murderers as individual psychopathic monsters disconnected from the social fabric that produces them, and thus these stories operate in a mutually beneficial relationship with law enforcement in general and the FBI in particular. The aberrance of serial killers is constructed via retrospective psychological analysis, typically focusing on their childhoods, rather than an analysis in critical socio-economic terms. Moreover, the construction of serial killers as a social threat disproportionate to their actual prevalence helps secure public support and governmental funding for the FBI and related organizations. Certainly, serial killer fandom undermines this conservative function, appropriating media construction of serial killers to different uses, including forms of sociocultural parody, examined in chapter 5.

Illustrating the disparity with which interest in serial killers has been addressed across academic frameworks, scholars from some disciplines have produced moralistic treatises on media sensationalism which go on to participate in the very sensationalism they condemn. A key example is Scott A. Bonn's *Why We Love Serial Killers* (2014). A criminologist and lecturer who sets himself up as an expert witness on serial killer enthusiasts, Bonn constantly condemns the media for their focus on serial killers—yet he advertises his exclusive interviews with said killers as a selling point of his book. He contends that a certain degree of interest in serial killers is normal, a fascination with the incomprehensible driven by fear and adrenaline and a desire to play detective, yet claims that fans constitute a "curious and obsessive world" of their own. He makes no clear distinction regarding what separates a fan from the normally-interested (other than "low self-esteem," apparently). He positions his book as a corrective to how mass media have made "morbid rock stars" of serial killers. Yet in his rhetorical use of declarations like "the Son of Sam legend is born," it is hard to characterize what he is doing here as any different.[2] At some points, Bonn invokes Émile Durkheim, suggesting serial murder as proceeding from social circumstances rather than individual consciousness, yet equally claims that "some acts of evil defy comprehension." Bonn's confused treatise—which notably perpetuates the construction of monstrous queerness, attributing Jeffrey Dahmer's crimes to a need for sexual gratification that "had no limits"—illustrates the need to apply consistent theoretical frameworks to interest in serial killers, whether focusing on self-declared fans or not.

Dirk Gibson's *Serial Killers and Media Circuses* (2006) is another example, supposedly a critique of the vast media interest surrounding serial killer cases since at least the nineteenth century. In a selling point from the forward, Gibson's material is presented in "such a way that the crime buff, interested in the gory details of strangulation, stabbing, torture, dismemberment, and even instances of cannibalism, will not be disappointed" (Wilcox 2006 in Gibson, ix). Gibson does make some notable points regarding the communal construction of the serial killer figure by the media, law enforcement, and indeed killers themselves, mostly via the letter-writing campaigns to newspapers that presaged the current relationship between social media and self-advertising criminal behavior. I will investigate how serial killer fandom treats this material in my discussion of media convergence.

---

[2] "Son of Sam" is a self-bestowed nickname for serial killer David Berkowitz, whom Bonn interviews. At the time of his crimes, he claims to have believed himself under the influence of some demonic force, and has now declared himself a Christian.

Serial Killing and the Media, Part 2: Killing, Sex, and Gender

The media construction of serial killers is highly dependent on their sex and gender, as well as the sex and gender of their victims. David Schmid has some notable observations on this point. He compares the reportage on Ted Bundy, a heterosexual man who killed a series of women; to that on Jeffrey Dahmer, a White gay man who murdered queer men of color; and that on Aileen Wuornos, a lesbian who killed men. He argues that true crime as a genre must exonerate heterosexuality by constructing Bundy as a totally anomalous straight man, an inexplicable exception who operated counter to everything we would expect of a heterosexual male: "True-crime narratives seek to relieve straight men of any guilt by association" (2005, 27, 178). This is particularly important considering that, in reality, the vast majority of serial killers are heterosexual men, and the vast majority of their victims are women. Feminist critics like Jane Caputi (1989) or Deborah Cameron (1994) would argue that the actions of Bundy are simply the ultimate expression of hetero-patriarchal hetero-capitalism: the peak of a pyramid supported by a normative social structure. Conversely, Dahmer's and Wuornos's homosexuality was utilized by the press as psychological explanations for their behavior: their queerness posited as monstrous, as telling "us," the posited straight reader, everything we "need to know" about homosexuality and lesbianism (Schmid 2005, 27). For example, Wuornos's lesbianism was consistently used as a justification or explanation for "man hating," and Dahmer's homosexuality was posited as having some sort of automatic link with "homicidal violence" (238). Bundy was constructed as an aberration, while "Dahmer had simply done what was expected of someone like him by being a murderous queer" (240). This discourse has material consequences, and actually contributed to the death of one of Dahmer's victims, whom police returned to his apartment despite his disorientation and visible injuries. In accordance with a popular assumption of gay relationships as aberrant and violent, police took Dahmer at his word that the boy was of age (false) and that their activities were consensual (obviously also false). Fan culture is often analyzed as a queer and feminine-leaning space (Lothian et al. 2007; Levin Russo 2013). Though this is obviously site-dependent and much more applicable to spaces like Tumblr and TikTok than murderabilia auction sites, it will be important to observe how serial killers are gendered across these spaces, and how that plays into their uses by fans.

In considering the easy acceptance of murder as entertainment, Jean Murley is particularly concerned with women's fascination with the genre. Women are the majority audience for true crime texts, and this is reflected in serial killer fandom. Murley observes that true crime and crime reporting deals primarily with "white, middle class killers and victims" (2), which is not at all reflective of real homicide statistics in America (or the UK; see also Horeck 2019). Murley is particularly interested in women's fascination with the genre. Like Schmid, Murley is critical regarding the qualitative distinction between receiving true crime texts in socially approved ways and a posited Bad Other of fannish interest, observing that "true crime is obsessed with full-on visual body horror: autopsy footage, close-ups of ligature marks and gunshot wounds on bodies, bruises or lividity on flesh, and blood pools, stains and spatters [. . .] causing some critics to refer to true crime as 'crime porn'" (2008, 5). Put into context like this, the faux outrage and horror over serial killer fandom in popular press accounts seems all the more unthinking and uncritical. From the release of Truman Capote's genre-defining *In Cold Blood* in 1966 to the multi-award winning Serial podcast (2014–present), consumption of true crime, always ubiqutous, has become almost respectable (Horeck 2019). So how does this relate to the phenomenon of serial killer fandom?

From True Crime Enthusiasts to Serial Killer Fans

We will now explicitly introduce the relationship—or sliding scale—between the more acceptable and popular forms of true crime fandom and serial killer fandom. Multiple academics have observed that women are significantly more likely to engage with true crime media than men are (Vicary and Fraley 2010; Browder 2006; Boling and Hull 2018; Schulenberg 2021). Reasons might include education—learning the ways and means of serial killers, in a bid to decrease one's chances of becoming a victim (Vicary and Fraley 2010, 82; Boling and Hull 2018; Schulenberg 2021), empathy (Schulenberg 2021; Browder 2006), a strong interest in abnormal psychology (Schulenberg 2021, 83), to vicariously cope with and process patriarchal violence, and/or to safely explore an interest in violence from which women are typically proscribed (Browder 2006, 292; Schulenberg 2021). Many women who enjoy true crime "feel that others perceived their reading habits as strange or disturbing" and express a sense of kinship and community upon finding other women who enjoy the same genre (Browder 2006, 933). Though

I would question how far an interest in true crime really is pathologized (cf. Horeck 2019), the important thing is that the women Laura Browder interviewed in her study of female true crime fans felt their interest to be stigmatized. Just as Jenkins and Bacon-Smith's Star Trek fans, analyzed in the first wave of fan studies, Browder's interviewees felt a sense of kinship, homecoming, or finding their communities upon meeting others who were equally invested in a then-stigmatized interest. Rhiannon Bury's (2005) soap opera fans reported a sense of community in their fandom that sometimes superseded interest in the text itself. Schulenberg writes, likewise, that fans of the irreverent female-hosted podcast *My Favorite Murder* feel a strong sense of communal support from their fandom, and experience para-social relationships with the hosts. Browder reports that the female true crime readers she interviewed identified with both the victim and the killer:

> Marla told me that "I can probably empathize and feel both what the criminal and the victim must be feeling at that moment, and I put myself into their shoes and think about what I would feel like if I were having these things done to me and I also do the same thing with the criminal." (2006, 932)

While these readers wouldn't call themselves serial killer fans, it is already clear that identification with murderers is not unique to self-professed killer fandom. Moreover, while true crime is generally considered a conservative genre, Browder notes that its modern form can be subversive in its critique of the patriarchal family structure (most female victims are killed by husbands or boyfriends). She suggests that true crime functions as a "dystopian romance":

> Many true crime books concern what happens to women who take romance novels too seriously: the genres talk to each other. A subgenre of true crime is the narrative of gullible women who are lulled by the romantic promises offered to them by psychopaths. (938)

In my consideration of serial killer fandom as textual poaching and discursive construction, I will consider how far serial killer fandom subverts conservative structures such as that of the primacy of the straight man, the valorization of law enforcement, and denigration of women. I will also return to this point in chapter 5, on sociocultural parody.

Kelsea Schulenberg does invoke a fan studies framework in her qualitative study of *My Favorite Murder* fans, who like many fandoms have evolved a collective noun, in this case, Murderinos. Schulenberg is aware of fan studies history and writes that the original direction of her work "pointed towards possible findings that would align with previous fan studies work on participatory culture (Jenkins, 2013) and fan behaviors like gift economy (Hellekson, 2009)" (2021, ii). Ultimately, though, her "findings tell a story fundamentally centered on journeying from feeling alone to no longer feeling alone" (ii), thus more aligned with Bury (2005) and Nancy Baym's work on affective communities (2000). I would actually consider the gift economy aspect of fandom—wherein fans gift each other user-generated content (UGC) based on their preferred texts without expectation of direct return, upon the understanding that the whole community benefits from the common practice—to be an aspect of an affective community rather than an alternative lens (see chapter 3). Indeed, this is how Schulenberg ends up treating gift culture as an aspect of affective community in her analysis, despite the statement quoted that seems to separate them. She explores Murderinos' UGC from a fan studies perspective, following Jenkins to analyze how analyze how "new tools and technologies enable consumers to achieve, annotate, appropriate, and rearticulate media content" and "promote DIY media production, a discourse that shapes how consumers have deployed those technologies" (2021, 21). Sarah Sacks also focuses on convergence culture and UGC as a framework for analyzing Murderino fandom (2017). In line with Line Clausen and Stine Sikjaer's observations on the participatory nature of podcasting as a genre, she acknowledges how "the hosts' inclusion of UGC promotes collaborative meaning making and knowledge" (2017, 35).

Serial killer fandom is likewise a participatory culture; it participates in the media construction of serial killers, and fans certainly do share UGC, with each other if not with official media channels. Schulenberg is primarily interested in how these activities support "friendship formation" and "foster relationships" (25). Her participants expressed very strongly that most people in their day-to-day lives found their fascination with murderers bizarre, and their fandom had significantly reduced feelings of isolation. Some of the fanwork Sacks documents in the Murderino community definitely straddles the border between fandom of the podcast and fandoms of the killers, such as Instagram art depicting murderers. In one case, a fan submitted a knitted "nipple belt" to the hosts, reminiscent of the belt of human nipples created by serial killer Ed Gein. Sacks interprets this act through a lens of resistive discourse, arguing that "what the fans appear to be doing here is transforming a threatening individual who represents the absolute worst of a patriarchal culture into objects to be laughed at, thus neutralizing their threat" (2017, 37–38). Yet such objects are polysemic, and meaning is context dependent. Maybe the creators just thought it was funny.

Acknowledging Sacks, Luna Stjerneby also considers *My Favorite Murder* fandom as a form of resistive discourse (2018). Like Sacks and Schulenberg, she invokes fan studies frameworks to do so. She is concerned with MFM fandom as resistive to patriarchal hegemony that positions women to be passive, polite, and accommodating even at the expense of our safety. One of the podcast's catchphrases is "fuck politeness," which Stjerneby uses as the title of her thesis. She finds awareness and self-protection through community to be of primary importance for the

> "sisterhood" of murderinos [sic] and sets out to investigate the discursive construction of particular gendered values within the community compared to those of "dominant culture" (which in this thesis will refer to dominant social norms of the Western world, particularly regarding gender). (2018, 4)

Her major research question is stated as, "How are hegemonic notions of femininity resisted and negotiated within the My Favorite Murder online fan-community?" (4), where hegemonic femininity is taken to be subordinate and passive. There are parallels here with my own work on fan communities as constructive of alternative discourse formations (Fathallah 2017, 2020). She suggests that the "carnivalesque laughter" invoked by the podcast's irreverent style "is humor marked by a satirical or mocking [attitude] against authority and hegemonic social hierarchies" (Stjerneby 2018, 32). Laughing at these awful situations defuses them of some of their power to victimize. But while the discourse formations constructed here do posit a somewhat alternative femininity—one based on self-protection, vigilance, and education—it is still a femininity within broad bounds of normative social structures. It is not particularly radical, confronting, or outrageous to state that women should be alert, informed, and self-protective. The femininities constructed in serial killer fandom—posited on a fascination with and attraction to the very violence MFM fans are attempting to evade—are rather more difficult to accommodate. On the other hand, I also found that fans of serial killer Aileen Wuornos utilized the narrative of her life to construct a different kind of resistant femininity: one based in identification with the abused killer, and retaliatory violence for men's abuse of women. Both these constructions of femininity need to be borne in mind and held in tension as I examine the data.

Naomi Barnes explores in detail the potentially blurred line and gatekeeping trends between serial killer fans and true crime fans in her article "Killer Folklore Identity Issues in the True Crime Community" (2019). The True Crime Community, or TCC, is an active and self-defined network spanning Tumblr, Reddit, and other websites. Though their activities look very much like those of a fan community, Barnes notes that "many members of the TCC object to the idea that they belong to a fandom" (154). Barnes utilized the Tumblr #TTC hashtag to recruit community members for surveys, asking questions concerning their interest in true crime, their activities around true crime media, and "whether or not they would consider themselves 'fans' of serial or mass murderers" (158). In accordance with earlier findings, more than 80 percent of Barnes's respondents were female—though I note that the Tumblr demographic skews female anyway. One of Barnes's respondents, bundyofjoy, asserted that TTCers were not a fandom, stating,

> A fandom is a community of people who enjoy the same things—they write fan fiction, create videos and fan art, they create OTPs, etc. Basically fandoms refer more to people who enjoy TV shows, movies, music artists. [. . .] If the true crime community were to do those things and consider ourselves a fandom we would be glorifying murderers and I not what we do. [. . .] A majority of the true crime community has made it well known that they do not condone the actions of the people they blog about. I think the best thing to call us is a community because [w]e're basically just a bunch of people who share the same interest in true crime. (2019, 159)

Barnes identifies this in sociological terms as "boundary work," and while from a fan studies perspective one might call it gatekeeping, the process is essentially the same. Yet she points out that TCC participants "utilize many of the basic techniques of Internet-based fandom" on their Tumblr blogs:

> Banners running across the top of a TCCer's homepage often display certain traits: an image of a killer used as a "userpic," insider references to the crime or criminal [. . .] Some usernames are explicit references to certain killers or crimes, such as: mycolumbineobsession, bundyofjoy, mrsjeffreylioneldahmer, richardrramirez, and dylannstormroofies. [. . .] It is difficult to reconcile both the community's rejection of the label "fan" as a socio-performance practice, as well as how the use of these names connoted a positive identification with the killers themselves. The common

> disclaimers, "I do not condone" at the top of a blog seems disingenuous when a user takes a killer's name as their own. (163)

Moreover, TCC members create and share the same kind of UGC that self-professed killer fans do: "the art, fanfiction, jokes, memes, etc" (164). Some serial killer fans simultaneously consider themselves TCC members and utilize the hashtag in their Tumblr posts. Other TCC members reject this forcibly. Barnes does, after all, acknowledge certain distinctions:

> Those who belong to various Killer Fandoms [. . .] tend to express a desire to feel closer to the killer on a personal level, obsessing over the minutiae of a killer's life. [. . .] While they do discuss case details and interact with members of the TCC, more often their focus is on physical attributes of the killers and they frequently express desires to either comfort the killers or engage in sexual encounters. (165)

Here I draw some definitional lines for the purposes of my study. A serial killer fan professes to be one, and/or expresses desire for/devotion to a killer, and is more focused on the killer than their victims. Serial killer fans may attempt to engage with serial killers at a personal level, via, e.g., letter writing, approaching them after apprehension, or collecting and requesting objects from them. They might write serial killer fanfic, and label it as such. They might create other forms of UGC celebrating serial killers. A TCC member might also create UGC, but states distinctly that she is *not a serial killer fan*, and marks out serial killer fans as a Bad Other. She might be equally or more interested in the victims of the crimes, their stories, and/or the detective work that led up to the apprehension of the killer as the killer himself. A serial killer fan may consider themself simultaneously to be a member of the TCC, but a TCC-only member would reject this. Serial killer fandom thus qualifies as a stigmatized fandom; TCC probably does not. Consider this Tumblr post, in which user v1ntage-p3psi1 neatly summarizes the lines that TCC community members tend to draw in defining the killer fan as Bad Other:

> What is okay:
>
> Being interested in true crime
>
> Wanting to find more about the killers
>
> Liking the killers but not excusing what they did

> Not idolizing or humanizing them
>
> What isn't okay:
>
> Literally wanting to suck off a serial killer
>
> Idolizing them
>
> Drawing fan art of them and making it all cute
>
> Shipping. The. Fucking. Killers. [. . .]
>
> Saying shit like: "omg the victims are dead they're not gonna care," they have families you uncultured swine. (v1ntage-p3ps1 2020)

"Liking the killers" is perhaps surprising and illustrates the debated nature of these lines. But then again, invoking a degree of sympathy or identification with serial killers is hardly unusual in professional media (see, e.g., Murley 2008, 5). With these definitions established, I will now explore the small amount of academic work there is on killer fandoms specifically, before introducing the frames through which I will analyze my defined object of study.

Killer Fandom in the Academy and in the Press

Some of the first academic work on so-called "dark" fandom specifically has been surveyed by Bethan Jones. I have chosen to avoid the descriptor "dark" in this text, unless quoting or referring directly to another academic's work, due to a) the inherent racism involved in casting anything perceived as negative as "dark" and b) the fact that we are speaking of serial killer fandom specifically, meaning there is no need for it.[3] Jones observes, as I have done, that early fan studies "focused on the positive aspects of fan behaviors and practices" in a deliberate effort to counter the pathologized and sensationalized perspectives of fans that appeared in the popular press (2020). Ryan Broll (2020) introduced the idea of "dark fandoms" in a journal article, but any further studies undertaken—such as Chelsea Daggett (2015) or Andrew Rico (2015) on the Columbine school shooter fandom—"tend [. . .] to be disparate analyses, taken as case studies of specific events rather than an overarching approach" (Jones 2020). Rico likewise noted that "dark fandoms remain rooted in the first wave [of fan studies] where these fans

[3] I thank Gus Hutchinson of the BTRN radio show *The C.O.W.S* for opening this discussion with me.

are dismissed as Others and their communities lack legitimization and acceptance by society" (2015). Jones also questions why the frames I have established to understand and explore fandom have not been better applied to killer fandoms, such as community identification, resistance to dominant narratives, or indeed trolling and irony, rightly arguing that "we can't afford to simply look at the audiences who engage in the "approved" versions of fannish production and involvement" and ignore what we find uncomfortable (2020). Daggett broached the idea of textual poaching (in suggesting that fans invested in the Columbine massacre construct an "alternative understanding [. . .] rooted in negotiated and oppositional readings of central news frames that solidified in early news coverage of the case" (2015, 46). Jones cites a user in a Columbine community on Reddit who wrote:

> It's a common thing for most communities about Columbine. Most people come here with widely spread narrative that Eric was a soulless psychopath and Dylan was a sad, sad boy. But then they actually research and see that it wasn't as simple. (quoted in Jones 2020)

Daggett's 2015 research showed a similar pattern of media reinterpretation:

> At first [. . .] I thought Eric and Dylan were terrible monsters to do something like that. As I researched, I realized that happy, healthy people don't just go and kill a bunch of their classmates and I started to humanize them more and more. That's the problem with this case [. . .] and why it keeps happening. They dehumanize the perpetrators. [. . .] If society cannot recognize that these sorts of crimes are committed by seemingly normal people they will continue to happen. (quoted in Daggett 2015, 64)

We observe then a form of textual poaching in the way that fans

> refigure news frames about Columbine to inject empathy and understanding into reading the motivations of Eric Harris and Dylan Klebold. Personally inflected interpretations lead these individuals to actively educate others about the shooting and potential ways to prevent future shootings. (Daggett 2015, 45)

This might be a somewhat sanitized interpretation on Daggett's part: Most killer fandom members are not potential school shooters, but nor is every member earnestly researching and studying for the sake of preventing them.

The error of assuming "earnestness"—in fandom as in online culture more broadly—is a key theme of chapter 5 of this book, on digital play.

It is also important to consider whether Daggett's respondents would actually consider themselves a member of a killer fandom, or something more akin to Barnes's True Crime Community members. Daggett argues that self-identification as a "Columbiner" (which sounds like the name of a fandom), rather than a person who is "interested in Columbine," is "a distinction based on members' primary association with more 'fan'-related emotion versus research" (48, 53). But she admits the distinction is in tension. Broll declares his study of the Columbiner community on Reddit a "study of one dark fandom," though again, he does not precisely delineate how he or his subjects define a fan. Like Daggett, he finds that:

> Columbiners express their fandom much in the same way as more conventional fans might: by discussing relevant characters, proposing fan theories, and debating the legacy of the shooting and shooters. (2020, 793)

Given the widespread media interest in and celebrification of extremely violent criminals, Broll contends that "rather than being seen as anomalies, these communities represent a natural progression of a cultural interest in dark artifacts and actors" (796). He goes on to argue that "the emergence of dark fandoms should not be seen as a surprise" (802). So far as this goes, I agree with Broll, as with Rico whose similar short study seeks to "challenge and expand the object of focus when we study fandom" (2015). Both writers see the pathologizing of Columbiners as a callback to the early pathologizing and stereotyping of media fans that fan studies emerged in opposition to, and point out how fan scholars have thus far largely avoided analyzing killer fandoms. Rico argues that popular media reinforces "the common perception that these fans are unpopular, disturbed, and inevitably murderous individuals—just like the idols of their fandom" and

> when examining fans of particularly challenging subjects like the Columbine shooters it appears that it is all too easy to play into the negative stereotypes of obsessive fannish behavior as disconnected from reality. [. . .] As a result, it seems that this and other dark fandoms remain rooted in the first wave where these fans are dismissed as Others. (2015)

He too describes Columbiners' activities as a form of textual poaching, repurposing appropriate media around the shooting, using such creative methods as drawing and painting. According to Rico, however, "confining Eric [Harris] and Dylan [Klebold]'s appeal to only psychopaths and aspiring school shooters would critically undermine what they can teach us about Western culture and, more specifically, about the field of fandom" (2015). A degree of empathy for a school shooter does not make one a budding shooter (though copycats do exist). Rico writes that "fans may appear to identify or even empathize with Eric and Dylan as social outcasts," and in this case, it is their own shared discursive construction of the shooters which is significant, rather than the historical facts of whether or not Klebold and Harris were systematically victimized at school. There are also other motives to consider, Rico contends: As fandom is no longer a scandalous category, the "lure of the forbidden" may have attached to those with particular objects, and some fans will pursue this for its own sake. Finally—and the reader should certainly bear this in mind regarding serial killer fandom, especially in chapter 5—some "might just be doing it for the attention—to incite reactions from the public" (2015). For some self-identified Columbiners, Rico observed actions which were clearly trolling: posting jokes on memorial pages, for example. After all, the widespread use of social media technology means that fannish activity no longer requires the time and emotional investment it once did (which again raises questions as to the definition of fandom, but as noted, for my purposes here I will abide by fans' self-definition). It takes minutes to create a Tumblr, minutes more to start reblogging posts, and seconds to post on a Reddit page. Even the creation of UGC and repurposing mainstream media is easy, fast, and accessible for millennials and Gen-Z raised in a digital culture.

Unsurprisingly, the profession of love for or attraction to serial killers has attracted particular attention in the popular media. A *New Statesman* article by Thomas Hobbs strikes a moral tone, condemning "warped memes mocking murder victims, or posts (especially in the case of Bundy) gleefully admitting a sexual attraction towards a serial killer" (2018). It is notable that there is still a market for such articles "discovering" something: Female fans turned out to support and express their attraction to Ted Bundy during his trial, and as is well known, he eventually married one. Richard Ramirez also married a fan, one of many who had written him letters in prison. The attraction even has a name: hybristophilia, a paraphilia wherein the knowledge that one's partner is capable of extreme violence has an erotic effect. Yet the popular press articles still present girls' attention to serial killers as some sort of uniquely shocking discovery, sometimes attempting to analyze in it pseudo-sociological terms, as Hobbs puts it, part of "a climate where serial killers have become pop culture icons" (as opposed to when?). Joshua Surtees (2016) does acknowledge that "back in the old days, before the internet and stuff, if you had a thing for a serial killer it was tradition to send him a love letter in prison. But times change" before a brief description of killer fandom, then admits his total mystification with it all. Some pieces take a more serious tone, playing into the concerned-pathologizing discourse familiar to early fan studies scholars and directed here specifically at the misguidedness of girls on social media. In the *Bitch Media* article I opened this chapter with, psychological explanations are sought, and experts consulted:

> Why are women, especially young women, stanning for these men, despite full knowledge of their twisted and fatal transgressions? There's not one core thread linking all women who have fallen in love with serial killers. David Schmid, author of *Natural Born Celebrities: Serial Killers in American Culture* and an English professor at the University at Buffalo, concludes that some of these women initiate a courtship with serial killers because they believe they can "save" them. "The savior complex is definitely an important part of the phenomenon," Schmid says. "Another element is the appeal of the 'bad boy' taken to its logical (if appalling) conclusion. Not surprisingly, many of the women who form these attachments to serial killers have also been in abusive relationships." (Willoughby 2017)

In this piece, Schmid posits that

> many of these women say that their relationships with serial killers are the safest/healthiest relationships ever been in. [. . .] Why? They always know where their men are and so those men can't cheat on them; because many of them are prevented from having any physical contact with these men, they can't be physically harmed/abused by them; they are essential to the emotional and physical well-being of these men, so these women feel needed. (quoted in Willoughby 2017)

How exactly Schmid knows this, whom he asked, and what gives him the right to speak on behalf of a huge variety of women, girls—and other people!—from a position of such authority is left unexplained. Note also how the special "concern" and moralization over things girls do reflects the construction and separation of "fangirls" as the Bad Other of the rational, critically engaged, and intelligent style of fandom (Hills 2012; Zubernis and Larsen 2012; Fathallah 2020).

Compare how a CBC radio article (2015) interviews a self-identified teenage female "Columbiner," who denies the label of fan, claiming that "to be a Columbiner is basically just having a huge interest in the Columbine shootings and being interested in the shooters," but admits that "a lot of people identify with the feelings of the shooters. So we kind of take comfort in it in a way, since a lot of us feel depressed and anxious, and they did too." The interviewer focuses on the young interviewee's "depression" before turning to an approved gatekeeper, journalist/researcher Dave Cullen, for comment. In an almost self-parodic opening statement, Cullen condescends, "First of all, I think it's great that you're [the radio station] giving her and people from that group a voice. I think that's really important, because I worry about those kids" (CBC Radio 2015). Cullen believes that Columbiners generally buy into the false narrative of Harris and Klebold as victimized outcasts taking revenge, which may or may not be the case, but presents no systematic research or analysis on how exactly Columbiners have constructed this discourse, and from what. This is why there is a need to bring the frame of textual poaching to killer fandoms: What matters here is ultimately what fans are constructing, how, why, and what that tells us about media culture and fan studies in general.

Adrian Chen is at least direct in his declaration that fans of spree killer James Holmes are "mostly teenage girls [. . .] die-hard James Holmes fans who gush supposed love for the alleged killer on Tumblr like he was a teenage vampire" (2012). His article takes a tone of mocking distance, stating that he has "yet to see any explicit fiction detailing James Holmes" romantic tryst with Ryan Gosling" but is "not looking too hard because [he'd] like to be able to fall asleep in the foreseeable future." He does acknowledge that some self-declared fans may be trolling, less invested in James Holmes than in making mischief on the internet, or indeed in fandom itself as a communal activity, arguing that "as the specificity of fandom has increased, fandom has become less about the cultural product it's supposedly obsessed with, and more about the very act of being a fan" (Chen 2015). This is certainly a possibility to be considered here. Some serial killer fans might just enjoy making memes, posting fanart and conversing around a shared media interest, or reflexive discussion of fandom as a practice—though this does raise the question of why they would choose to congregate around a serial killer text specifically. Chen suggests it is the very oddness or taboo nature of the subject matter, as "nothing brings a fandom together better than their weird passion being mocked by outsiders. Now that fandom is largely about the act of being a fan, this mockery can be the very thing the fandom is after." This seems to be a factor in Murderino fandom, as the hosts stress frequently how odd outsiders find their obsession with murder, and "paint fans as [a] knowledgeable in-group" (Sacks 2017, 45). Sacks argues that "this kind of discourse perpetuates an idea of [hosts] Karen and Georgia [and the listeners] as 'authentic outsiders' whose niche interests separate them from mainstream culture" (46). Subcultural studies has long pointed to the draw of the "alternative" and "authentic" as opposed to a posited mainstream that is considered mundane and inauthentic by comparison (Thornton 1995; Hills 2002). I also observe that Browder's participants conceived of themselves as confronting the true, depressing, violent nature of society via their interest in true crime, as opposed to those who choose to avoid thinking about it (2006). One even suggested that women predominate in true crime fandom because women are more likely than men to "live in the real world" (932). Browder's participants conceived their reading of true crime narratives as an "existential encounter with the truth—and saw bravery in their own refusal to avert their gaze" (932). So if true crime fans who would not define themselves as serial killer fans self-identify through the "different" and taboo nature of their interest, as perhaps more authentically engaged with gritty reality, I must consider whether and in what ways being cast as the Bad Other of the True Crime community consolidates serial killer fandom as an identity, and with what effects. This is explored in chapter 3, on affective community.

Four Frames from Fan Studies: Methodologies

I will now introduce the four frames through which I will address serial killer fandom in the coming chapters. To be clear, I am not suggesting that this is a comprehensive review of fan studies theories and methodologies, which would be far outside the scope of this book. Moreover, there will necessarily be some overlap between the frames in their practical application. Nonetheless, I will now give a general outline of the four major fan studies frameworks that will structure chapters 2–5 of this book.

1. Textual Poaching and Convergence Culture

Henry Jenkins's 1992 *Textual Poachers* is considered an inaugural work in fan studies scholarship. As noted, this book was written in part to counteract prevailing prejudices against media fans as being passive, silly, immature, or otherwise lacking as properly functional adults. A lot of these stereotypes focused on *Star Trek* fans, and so did Jenkins. He used the term "textual poachers" to describe fans' active processes of meaning-making from their desired texts, taking and building creatively on what they love, ignoring and transforming what they dislike. Camille Bacon-Smith (1992) discussed *Star Trek* fandom as a resistant women's culture based on the appropriation and recreation of masculinized hegemonic culture. Bacon-Smith's *Enterprising Women* was significant for its appreciation of women's labor, subcultures, and subcultural creativity, but could be criticized for perpetuating a sort of soft pathologization of women and girls as wounded victims perpetually in need of healing. Hers was the first book to focus on slash (pairing same-sex characters in homosexual relationships in fanfiction or UGC, at that time a very secretive practice). Her explanations for slash are more or less all rooted in the psychoanalysis of healing gendered trauma from the perspective of female oppression—which may, at times, be the case—or it might be that slash fans are fully self-realized, happy, adult women who find the idea of same sex partnerships attractive. Or a bit of both. The poaching metaphor is adapted from Michel de Certeau (1984), who stressed that the "poachers" of culture are in a relatively powerless position compared to those who own, control, and broadcast it—so the reader may observe immediately that the metaphor has dated, and is based primarily on a broadcast-to-consumer media model and a far less diverse media landscape. Jenkins acknowledged this in his 2006 work, *Convergence Culture*, which depicted a media field based on narrowcasting, audience selectivity, and the active interaction of audiences with texts via UGC and social media. Obviously, these tendencies have only increased; Jenkins cautioned that he did not wish to predict the future, but it must be admitted that *Convergence Culture* was fairly prescient in a socio-technological sense. The book can be fairly criticized for glossing over issues of access, equality, and education when it comes to new media, and for its too-easy slide from media participation to participation in citizen politics. Jenkins's later work is very much focused on what he calls "participatory culture" and "spreadable media" (Jenkins et al. 2013).[4] Acknowledging the fan studies frame, Clausen and Sikjaer write:

> When Jenkins talks about spreadability, he is not interested in distribution in the traditional sense, which has customarily been measured through the sum of people who watch a movie on TV, or the number of tickets sold at a movie premiere. Instead, he sees it as a process where "a mix of top-down and bottom-up forces determine how material is shared across and among cultures in far more participatory (and messier) ways," or put more simply, the capability of media being spread (Jenkins et al. 2013, 1). According to Jenkins, networked communities play a significant role in how media circulates. (2021, 158)

Now clearly, this is a significant lens through which to understand serial killer fandom. But I must develop it a little. For me, the biggest weakness in the participatory culture argument is that it ignores questions of labor, economics, and the re-appropriation of fan culture by media industries. In a very real sense, corporations can now sell fan culture back to fans, inviting contributions such as game modifications, fanart, and fanfic, then repackaging and redistributing it in commercial forms (Pearson 2010). It also creates a system whereby media industries promote and monetize the kinds of fan production they like, and ignore, denigrate, and marginalize that which they don't. As Kristina Busse put it:

> The fannish community [. . .] might have to disavow those parts that do not please the owners of the media product. Certain groups of fans can become legit if and only if they follow certain ideas, don't become too rebellious, too pornographic, don't read the text too much against the grain. That seems a price too high to pay. (2007)

Suzanne Scott has done significant work on this phenomenon and its intersections with how fannish practices are gendered; I'll discuss this in the introduction to chapter 2. Serial killer fandom is different because, firstly, it is not based on a media franchise with an owner, and secondly, because it is not so easily recuperable by media industries, except perhaps as fodder for clickbait articles. But on the other hand, there is already a serial killer industry, and an industry for entertainment via real-life violence. Murderabilia is openly sold online. The more tenuous marketability of serial killer

---

[4] "Participatory culture" may be part of the subtitle of *Textual Poachers*, but it is Jenkins's later work that really develops the concept.

fandom, as opposed to more traditional fandom, needs to be remembered in any discussion of convergence and participation. Moreover, as I have argued in my last book (Fathallah 2020), there are occasions when metaphors like poaching and even convergence—which are based on fans appropriating and modifying extant discursive structures—are less appropriate than a perspective where textual definition actually begins with fan culture, and is then reappropriated and reinforced by the media industry. There, I illustrated the case of the music genre emo(tional hardcore). Emo had no stable definition until fans utilized new media to make one, which was then reappropriated, legitimated, and recirculated by the music press. How far does serial killer fandom invent its own objects, and how does this relate to the construction of serial killers in professional media? How does this UGC relate to the largely conservative impetus of professional crime media, in terms of the construction of law enforcement, patriarchy, and violence?

2. Affective Communities

From the outset of fan studies, it was clear that friendship and relationship building, both online and in person, were important factors in fandom. When Rhiannon Bury published her *Cyberspace of their Own* (2005), she was reporting on research on UseNet lists from the late 1990s. She studied women's engagement with the *X-Files* via the coyly named "David Duchovny Estrogen Brigade (DDEB)" mailing list—so-called to mock the way general fan spaces had side-lined female fans as only being interested in a male actor's attractiveness. She also studied a *Due South* list devoted to slash in the early 2000s. On this list, fans discussed the show, their experiences as (female) fans, and several other topics. Bury found that the participants bonded over their shared texts and their experiences as fans and as women in the world, and formed enduring friendships and relationships. While this is undoubtedly true of some fannish experience, I must acknowledge that fan culture and the internet in general from the late 1990s and first few years of the twenty-first century are barely recognizable today. Websites are much more connected. Fan culture is much more visible. Far more people are online, and barriers to technological engagement are much lower. Users dip in and out of communities more easily. Twenty years ago, Nancy Baym (1998) found the term community appropriate for online groups—but is it now? Does it make sense to speak of all the fans of a large media property as a community, though they may never meet each other nor even frequent the same websites? If not, where does one draw the boundaries of a community? As Stjerneby writes on fans of the *My Favorite Murder* podcast:

> Some fans may believe the fandom they are a part of is a community, while other fans may not. It may be problematic to speak of all MFM fans as one unified community due to fans being spread out in different clusters on different online platforms and the hundreds of subgroups which all have their own specific additional interest besides the podcast itself. (2018, 28)

At the outset of this research, I thought that the more secretive, taboo, and restricted spaces of serial killer fandom may render it as one of the few spaces where the term "community" in a stronger sense is more appropriate. However, my findings (see chapter 3) did not really support this. Stjerneby goes on:

> Baym (1998) refers to Benedict Anderson's (1983) argument that online communities are "imagined communities," a theory which has led many computer-mediated communication (CMC) scholars to research the "style" in which a given online community is imagined [. . .] Baym argues that the "style" of a community "is shaped by a range of preexisting structures, including external contexts, temporal structure, system infrastructure, group purposes, and participant characteristics" (Baym 1998, 38). These structures culminate into a set of systematic social meanings [. . .] hence enabling an emergence of "group-specific forms of expression, identities, relationships, and normative conventions" (Baym 1998, 38). (Stjerneby 2018, 28)

Most fandoms, at present, are probably too diverse, too widespread, and too various for attributes like "style" to apply in any meaningful way, not least because communicative styles are heavily structured by the site or app they occur on. Other academics have posited that fan communities are bound by a "gift economy" (Hellekson 2009), wherein fans gift their time, skill, and textual creations to other fans without expectation of direct return, but on the understanding that this practice benefits the community as a whole. Tisha Turk calls this "circular giving," which is rarely one-to-one. The default is one-to-many, as each created gift is available to all. In a taboo fandom, a scholar might posit that gifts are created and shared with less expectation of communal return. For one thing, there are fewer members to create gifts. For another, one might imagine serial killer fandom to have a greater percentage of lurkers than active participants, reluctant to leave digital traces. How will this affect the gift economy of serial killer fandom?

3. (Sub)cultural Capital

The theory of cultural capital is developed from the work of sociologist Pierre Bourdieu (1984). It means, in short, to accumulate the sort of knowledge, habits, and ways of expressing oneself that are socially beneficial within a particular milieu. Bourdieu was primarily discussing class, but Sarah Thornton (1995) then demonstrated how subcultures develop and accumulate their own forms of cultural capital—expertise, facility with the topic of interest, and the ability to create and distribute UGC with skill, for example. In Thornton's own work on subcultures, cultural capital depended on having and demonstrating the correct "tastes," showing oneself to be an informed consumer, and denigrating casual participants (usually women). Subcultural capital is often expressed in gatekeeping (you can't be a real fan if you don't know about . . . if you haven't been to . . . if you don't own a . . .). A wide range of fan studies scholars have utilized this framework to study how fandoms operate; see Matt Hills (2002), Milly Williamson (2005), or R. M. Milner (2011) for examples. High subcultural capital elevates one's position in comparison with other fans and may even lead to association with the object or producer of one's fandom. Williamson (2005) demonstrated how some fans of Anne Rice, the author of *Interview with a Vampire*, gathered through expertise, knowledge accumulation, and persistence sufficient subcultural capital to associate with the author in prominent positions running fan activities—which then of course increased their subcultural capital manifold. How will subcultural capital operate in serial killer fandom? How will it be gathered and displayed? Expressed? What relation does it bear to other, more official forms of capital? How will it tie into the collection of serial killer memorabilia, whose cultural and commercial value very much turns on its authenticity? These form the main questions of chapter 4.

Activities that are culturally perceived as feminine lack in subcultural capital in many fan cultures (Larsen and Zubernis 2012; Fathallah 2020). Too-enthusiastic expression of sexual interest, performed lack of rationality, or behavior generally considered excessive depletes subcultural capital—and this is gendered, because behaviors associated with the body rather than the mind are discursively coded as feminine in Western cultures. The derivation of the pejorative term "hysteria" (from the Greek hysterus: uterus) might be the ultimate illustration of this tendency. Will the same be true of serial killer fandom, or will the subject itself be unusual enough that the expression of sexual interest in serial killers is actually a method of accumulating subcultural capital?

4. Playing Fans

The final frame I will engage is the most contemporary, and taps into some of the caveats raised by writers like Rico above. It might be mistaken to assume that self-professed serial killer fans are particularly serious about their online activities. Paul Booth argues that the contemporary internet is characterized by a "philosophy of playfulness" (2015, 2017) and that fans are, to a large degree, playing. Many might think it play in bad taste—but bad taste humor is hardly new or unique to the internet or to media fandom. Joking about atrocities is a fairly constant cultural practice. Booth writes:

> What is a "philosophy of playfulness?" [. . .] The contemporary media scene is complex, and rapidly becoming dependent on a culture of ludism. Today's media field is fun, playful, and exuberant. More so than at any other time, the media we use in our everyday lives have been personalized, individualized, and made pleasurable to use. We play with our media; it is malleable in our hands. The field of media studies needs to take into account this philosophy of playfulness in order to represent the media texts created by fans not just as individual fan fiction, fan videos, fan songs, or fan research, but rather as pieces of what fans use as a larger multivocal media "game." (2016, 8)

Playing with serial killer media is not a "nice" or palatable game, but it doesn't necessarily valorize serial killers in the way popular critics have imagined. Aja Romano observes that many fans of school shooter T. J. Lane insist their "fascination is laced with irony," and quotes a participant:

> We're making fun of the little shit prick. even the girls who think He's ~so fine~ know he's a complete piece of shit and nothing's gonna change that. not even his fine, soft, newborn baby deer features. (quoted in Romano 2014)

On one hand, this participant admits that there are female fans attracted to Lane—even as they are mocking him. On the other, s/he claims a recognition that ultimately, such fans recognize that he is a "piece of shit." Again, this pushes at the boundary of how one defines fandom—but self-professed fans of all kinds of media mock and insult it and its creators regularly, so again,

I believe I must retain an iterative perspective, and take those participants who claim to be fans at their word. All fandoms can contain a degree of irony. Whitney Phillips and Ryan Milner (2017) believe "ambivalence" to be at the root of much online culture and creativity: Ambivalence is not indifference, as the term is often misused. The clue is in the prefix "ambi-," meaning both, on both sides, in both directions. Expressions of online culture have multiple meanings, both serious and flippant, often signalling in multiple directions. Further, Booth conceives of fannish play as generally *not* transformative, as Jenkins et al. would have it, but rather as operating *inside* certain pre-set boundaries, boundaries drawn by the media industries. In chapter 5, I will suggest that contrary to journalistic admonishments, much serial killer fandom does just that. Online fans did not create the serial killer industry. They might *stretch* its boundaries, but they don't particularly oppose it.

The first three frames established by fan studies tend towards a particular kind of fannish activity—creative, communal, productive, and now, digital. They ultimately derive from the valorization of fan studies phase—and there has lately been a certain widening of these lenses towards the revaluation of less celebrated forms of fandom, such as those based on consumption and curation, cosplay, or ephemeral performance. There is also a great deal of attention paid to the convergence between fandom and professional media in all its forms—convergent, exploitative, opportunistic, or otherwise. Much of the activity of serial killer fandom fits, at first glance, quite easily into these frames—the textual poaching, the UGC, the habits of collection—and the media construction of the serial killer as celebrity fits quite neatly into the idea of the distributed, readerly, eminently poachable, and interpretable popular text. And yet, when I turn to the concept of fandom-as-play, I will observe that it is mistaken to draw a binary between serial killer fandom and received, official media concerning serial killers. If online culture *is* ambivalent (and I think it is), scholars should avoid attempting to categorize instances of fandom as either "resistant to" or "complicit with" broadcast media. How far, then, can serial killer fandom be understood through a fan studies lens? What will the findings tell us about popular engagement with serial killers more generally, or about fan studies in general? Is there a qualitative difference between a serial killer fan and a true crime enthusiast, or is the line merely a site of discursive struggle that might land anywhere on a spectrum at any particular moment—and ought this inflect the way we think about our cultural obsession with true crime? Those are the key questions of this book.

I now turn to chapter 1 for my historical retrospective on serial killer fandom, beginning with media sensations around Jack the Ripper and H. H. Holmes. As noted, these killers' crimes were committed long before the term "serial killer" was coined, but they have since been integrated into a well-established discursive framework, and moreover initiated the kind of public and media fascination to which I begin to apply at least some of my theoretical frameworks. Due to the lack of data and the very different media contexts, it is difficult to be systematic about this, but the chapters following will provide a systematic application of the frameworks described, building off the historical insights I have gathered.

CHAPTER 1

Fanlike Engagement before Fan Studies

Personators, Collectors, and Groupies

Most famous serial killers have had fans. Of course, the term "fan" here is immediately complicated by the fact that it now evokes the whole field of fan studies and a range of definitions around what fans are and do—not to mention the fact that prior to online fandom, information on people's engagement with serial killer media is less reliable. Nonetheless, I have noted distinct patterns of behavior, ways of writing, and modes of reception around serial killer media dating to at least Victorian England that I recognize as forms of fannish engagement. In this chapter, I'll look at some of these patterns, and while bearing in mind that the application of academic lenses retrospectively is always complicated by context, consider what can be learned about what one might call the "pre-fan studies fandoms" of serial killers, in order to carry these insights into my analysis of serial killer fandom today. I will bring to bear the major concepts outlined in the introduction (textual poaching/media convergence, affective community, (sub) cultural capital building, and fandom as play), offering supplemental insights from other fan studies theory where appropriate. Most of this supplemental theory applies best in a pre-digital or extra-digital context, for it concerns the collection of material artefacts, fan tourism, and cosplay; but all of these processes have digital manifestations and continuities. For the purposes of this pre-history, we will have to look beyond explicitly self-identified serial killer fans—largely because these are much, much harder to identify before the internet, and would yield only idiosyncratic results. For the sake of establishing a broader and more substantial basis for the theoretical insights we will bring to the next chapters, we will investigate fannish behavior around nineteenth and twentieth century serial killers, for which there is a wealth of data. Of course, it won't be possible to cover examples from every popular or famous serial killer. Therefore, after opening with the emblematic Jack the Ripper and H. H. Holmes cases, I have focused these examples around four of the most popular serial killers with online fans: Ted Bundy, Richard Ramirez, Jeffrey Dahmer, and Aileen Wuornos. This particular cross-section also allows me to make some instructive comparisons regarding responses to serial killers of different genders and sexualities, a theme that will extend to coming chapters.

According to Alexandra Warwick, "the Whitechapel murders [of Jack the Ripper] represent both the inaugural event in serial killing and the narrative accounts of it" (2007, 74). The corpus of "fictional and non-fiction literature devoted to the murders" is vast enough to have gained the portmanteau "Ripperature" (Irwin 2014). Some excellent work with both primary and secondary sources has documented fannish engagement with the unknown killer popularly called "Jack the Ripper," from the contemporary media frenzy and the fashion for Ripper "personation" continued in cosplay to this day, to the "sensationalized television documentaries and tacky memorabilia sold in East End pubs" up to the present (Curtis 2001, 259). Peculiarly, "Jack the Ripper" is both an exemplary and an exceptional serial killer. He is exemplary because his are the crimes to which pretty much every serial killer of women has been compared since. He is exceptional because he is anonymous: a "floating signifier" (259) to which fantasies around killing—and race, and sexuality, and gender, and class—can be attached and detached with far more flux than they can around killers with a face and a real name. The press speculated broadly that he might be one of three "types" metonymically representing *fin de siècle* fears: a vicious aristocrat (symbolizing the power and perversion of the upper classes); a mad doctor (symbolizing fears around the relationship of a bestial human nature to a veneer of civilization and modernity); or a foreigner, usually a politicized

Jew (see Frayling 2007). His crimes have particular multi-accentuality, of which the London press took full advantage. In John Fiske's terms, I would call this a "producerly text" (1989, 104).

The construction of Jack the Ripper needs to be understood in the context of the "New Journalism" associated with 1880s Britain. At this time, basic literacy was increasing rapidly; cheap, readable, and disposable papers were a booming industry. According to L. Perry Curtis Jr., "the advent of the penny paper enabled workers to buy a daily or weekly paper on a regular basis without having to forego their pints of bitter or plugs of tobacco" (2001, 56). In these texts, scholars observe the rapid expansion of features now associated with tabloid or popular journalism, including "a heavier emphasis on crime, scandal, disaster, and sports along with bolder and more lurid headlines and subheads" (61).[1] In his extended study Jack the Ripper and the *London Press,* Curtis analyzed the ongoing contemporary coverage of the murders—and the social effects associated with them—across fifteen London newspapers, including three East End weeklies, "chosen with an eye to striking a rough balance between the morning and evening, the daily and weekly, and the Tory, Liberal and Radical Press" (2001, 16). Papers across this spectrum contained "clinical details of bodily injuries that Victorian newspapers served up to readers in an almost pornographic manner" (cf. Murley 2008 on crime porn). Curtis quotes Joseph C. Fisher on a "synergistic response to the Whitechapel murders in the press as well as the metropolis," akin to the triadic relationship between "the public's insatiable desire for news, the media's commercial interests in providing it, and the [serial] killer's need to publicize his invincibility" (7).

It is tricky—and probably not particularly valuable—to speculate on the Victorian readers' personal motivations for their fascination with Jack the Ripper, but two fandom-related perspectives are established beyond doubt: firstly, that Jack was a sensation and a celebrity, and secondly, that "Jack the Ripper" is and always has been a collective, collaborative, cultural invention (Warwick 2007, 72). The Whitechapel murderer is not synonymous with Jack the Ripper. Notes by contemporary police, now housed in the London Crime Museum, indicate that the Whitechapel murderer was Polish barber Aaron Kosminski, readily identified by a reliable witness who refused to testify in court (Benetto 2006). Kosminski was institutionalized in insane asylums from 1891 until his death in 1919. "Jack the Ripper" is a product of

---

[1] The term "New Journalism" is also associated with the crusading investigative style of reporting pioneered by William J. T. Stead of the *Pall Mall Gazette*.

what one might call "proto-convergence" between the media and the newly literate public. Reportage on his celebrity is plentiful, dramatic, and probably to some extent hyperbolic:

> In the autumn of 1888, reporters dwelled on the "thrill of horror" that ran through the country as a result of the atrocities taking place in Whitechapel. After dipping his pen in purple ink, one journalist wrote: "Horror ran through the land. Men spoke of it with bated breath, and pale-lipped women shuddered as they read the dreadful details. People afar off smelled blood, and the superstitious said that the skies were of a deeper red that autumn." (Curtis 2001, 77)

There is further concrete evidence of Celebrity Jack, created by a whole mass of people inside and outside of the media. This includes the immediate addition of tableaus depicting his crimes to London waxwork museums, some of which were, according to the local magistrate "revolting in the extreme" (76). Meanwhile, at the site where victim Annie Chapman was murdered, one enterprising local started charging visitors a penny simply to enter the yard where she died (123). "Crowds of sightseers" at Whitechapel were entertained by a pavement artist's "graphic representations of the murders" (Schmid 2005, 34) while "a local woman did a lively trade selling swordsticks to members of the crowd" (34). This appears very much like an intersection between "dark tourism" (Foley and Lennon 1996; Lennon and Foley 2000; Wilson 2008; Farmaki 2013) and fan tourism (Williams 2017; Geraghty 2018; Zubernis and Larsen 2018). "Dark tourism," now a well-established field of study, refers to the commercial or noncommercial visitation of sites where atrocities and/or tragedies have taken place. The term was coined in 1996 by Lennon and Foley, but variations on the practice seem to be fairly ancient (Hartmann et al. 2018). Murder sites are a classic destination of so-called "dark" tourism, as are prisons.[2] Steenberg describes tourism to the scenes of crimes as an "example of an intersection [of these fandoms] with the kinds of fan practices normally associated with more socially sanctioned forms of celebrity" (2017). Motivations for "dark" tourism are probably as diverse as their tourists, but might include the contemplation of death and suffering, schadenfreude, a desire to empathize with victims, and/or a desire for education in a kinetic, sensory form (Farmaki 2013, 283).

[2] Again I must register my objection to the descriptor "dark" used to mean "negative," but that is the term commonly used in these texts.

Fan tourism, as it sounds, is the practice of visiting sites associated with fans' preferred media properties and/or celebrities. Ripper Tours remain a popular and thoroughly commercialized attraction of Whitechapel up to the present: TripAdvisor boasts a multi-page selection of "Ripper tours." According to Lincoln Geraghty, "media fan tourism is about passing through different tourist spaces and finding meaning in the act of being present, taking photos, and performing as a fan within those spaces" (2018). Fan tourists describe their experience in sensory, spatial terms, such as getting "closer to the story" or making a "connection" (Reijnders 2011, 245). Obviously, the earliest Ripper tourists were not taking photos, but they were performing in a fanlike way, getting "closer to the story" via the enthusiastic contemplation of the celebritized killings and the collection of unofficial merchandise. Geraghty writes that fan tourist sites are both "constructed and natural, subverted and official, consumed and constructed, creative and hierarchical" (2018). Some of these properties apply to the Jack the Ripper case. The yard of 29 Hanley Street, where Chapman was murdered, is the "natural" destination of those wishing to participate experientially in the phenomenon of the day. It is also constructed, opportunistically, as a tourist site one must pay to enter. It is the officially constructed scene of a crime, and the subversively consumed scene of voyeuristic entertainment. It is creative in the sense that onlookers project their fantasies and fears regarding the killer and victim. It is almost a kind of physical enactment of media convergence, where onlookers brought their own fascinations and fantasies to the mystery playing out in the press. Curtis writes that

> the impenetrable mystery of the Ripper's identity and motives created a huge vacuum into which all kinds of cranks or crazies as well as many ordinary, rational people rushed with their ideas and fantasies. (2001, 251)

While the reader might object to the easy demarcation between "cranks and crazies" and "ordinary, rational people" (the serial killer fans and true crime enthusiasts of their day?), notice the spatial metaphor. People physically inserted themselves into the spaces associated with the Ripper, and so into the narrative.

Two other terms frequently associated with fan tourism are "pilgrimage" and "performance" (Williams 2017; Zubernis and Larsen 2018). "Pilgrimage" captures the emotional dimension of the physical movement, the crossing of a boundary between space that is mundane and everyday and space that is—if not precisely sacred—endowed with special emotional qualities. "Performance" relates to the sorts of actions fans use to inscribe and/or record their presence at special places. Lynn Zubernis and Katherine Larsen remark that

> inscribing one's name at a tourism site is as old as tourism itself. Byron etched his name into a pillar of the temple of Poseidon in Greece and Charles Dickens etched his name on a window at Shakespeare's birthplace in Stratford-upon-Avon. (2018)

Scholars do not know precisely how onlookers behaved at semi-official Ripper "scenes" like the places of the murder, but we do have multiple reports of Ripper "performances," or "personations," which we can connect to the fannish practice of cosplaying, or dressing up as a favored character. The term "play" in cosplay carries overtones of both play in the sense of pure fun and jollity, and play in the sense of performance and acting: to play a role. Paul Booth (2015, 2016) considers both as aspects of fannish play.

Sophie Duncan argues that "the Ripper murders and their 1888 coverage re-theatricalized not only London, but many provincial towns," both through the many professional plays based on or interpreted through the Ripper story, and through "extra-theatrical, popular performance 'scenarios' by civilian men" (2019, 190). Men in London used costume and performance to imagine themselves into the whole cast of characters: "the plain-clothes detective, the Ripper's female victims, and the Ripper himself" (190). The contemporary verb for such performances was to "personate." Here is a fascinating departure from our modern usage of "*im*personation," implying that in dressing and behaving as these semi-real, semi-imaginary characters, the performer is not so much partaking in a falsehood as *embodying a character into being,* in line with the Butlerian idea of performativity. Recorded detective "personations" include that of a sailmaker of Ipswich who "gave out that he was a detective from Scotland-yard," apparently walked around offering people "undecipherable [*sic*]" messages, promising that "the murderer would call [. . .] and upon being confronted with the written paper it would have a strange effect" (195). Other men engaged in "Ripper-baiting": dressing in female clothing and loitering at likely hours in the appropriate Whitechapel locations. This was one tactic used professionally by police and journalists, but other motives are unknown. In 1889 one Edward Hamblar was arrested for "disorderly conduct and being dressed in female attire," specifically a hat, veil, "dress, two flannel petticoats, and a dress improver" (198). Multiple men of course claimed to be Jack, and/or threatened to "do for [women of their acquaintance] the same as 'Jack the Ripper' had done for the others [. . .] some night when she little thinks of it." "Do a Jack the Ripper" or "play Jack the Ripper" seem to have become threatening idioms to some extent, recorded in letters and divorce proceedings (199–200). Some men—including perfectly nonviolent ones—utilized costumes and props as a part of their Jack personations. George R. Sims was a journalist, author, and collector of mortuary photographs. Duncan notes that he recollected with relish his experience of going "to the Pavilion Theatre, Whitechapel" late at night, carrying "a long Japanese knife of a murderous character for melodramatic purposes" in a "black bag," continuing,

> I often wonder what would have happened had someone cried out, "That's the Ripper," and my black bag had been opened. [. . .] On the occasion when I carried the black bag and Japanese knife I [. . .] was standing among the people, close to the very spot where one of the worst murders was committed. (201)

Is this cosplay? It sounds like it, with the props carefully selected for the theatrical impression, but the audience for whom fan cosplay is typically performed can only be imagined, lest the player find himself in real-life trouble. Lamerichs argues that "cosplay emphasizes the personal enactment of a narrative [. . .] a form of fan appropriation that transforms, performs, and actualizes an existing story in close connection to the fan's own identity" (2011). It is a liminal experience, incorporating aspects both of the self and the Other, mixing properties of the self with properties of the character one is performing. Ellen Kirkpatrick argues that cosplay "exemplifies a moment" of "embodied translation, during which the fan transfers the character from a limitless fictional landscape to the fan's delimited physical one" (2015). Given the amount of speculation and mystery surrounding Jack the Ripper, the fears and anxieties and contemporary bogeymen he represented (a mad doctor? an evil aristocrat? a foreign Jew?), one can certainly imagine the personations as a sort of delimitation—the endless landscape of possibilities narrowed to the personator's body, brought within his control.

If cosplay involves elements of both the player and the character, here is a first demonstration of how Jack the Ripper was collaboratively invented through a proto-convergence culture. There is also a wealth of textual evidence for this process. The second way I observed the public creation of Jack is through what one might call proto-textual poaching: a vast and rapid uptick in public letter writing for publication on the subject of the killer, who he was, what his motives were, what sort of character he was—and of course, claims to be him. Initiated from the very first murder, that of Annie Chapman, hundreds of readers likewise "wrote themselves into the Ripper story, and in the process left some clues about their own desires, fantasies, and fears" (Curtis 2001, 239). Curtis coded a sample of 241 readers' letters published across five newspapers, and found that their topics fell into five overlapping categories: "detection, law and order, suspects, moral and social reform, and miscellaneous" (241). Emphasizing that multiaccentuality of serial killing that Schmid observed, many writers took a moralistic posture, reproaching the public fascination with sensation-horror, blaming "journalists, novelists, and theatre managers" for pandering to the "'the foul and seamy side of human nature'" (248). "'We have set up King Horrors,' complained one writer, 'and we must bow down and worship him'" (248). Perhaps most interesting to my purposes are the hundreds of letters claiming to be from the Ripper himself. The missive signed "From Hell" is probably the best-known of these. Of almost equal fame are the "Dear Boss" letter—this is the first in which the writer names himself "Jack the Ripper"—and the "Saucy Jacky" postcard, in which he signs off as the above. There is no evidence that any of these missives were actually from the killer, though a linguistic forensic expert established in 2018 that the letter and the postcard are almost certainly by the same writer (Nini 2018). In any case, both the police and the press were inundated with "Ripper Letters," claiming either to be The Ripper or an associate:

> Written in different hands, most of these manic messages threatened more butcheries to come. Thus the *East London Observer* (Oct. 13) published a letter from "George of the High Rip Gang," boasting that he would now commence cutting up "gilded" women or duchesses in the West End, while his "pal"—"jocular Jack"—continued his work in the East End. As he put it, "Oh, we are masters. No education like a butcher's. No animal like a nice woman—the fat are best." (Curtis 2001, 145)

This might be compared to the fannish practice of online roleplay, a form of digital play in which fans assume the personas of their favorite characters or celebrities to create Twitter accounts, journals, or other roleplaying platforms in their name. Nor was this textual form of "personation" limited to men. In 1888,

> the police actually caught one of the Ripper letter writers, who turned out to be a "good-looking, respectably dressed," twenty-one-year-old seamstress named (appropriately) Maria Coroner, from Bradford. A search of her lodgings yielded copies of several Jack the Ripper letters in her handwriting, addressed to both the Chief Constable and a local newspaper, indicating Jack's intention to "do a little business" in Bradford. (Curtis 2001, 172)

As in some contemporary forms of textual poaching, readers took from the media narrative and wrote themselves into it—for attention, for entertainment, for reasons known only to themselves. Most of them are intensely melodramatic: Clive Bloom describes them as a form of confession narrative heightened to the level of fiction via black humor and the invention of a Cockney, slang-using persona (Bloom 2007, 94–95). When the papers couldn't get Ripper news, they made it. In November 1894, the *Gazette* published "several macabre stories, one of which consisted of a long letter written by 'Jack the Ripper's Pal'" (Curtis 2001, 207). Perhaps most fascinatingly of all, in 1894, the sensationalist newspaper the *Sun*[3] actually managed to publish the first Ripper fanfic. Pitched as a piece of investigative journalism, an anonymous staff reporter known only as "WK" supposedly traced the "real" Ripper to Broadmoor, an asylum for the criminally insane, and promised to extract his final confession, exclusively for the *Sun* (Bloom 2007, 92–93). Of course there is a question of where roleplay becomes fanfic, but this is a real, verifiable historical example of a first-person fictional narrative in which our hero meets a real-life serial killer, a genre that dominates the serial killer fanfic on Wattpad to this day.

Though the bulk of surviving press on Jack the Ripper is naturally British and London focused, journalists in New York also produced a large body of newspaper reports and Ripper-based dime novels. After 1894, I found frequent comparisons with America's own first celebrity murderer, one Herman Webster Mudgett, better known as H. H. Holmes (Schmid 2005, 44). David Schmid writes that "the Holmes case was one of the first high-profile instances of serial murder in America, and the intense media and public interest in Holmes rapidly made him into a star of American popular culture" (49). Schmid documents that for many commentators, the technology-obsessed, entrepreneurial Holmes represented "the dark side of frontier individualism, a man who, by defining progress in violent terms, was willing to use anyone to achieve his goal of self-(re)generation" (51).

---

[3] Not to be confused with the contemporary British tabloid *The Sun*.

Mark Seltzer explores the complex collision of technology and primitive forces at work at the scene of the Chicago 1893 Columbian Exposition, a short distance away from which Holmes had constructed the hotel where he killed an unknown number of people via a network of traps, trapdoors, gas chambers, and other fatal technologies—at least, according to the press (2013, 237–50). The actual facts of the Holmes case are difficult to verify, and the killer took them to his death. "The technophilic city of light and life and the tech-noir factory of death" (237) were a readymade press phenomenon, inciting an intense and public conversation over American identity, modernism, technology, individualism, and self-invention.

Thus we can understand how, despite the fact that Holmes was caught and had a verifiable identity, both he and the Ripper served as cultural constructs embodying the *fin de siècle* fears and fantasies of their respective cultures. The response to Holmes "combined horror with fascination, even admiration" (Schmid 2005, 53). Holmes was intensely self-conscious of his own celebrity, as Schmid documents. In his final confession, he claimed to have killed a total of twenty-seven people both in the Chicago hotel and elsewhere. Many doubted this, both because he was "being paid a handsome sum by a newspaper for this confession and because they preferred to let their imaginations run riot and attribute hundreds of murders to Holmes, turning him into the devil incarnate" (54). Holmes participated in the iconography of monstrosity that began to be attributed to him, claiming in his prison writings that his face and features were literally changing to resemble Satan. He published his own account of his crimes, "to compete with the flurry of books that appeared about him" (55). He sold his confession for thousands of dollars. What exactly he planned to do with those dollars is a mystery, given that he was already sentenced to execution, but neatly demonstrates how "Holmes was inextricably both murderer and businessman" (Schmid 2005, 57) to the last, an *American Psycho* predecessor for the turn of the century. The American answer to the London waxworks were dime museums, which rapidly adapted to advertise "artifacts and photographs of Holmes, his victims, and his crime scenes [. . .] a large pile of human bones, a human skull, and a miniature replica of the Castle in Chicago" (Boswell and Thompson 1955, 46). Though early attempts to convert the so-called "murder castle" into an actual tourist attraction were thwarted, its excavation attracted the very same kind of fannish tourism that the Ripper's crime scene did. Schmid quotes a witness report from the *Chicago Daily News* in 1895:

> "Cyclists, evidently away on a day's outing, dismounted and left their steeds in the alley back of the castle while they fought with the street gamins for advantageous loopholes in the wooden sidewalk, through which they could peep at the men digging in the soft mud of the cellar. By 9 o'clock fully 100 men, women and children were lying flat on the sidewalks above the cellar peering in through every conceivable crack or knothole." (Schmid 2005, 58)

Once again, it would be fruitless to speculate on the exact motives of such onlookers. But observe the descriptions of physical actions: digging, peeping, peering. There seems to be a trajectory of the physical body towards the "heart" of the story, a movement to insert the self into the narrative, to "get closer to the story" as Reijnders's participants described (2011, 245).

We have already set the groundwork for many insights into fannish behavior around serial killers that predate fan studies. In the twentieth century, though, there is arguably a shift in the popular press portrayal of its serial killer celebrities. Jack's and Holmes's celebrity was based in monstrosity and sensation-horror. According to Vronksy, the imagery of monstrosity and horror yields in the second half of the twentieth century to a "new postmodern serial killer role model" (2004, 6), specifically associated with Ted Bundy. Fox and Levin write that the "human monster" that was once so common in media images of serial killer imagery had yielded to a "more modern image [that] describes these killers as unusually handsome and charming" (2005, 107; see also Wiest 2011, 39). However, the process is not neat or strictly chronological. As I will observe when I come to discuss Jeffrey Dahmer, the monster discourse did not die out, nor has it. Discourse, after all, is always in struggle and flux. It would be more accurate to state that the later twentieth century produced a new *option* for constructing serial killers: the "psychopathic or sociopathic personality" (Murley 2008, 33). The psychopathic sex symbol came to full fruition and public attention around the trial of Bundy, one of the most popular serial killers with online fandoms today. Both Bundy and Richard Ramirez had "fans who flock[ed] to courtrooms during trials and prison visitation rooms after convictions, and [. . .] receive[d] a substantial number of letters, visitors, and even marriage proposals" (Wiest 2016, 331). They have been the subjects of countless interviews, documentaries, foreign and domestic publications, and "their autographs, photographs, and even hair clippings draw large sums at auction" (331–32). Before I turn to examine the Bundy case in more detail, I must make a brief side-foray to introduce this topic of buying and collecting such "murderabilia" from twentieth and twenty-first century serial killers.

The collection of memorabilia—or murderabilia, as it is here called—relates of course to the fannish practice of collecting artifacts, both official and unofficial, associated with favored texts. As the practice of collecting murderabilia is conducted primarily online, I will discuss it properly in the chapter on cultural capital, through which lens it is best viewed. But this practice has a long pre-digital history. Ruth Penfold-Mounce compares it to a practice common in the 1700s, wherein people kept the fingerbones of executed criminals as a charm against running out of money (in Damon and Fiennes 2019, episode 6). Penfold-Mounce also relates cases from the nineteenth and twentieth centuries wherein doctors performing autopsies kept body parts from convicted criminals. While the contemporary collection of body parts, writings, and objects connected to serial killers is obviously not quite the same, Poppy Damon and Alice Fiennes argue that people retain a kind of magical thinking around these artifacts. Many of us hold an implicit belief that abstract properties, be they evil, charisma, specialness, or something else, can be transmuted through the body part or object that has touched the body of a serial killer. This is an example of a phenomenon known as the "law of contagion," which psychologist Paul Rosen summarizes as "once in contact, always in contact" (Damon and Fiennes 2019, episode 1). The murderabilia collectors that Damon and Fiennes interview value the authenticity of their products, and dealers go to great lengths to certify that their items for sale are real. There is, naturally, a booming market in counterfeit murderabilia. Sometimes, interviewees speak of the killers whose objects they possess with absolute awe: Eric Holler, a significant figure in the establishment of the murderabilia industry who I will revisit in chapter 4, describes the feeling of receiving a letter from "Richard fucking Ramirez" in "starstruck" terms, reflecting on his "groupies" and describing him as a "fucking legend" (episode 1). The UK and several US states have laws in place to prevent criminals from profiting directly from their crimes, but this has not always been the case. John Wayne Gacy, for example, successfully sold paintings from his prison cell until 1985. His artwork continues to be auctioned. In any case, there are always workarounds: Holler conducts many of his transactions with imprisoned serial killers via an understanding that should they post him saleable murderabilia, he will "take care" of them financially in the form of "gift[s]" (episode 1).

The six episodes of Damon and Fiennes's *Murderabilia* podcast (2019) throw up a lot of themes that murderabilia and other fan memorabilia collectors have in common. Dorus Hoebink, Stijn Reijnders, and Abby Waysdorf write that "fandom is about more than reading and writing; it is also about touching, smelling, controlling, and collecting the objects of fandom" (2014). Cornel Sandvoss argues that "fans give their consumption an inherently private and personal nature that removes their object of consumption from the logic of capitalist exchange" (2005, 116). For murderabilia collectors and fans alike, owning a material and physical link to the object of their fascination allows the insertion of the self into a larger narrative, allows the fan to mold an experience of that narrative via manipulation of the collection, and allows one to build and experience one's identity through it (Hoebink, Reijnders, and Waysdorf 2014). Damon and Fiennes discuss how private murderabilia collections differ or compare to museum collections. Predictably, the owner of the Hastings "True Crime Museum" argues for a didactic purpose to his public display, but his murderabilia collection is equally woven into his local and personal history, given that he received the beginnings of his collection through family history and contact with local murderers (Damon and Fiennes 2019, episode 3). The podcast hosts find themselves affected by the desire to touch, experience, and somehow understand the "authentic" experience of holding and touching real, material murderabilia, and are disappointed to discover that the letter from executed murderer Sean Sellers which they purchase online is in fact a photocopy. Geraghty (2014) and Hoebink, Reijnders, and Waysdorf (2014) all note that fan collection of memorabilia is an overlooked aspect of fan studies, which Geraghty attributes to "its basis in consumption rather than production" (2014, 2). Consumption is devalued in academic discourse. Fascinatingly, Jack Denham (2016) has written that once the serial killer moves from consumer (of people) to object of consumption (via their body), moral condemnation tends to transfer from the object of consumption—which is now the killer—to the ever-hungry consumer, the buyer, the collector, the hoarder. Again, I will explore this in chapter 4, in a discussion of contemporary murderabilia collection via the internet. I will be concerned with the authenticity of the material object, specifically its relationship to subcultural capital, and how this connects to the posited authenticity of the (wo)man outside the law. I will also be attentive to the objects' investment with meaning by the consuming collector. Murderabilia auction sites, including Holler's Serial Killer Inc, will be an important focus for this study.

For now, I must continue to set the groundwork via an examination of the pre-digital history of serial killer fandom. The celebrity psychopath of the twentieth century was created through the media surrounding Ted Bundy in particular. The contemporary media made much of the dichotomy between Bundy's civilized persona and the brutal facts of his crimes. AP News described him as a "charming killer" who "seems one of us" (Berlinger 2019a, episode 1). Bundy's outrageous, self-orchestrated trial, the first to be broadcast live on national television, has recently gained new popularity and attention via its heavy inclusion in writer-director Joe Berlinger's Netflix documentary series *Conversations with a Killer: The Ted Bundy Tapes* (Berlinger 2019a). Berlinger made this documentary simultaneously with the Zac Efron vehicle *Extremely Wicked, Shockingly Evil and Vile* (2019b), a biopic that essentially cuts re-enactments of the court scenes and historical footage with depictions of Bundy's private life based on an autobiographical book by his then-girlfriend Elizabeth Kloepfer. The biopic's title is taken from the judge's closing statements to Bundy, describing his crimes. In the next breath, the judge expressed regret at the path Bundy chose in life, told him he would have made a good lawyer, and admonished, "Take care of yourself. I don't have any animosity to[ward] you, I want you to know that" (2019a, episode 4; Yes, this really happened). Bundy seems to have had a similar effect on many people around him, and the *Bundy Tapes* recreates and reinforces the celebrity he enjoyed at the time of his trial. Reflecting on his eventual success in getting Bundy to talk (albeit in third-person) about his crimes, journalist Stephen Michaud admits, "I was there to tell his story" (Berlinger 2019a, episode 1). And the *Bundy Tapes* are *his* story, giving Bundy plenty of space to pontificate on the nature of history and fiction, recounting the press fascination, interviewing former associates discussing his chameleon-like ability to change his appearance. Even at his execution, investigative journalist Hugh Grant Aynesworth maintained that Bundy was "entertaining" with "a good sense of humour" despite being "a very devious, mean son of a gun" (episode 4). Attorneys on both sides of the case marvel at his audaciousness, his sheer force of character. This serves the conservative function of eliding the mistakes made by law enforcement in apprehending him. He was, after all, *just so special*. Some of the material I present in chapter 5 will parody this conservative function of crime texts.

Bundy, of course, did have multiple female fans attend his trial, who claimed to be "fascinated" by him, to the point of adopting the seventies fashions his victims favored. These included hoop earrings and shoulder-length brown hair with a center parting. Unlike the Ripper-baiters, these onlookers weren't attempting to assist law enforcement. Some believed him guilty, others did not (including his new girlfriend, Carol Boone, to whom he somehow managed to propose mid-trial). Bundy's trial set the template for the new type of celebrity criminal, and the press continued to construct him as a celebrity after his conviction. Having been re-apprehended after a prison break (his second), he was filmed returning to prison surrounded by reporters with flashing cameras, smirking conspiratorially at his public. Bundy's extreme star-power was most apparent at his execution by electric chair, one of the first major news stories to use satellite trucks for reporting. The execution was celebrated across America. Students from Florida State University—one of the institutions from which Bundy selected his victims—hung an enormous banner outside a fraternity accommodation reading "Watch Ted Fry/See Ted Die!" (see figure 1).

Figure 1. Celebratory banner at Florida State University (Public Domain image by Donn Dughi).

At the prison itself, a huge crowd had gathered with the news vans, and the atmosphere was carnivalesque. Onlookers drank, sang, cheered, and held up homemade signs reading "Hey Ted, this buzz is for you," "Burn Bundy Burn," and similar slogans (Berlinger 2019a, episode 4). Much of the crowd was comprised of Florida State students, who would have been, as Michaud observed, no more than ten at the time the crimes took place. Michaud considered the event an "excuse to get drunk and whoop it up" (Berlinger 2019a, episode 4). Folklorist Rachelle Saltzman reported:

> Visual representations and mock enactments of Bundy's execution while the event was occurring accompanied the word play [on the signs]. On the back of one truck was a life-size inflatable doll strapped into a chair and wearing a black ski mask topped by a chrome hubcap and a pair of antennae (Lyons and Trei 1989, 7a). Vendors hawked electric chair pins, and one spectator repeatedly staged a hanging with a doll while another carried a coffin. Some spectators wore imitation execution hoods (Davis 1989, 8a). Still others "sported aluminum-foil imitations of the electrode cap that was soon to be attached to Bundy's head to send the fatal surge of electricity to his brain" (Lyons and Trei 1989, 1a). (Saltzman 1995, 108)

Here is another form of cosplay that can be understood as the insertion of the self into a prominent public narrative. There is no discernible statement or meaning to the costumes: They are, as Joel Gn (2011) contends cosplay can be, pure spectacle. Gn likens this kind of cosplay to

> Baudrillard's (1994) conception of simulation or simulacra, whereby objects are simply copies without an original referent. This means that through the consumptive act in cosplay, the image becomes a disembodied sign that acquires its own material force (1994, 6). (2011, 587)

I will return to this idea of signs without referents in chapter 5. Moreover, the folkloric analysis aligns with an idea that the folklorists and anthropologists have put forth—the idea of the execution as Bakhtinian carnivalesque space. In this delimited space, licensed by authorities as set aside from ordinary life, social norms are suspended. Meaning, logic, rationality, and logos are discarded. Spectacle reigns. Saltzman found the atmosphere "festive [. . .] reminiscent of rowdy eighteenth- and nineteenth-century public hangings" (102). Once the execution was announced, fireworks were released (107). When the hearse removed Bundy's body, the crowd cheered and ran after it, as though for a celebrity limousine. It was even white (Berlinger 2019a, episode 4).

Fan conventions, gatherings, and spaces are likewise analyzed in carnivalesque terms and have been since Jenkins (1992; cf. Freund 2006; Booth 2016). Lynn Zubernis and Katherine Larsen argue that

> realworld fan spaces function both as liminal spaces and as sites of performance, play, veneration, and community norms [. . .] The circumscribed space of conventions has been described as a sort of "magic circle," within which fans all understand and share the event's parameters and norms (Huizinga 1955). (Zubernis and Larsen 2018)

Fan convention space particularly is described as a transitional space of temporary transgression, one that "encouraged open and creative expression within that space, even of behavior and ideas which would be censured in the broader culture" (Zubernis and Larsen 2018). Most people would not normally find it acceptable to admit they are happy to see a man die, especially if they work in law enforcement. Yet Lyons and Trei quote police offer Bob Duha at the execution as observing, "I went to this [execution] thinking it would be a solemn occasion, [. . .] but everybody's making this into a tailgate party and I'm a party animal" (1989, 7a). The idea of a magic circle will return in chapter 5, when I consider fandom as play.

Bundy's was the first case in which the mainstream media professed their consternation with serial killer "groupies," a term obviously borrowed from moral panics over young women's engagement with music. The term was revived for the trial of Richard "The Night Stalker" Ramirez in 1989–90. Ramirez murdered thirteen people across the Los Angeles area from 1984 to 1985, breaking into their homes apparently at random, and was also convicted of multiple rapes and molestations. A 1990 report for KRON 4 news interviewed several women who attended the sentencing. The featured participants are dressed in a somewhat gothic style, preferring dark clothes and sunglasses, perhaps in alignment with Ramirez's professed Satanism. "*They* are the women in black," intones reporter Chuck Coppola, "admirers of Richard Ramirez's" (KRON 4 2014 [1990]). Some defend Ramirez's character and claim he has been nice to them; others profess simple fascination with the audaciousness of his crimes and the length of time he evaded capture. Interestingly, the report seems to cast the women as the new criminals: "From Los Angeles to San Francisco, *they* stalk Ramirez" The stress is always on "they"—the anomaly, the Bad Other. *We* are legitimately, indeed professionally, fascinated by Ramirez; *they* are the freaks who want to sleep with him. I return here to Jack Denham's (2016) argument, that the "consuming fan" takes on the monstrousness of the consuming serial killer, who becomes a passive object. (Though Ramirez was obviously still alive at the time of this report, he is pictured in handcuffs as the fans "stalking" him are described; effectively, he is contained and neutralized). The press also made much of two women who were having an apparent feud over Ramirez's affections, with the *Current Affair* program dubbing him the "Death Row Romeo" (The Uncombed One 2017 [1990]). In the Netflix documentary series *Night Stalker: The Hunt for a Serial Killer,* reporter Tony Valdez remarked, "In all my years of covering trials in Los Angeles, I never saw a defendant with more sex appeal than Richard Ramirez. [. . .] [He had an] animalistic magnetism, [a] charisma women found attractive" (Russell and Carroll 2021, episode 4). *The Los Angeles Times* reported on a woman who attended his trial in a "skin-tight black spandex jumpsuit" and "smiled and waved" at the murderer (Timnick and Lee 1989). Many of the participants in the *Night Stalker* docuseries who are positioned as normal, rational, and sane attest to Ramirez's charisma and qualities of "specialness." "I remember when he walked through the door," states a crime scene technician: "He was tall and slender, he had these dark eyes" (Russell and Carroll 2021, episode 4). Her response when he looked directly at her was to think, "wow," she recalls—before going on to elaborate on her perception of "evil" in him. Police officer Gil Carrillo attests to a sensation of fear and awe at having Ramirez confined in an interview room: "If this guy starts to float around this room I'm outta here [. . .] [I thought] this guy's gonna levitate" (episode 4).

Ramirez also had explicit male admirers, though of course they are never called groupies. I have already mentioned murderabilia collector Erik Holler, who hailed Ramirez as a rockstar and considered Ramirez's in-court declaration of "Hail Satan" to be "fucking awesome" (Damon and Fiennes 2019, episode 1). Ramirez also had a penchant for drawing pentagrams on his palms: In the *Night Stalke*r documentary series, a trial witness recalls finding herself waiting outside the courtroom next to a boy with a pentagram tattoo. She refers to him as "somebody who looked up to" Ramirez, rather than a groupie (episode 4). The *Night Stalker* documentary likewise stresses Ramirez's charisma, introducing him via voiceover recordings that are initially unidentified—except that they are captioned in purple font, matching the font of the title screen, hinting towards their origin—and their uniqueness. They aren't unique—Ramirez's justifications and explanations are the standard self-aggrandizing melodrama, casting himself as the simple expression of human evil, sometimes "in alliance with the evil that is inherent in human nature" (episode 1), or at other times above all dull plebian society, "beyond good and evil" (episode 4), and so on and so on, the authentic man outside the law. Again. Ramirez's discussion of Satan and Satanism as his motivation and as a "stabilizing force" in his life provides the audio for real crime scene photography (episode 2), thus imposing his narrative and interpretation over that of the victims and their families. *Night Stalker* does make space for the victims—some of his survivors give their account of events, as do the families of those he murdered—but Ramirez, whose identity is not fully revealed until the final episode of the docuseries, remains the focus, the mystery and the star. Ramirez was actually apprehended by a group of citizens who saw him recognize his own photograph in the newspaper and attempt to flee. As he was transported to prison, a huge crowd gathered, screaming, cheering, and jumping up and down—supposedly for the police, though the arresting officer admits that the woman who lifted her shirt to show her breasts did so specifically for Ramirez (episode 4). Compare the crowds that gathered around Bundy's execution—supposedly for the victory of law. In sum, Bundy and Ramirez both attracted quite the range of fan-like engagement—but it is female behavior specifically that is pathologized. Reporter Laurel Erikson in *Night Stalker* describes a "clown car of these women" when discussing Ramirez's admirers, while a local resident declares them "the dumbest bitches ever" (episode 4). Compare the pathologization of "fangirls" as opposed to any other kind of fan.

Bundy and Ramirez are two of the most popular serial killers with present-day fans online, and both attracted high degrees of contemporary fanlike behavior. When I turn to Jeffrey Dahmer—almost if not equally popular in present-day online fandom—the picture is quite different. As Schmid demonstrated convincingly, "Dahmer's fame was qualitatively different from Bundy's" (2005, 220). So much contemporary media on Bundy had a tone of near admiration to it—as did the judge who sentenced him. Bundy's excellence at serial killing was a key point of discussion: A veritable expert at murder, detectives, journalists, and criminologists consulted with him extensively after his apprehension on the motives and patterns of other serial killers for the insight he'd be able to provide. Granted, this was partly an appeal to his narcissism designed to derive a full confession—Bundy initially spoke about his crimes entirely in the third person, opining like a theatrical professor on the sort of person who would have done such things—but it solidified his cultural status as an expert, professional, and above all, accomplished character. Jeffrey Dahmer was afforded no such authority. His tragic, monstrous queerness, combined with his cannibalistic tendences (exaggerated, but true) precluded this. Dahmer was the cultural monster Bundy wasn't. Newspapers were obsessed with the fact that he had consumed human flesh—and apparently compared the taste to "filet mignon" (Tithecott 1995, 6). The contemporary term for Dahmer's crimes was "homosexual overkill"—as opposed, one contemporary journalist commented satirically, to "'good old heterosexuals' [who] 'kill people just the right amount'" (122).

Dahmer had few contemporary fans in the traditional sense. He was certainly a celebrity. At his trial, the sisters of two of his victims protested that, while Dahmer's face was everywhere, their brothers were forgotten (Tithecott 1995, 167–68). But he did not have many fans who behaved in the identifiably fannish ways I have documented above, so far as I have been able to ascertain. Phyllis Chesler does report a "growing number of women supporters" at his trial, some of whom "reportedly formed a Jeffrey Dahmer fan club" (1993, 963), but they never seemed to receive the publicity that Bundy's and Ramirez's fans did. In any case, it can be argued that if Dahmer had fans, they were far fewer, less visible, and less vocal than the fans of Bundy and Ramirez. He had admirers, typically homophobes: "Sales were brisk for a poster issued by the Oregon Citizen's Alliance that read 'Free Jeffrey Dahmer: All he did was kill homosexuals'" (Tithecott 1995, 10). An organizer for the Lesbian Alliance of Metro Milwaukee reported to Martha A. Schmidt that "we get a lot of phone calls here. People saying, 'I think Jeffrey Dahmer is a wonderful person. He did the right thing. Get rid of those queers'" (Schmidt 1994, 88). A lesbian social worker recalled hearing people on the street call Dahmer a hero. In the sphere of performativity and roleplay, the president of the Gay/Lesbian International News Network received the following answering machine message: "Hello, this is Jeffrey Dahmer. I want your head in my refrigerator. Call me" (88). This admiration is more about hatred of queer people than affection for or interest in Dahmer (who was, of course, queer). So far as Dahmer is depicted now, portrayals tend toward pity and interest—not empathetic, but to a degree, sympathetic, thus playing into the trope of the tragic queer and queer death. The *Biography* episode "Jeffrey Dahmer: The Monster Within" (Harris 1996) depicts its subject as a tragic Jekyll, struggling futilely to contain his inner Hyde, finding soon after "his first murder" that "only alcohol erased the horror and violence" in his mind. At his arrest he is described as "whining . . . like a baby crying noise about him." More grotesque than guilty, as the arresting detective reports,

Dahmer cried, "went into a rage," and appealed to be allowed to kill himself. The prison chaplain describes him as "like a little boy." His construction could not be further from the charismatic ringmaster of the *Bundy Tapes*, yet even Dahmer seemed to be aware of the immediate celebritization that was about to overtake his trial, telling the detective: "When I tell you what I'm gonna tell you, you're gonna be famous." But Dahmer—the tragic, monstrous queer killer/victim—certainly has fans now. He is one of the most popular serial killers on the internet. Thus the contemporary fandom of this queer killer forms an important point of contrast to Bundy and Ramirez.

Another queer serial killer who appears to have *gained* a fandom in the contemporary sense is Aileen Wuornos. Wuornos was a lesbian sex worker who was systematically abused more or less from birth, and went on to kill seven male clients between 1989 and 1990. Though she initially testified that each time she had been in fear for her life, that each man had tried to rape her, her story changed a great deal, sometimes claiming to have killed in cold blood, "real nasty" (in Schmid 2005, 240). Wuornos killed in a way that is unusual for women: She killed strangers, outdoors, with a gun (Rogers 2010, 56). In short, she killed like a man. Kyra Pearson argues that the media masculinized Wuornos in order to make her intelligible:

> Reporters introduced the public to its "first female serial killer" through biographical information. While characterizations of her as an anomalous female killer classified her as a murderer who should not, by definition, have existed, biographies about her life preceding the murders suggested that her killing was inevitable. Though contradictory, these claims mutually reinforced one another by drawing upon criminality as a gendered category. The logic was: she was anomalous because she killed like male serial killers do, and her killing was inevitable because Wuornos's upbringing had predisposed her to a life of crime, invoking criminality as a category that seemingly confirms masculinity. (2007, 265)

Unlike Dahmer, Wuornos did have public, vocal defenders at and shortly after her apprehension. These were mostly feminists, who maintained her "right to self-defense" (Chesler 1993), highlighted her history of trauma and abuse, and pointed to the discrepancies between her trial and the trials of Bundy and indeed of Dahmer. Dahmer was at least "able to command a private lawyer" and had the support of his family in court (963). Wuornos had no such resources. Bundy was offered a plea bargain; Wuornos was not (963). Several lawyers offered to defend Bundy pro bono. Wuornos's public defender was more interested in negotiating a film deal than defending his client. Some of her contemporary defenders sound like admirers: Phyllis Chesler refers to Wuornos's acts as "Everywoman's most forbidden fantasy and Everyman's worst nightmare" (934). Feminists like Chesler are concerned primarily to situate Wuornos within the context of systematic abuse that the judicial system ignored, and in doing so, they sometimes posit her actions as justified: "Was a quarter-million johns all Wuornos could take before she cracked, or, dare I say it, experienced a momentary flight into sanity?" (958). This reads like a radical feminist take on Trilling's observations of insanity-as-authenticity, or so-called insanity as the natural response to a society that is itself completely insane (1972). For Chesler, society's treatment of women—particularly poor women, sex workers, and lesbians—is insane.

Wuornos remains at some level another tragic queer: Nick Broomfield's pair of documentaries *The Selling of a Serial Killer* (1992) and *Aileen: Life and Death of a Serial Killer* (2003) focus on her exploitation before and after her crimes. His work makes it clear that every single person around Wuornos, from her lawyers to her born-again Christian adopted mother, was intent on profiting off of her. Indeed, Broomfield has been accused of continuing this exploitation (see Schilt 2000), regardless of his sympathy for Wuornos; he is still a comparatively wealthy, comparatively powerful man gaining money and status from her life story. That said, Wuornos did not perform like a tragic queer. Dahmer was contrite and miserable in court, apologizing to his victims' families and professing that if he could give up his own life to bring them back, he would. After her sentencing, Wuornos admonished the court, "I'll be up in heaven while y'all rotting in hell" and told the jury, "May your wife and kids get raped. Right in the ass" (in Broomfield 1992). Shortly before her execution, she appears in Broomfield's documentaries to have become completely out of touch with reality, claiming that organization (the prison system? the judiciary?) is manipulating her brain through technology inside her cell, and moreover, that the police deliberately made her into a serial killer, and were surveilling her before she ever killed. She then compares herself to Jesus and informs the public that we are all about to be "nuked" (2003). There is absolutely a pathos here, but Wuornos remains an elusive and "difficult" figure who evades categorization:

> She is more than just victim, and more than predator.
> She doesn't fit comfortably into either the "serial" or "spree" murder categories.
> She is and isn't a lesbian. She is not the media's monster,

> and is also a little too broken to be the feminist vigilante we need . . .
> She is, absolutely, an outlaw. (Gottlieb in Robinson 2014, 142)

Though sensitive to the claims of exploitation that have been made around Broomfield's work, Christine Rogers (2010) appreciates it for breaking Wuornos out of the typical modes of narration used for violent women: victims, mad, or bad. Sometimes Wuornos seems mad—sometimes she is rational. Sometimes she seems vicious, vindictive—at other times she is professing her love and thanks for the documentary maker. Sometimes she is a victim. Sometimes she is wishing for the jury's children to be anally raped. Indeed, the Charlize Theron biopic *Monster* (Jenkins 2003) has been rightfully criticized for oversimplifying Wuornos, portraying her as reluctant prostitute who is a "fool for love," pushed back again and again to a life of crime by her nubile young (fictional) lover (Rogers 2010, 58). Rogers wrote that Wuornos inspired a special public hatred, in contrast to the near-admiration male serial killers seem to elicit. This is no longer the case. For as Murley acknowledges, the internet has also opened up the consideration and reaction to crime to a much more diverse range of voices than have dominated the official professional genres (2008, 133–49). For example, in 2019, the extremely popular hip-hop artist Cardi B used a promotional photograph inspired by a famous picture of Wuornos, in which Wuornos holds up her own handcuff chain to her neck. Cardi B, a former sex worker who has stated that she stripped to escape domestic violence, tweeted the photograph of herself imitating the pose as part of a promotional drive (Barret-Ibarria 2019). Fannish response was immediate: "Yea props to Aileen Wuornos!!" one fan replied. Fandom for the rapper and fandom for the serial killer with whom she is identifying collide. "This is so political," tweeted Black lesbian activist Dani Love: "I actually strongly support this. I respect it. I'm actually mind blown by this" (in Barrett-Ibarria 2019). Online clothing shop proprietor and designer Eric Lee created a "t-shirt juxtaposing that iconic image of Wuornos in handcuffs with Hillary Clinton's presidential campaign slogan 'I'm With Her.'" It remains one of his most popular designs. Lee states:

> I was fed up with the phony agendas of neo-liberal politics. [. . .] Career politicians that pretend to give a shit about poor people while supporting legislation that kills them. I wanted to say something about it and happened to be reading a lot about Aileen Wuornos at the time. She was the definition of disenfranchised. (in Barrett-Ibaria 2019)

Drag performer Willam Belli created a parody song named "Aileen" to the tune of Dolly Parton's "Jolene," which contains the lines "She hated men just like I do / But she had the balls to follow though" (Belli 2018). Fandom of Aileen Wuornos, then, seems to be qualitatively different from the other kinds of fandom so far encountered, and the findings will bear this out. It is more like fandom of an idea than a person—the idea that structural violence against women and girls deserves to be met with violence, and if a few johns have to die for that, so be it. This is certainly less supportive of conservative and patriarchal ideologies than the traditional "special mysterious genius psychopath finally caught by dogged investigators" myth that texts around Bundy and to a lesser extent Ramirez tend to uphold—but then, the source texts on Wuornos, like the Broomfield documentaries, are distinctly less conservative than the *Bundy Tapes*.

I have now established a range of fannish behavior around nineteenth and twentieth century serial killers, existing before scholars began to consider fandom as community or fandom in digital space. I have observed solid evidence of popular imaginative engagement with serial killer media as a form of proto-convergence, of textual and performative play, of the insertion of the self into public narratives and constructions of these killers. I noted especially the pathologizing of female fannish behavior, as opposed to more professionalized and legitimized forms of male "interest." Finally, I observed that famous queer and female serial killers Dahmer and Wuornos did not attract the sort of fannish behavior that Bundy and Ramirez did, but have in recent years attracted fanbases on the internet. Next, in chapter 2, I begin the systematic application of fan studies lenses to online serial killer fandom, starting with the work of Henry Jenkins.

CHAPTER 2

Textual Poaching to Discursive Formations

Serial Killers and Fannish Creation

Henry Jenkins's *Textual Poachers* (1992) is considered a foundational text for fan studies. A twentieth anniversary re-issue with an author interview and an edition of the *Journal of Fandom Studies* dedicated to its influence bear witness to its enduring presence as a touchstone in our field (Jenkins 2013; Larsen 2014a). Jenkins himself is always the first to acknowledge that the theory has dated in fundamental ways, and, moreover, that the book contains significant weaknesses, but without it fan studies as we know it would not exist. Its key tenet is that fan audiences "poach," or take from the texts of corporate media whatever aspects are of interest to them, and rework those aspects in innovative, communally informed, and communally interpreted ways.

The lens of textual poaching has been developed both by Jenkins and others into a less top-down approach, in keeping with the current landscape of media convergence and active meaning-making processes of fans. In this chapter, I applied these lenses across a range of fannish sites, including the major fanfic archives the Archive of Our Own (AO3), Fanfiction.net, and Wattpad, as well as the multimedia sites YouTube, TikTok, and Tumblr, on which creative fanwork has a strong presence. I also incorporate some of my own insights regarding discursive construction by fans, exploring how far fans actually create the objects of their interest amongst their own communities. I found that the older poaching model was, in many ways, more suited to this relatively small and stigmatized fandom than the model of media convergence, but that a discourse-analytic approach that accounts for fannish construction serves as a necessary corrective to viewing the process as primarily (or entirely) top-down and derived from media corporations.

When Jenkins was writing, it was easier to think of fandom as comprised of relatively contained subcultures, largely pre-internet and reliant on zines, word of mouth, and physical meeting places. Like his contemporaries Camille Bacon-Smith (1992) and Constance Penley (1997), who both utilized the poaching metaphor, Jenkins was actively and deliberately working to counter contemporary stereotypes of fans as pathological, isolated, obsessive, juvenile, and pitiful—the stereotype that fans have "no life." He also introduced the idea of the "aca-fan," the researcher who, far from standing objectively and looking (down) upon their subjects, occupies a hybrid identity as both fan and scholar. In an introductory interview to the new edition, Jenkins stressed the importance of the fannish subculture in both producing and interpreting texts:

> When my mentor, John Fiske (1992), said he was a "fan," he meant simply that he liked a particular program, but when I said I was a fan, I was claiming membership in a particular subculture. Meaning-making in Fiske was often individualized, whereas in my work, meaning-making is often deeply social. (2013, xiv)

The meanings which fans poach and create often differ emotionally, socially, and politically from those of media producers, and may privilege pleasures traditionally thought of as feminine (relational, sexual, emotional) in the face of androcentric media. "Slash" (the queer pairing of canonically straight characters) was easy to read politically at a time when queer pairings in media were either absent or a joke. Slash communities remained a relatively secretive sub-section of larger fandoms (Bacon-Smith 1992), and as Lucy Bennett observed:

> Within *Textual Poachers*, a tenet that proved influential towards my work is the concept of fans reading a text in the "correct" way that is dependent on the relevant fan culture and community. Exploring the processes at work between fans and the fan text, Jenkins argued that this "right way" of reading and approaching the text as a fan or object of fandom is determined and enforced by normative fan identity. (2014, 14)

In approaching the poaching habits of serial killer fans, the observation of interpretation being determined by fan identity seems as true today as it did at publication. Serial killer fans have particular ways of reading and appropriating texts which resonate with each other and are shunned by communal outsiders, specifically, by other kinds of fans. Thus, aspects of the poaching idea still resonate, particularly when scholars apply it to contemporary forms of fan creativity like GIF-creation, vidding, and gaming practices (Hautch 2018; Walliss 2010; Nguyen 2016; see also Zhao 2019; Matthews 2018; and Palmer 2021 for more recent engagement with the model). Larsen suggests that perhaps the best evidence of poaching's importance is the fact that we now take so many of its principles for granted: "Of course fan cultures are participatory; of course that participation often involves cultural critique; and of course fandom involves renegotiating the terms of engagement between fans and producers" (2014b, 3).

But the idea of fans as relatively powerless, industrially voiceless nomads largely cut off from the processes of media production had become dated as early as the mid-2000s. In acknowledgement of this, Jenkins published *Convergence Culture.* The media environment has absolutely transformed over the past thirty years, leading Jenkins to acknowledge that it's best to read *Poachers* as a "time capsule which captures a particular moment of transition within fandom—the beginnings of the end of the era of print zines, the beginnings of the era of digital networks" (2013, xx). His use of the phrase "convergence culture" represents a shift in the relations between audience, technology, and producers, as he argued that "fandom is one of those spaces where people are learning how to live and collaborate within a knowledge community" (2006, 134). This learning takes many forms, from increasingly direct engagement with media producers and production to the creation and participation in communities of collective intelligence via database building, knowledge sharing, and creative collaboration. These cultural shifts are enabled by increasing digital connectivity, the development of more advanced and user-friendly tools to create and edit media, and economic models favoring multimedia narratives using mixed modes of broad- and narrowcasting.

As the findings below show, serial killer fandom seems to fit rather better into the older model—where fans are poachers, relatively powerless, subordinated, and pathologized by the broader culture. They often have little to no involvement with media production and no particular engagement with media producers. One criticism of Jenkins's views in *Poachers* centered around ideas of labor and reward: in sum, the school of thought that as users/viewers dissect media, create content, review, respond, hashtag and tweet, we are not so much poaching the fields as tilling them (Andrejevic 2013). We are performing free labor, which adds value and creates revenue for copyright holders (Andrejevic 2008; Lothian 2009; Milner 2009). Jenkins recognizes these criticisms, and draws a distinction between

> participatory culture (a broad movement which takes many different forms across history), fandom (a specific kind of participatory culture with its own history and traditions), and Web 2.0 (a business model which seeks to capitalize and commodify participatory culture). (2013, xxii)

At first glance, serial killer fandom might seem to rebut these criticisms of the *Poachers* model and demonstrate its continued applicability. It is fairly difficult for the media industry to profit from and reappropriate TikTok videos admiring the sexiness of Richard Ramirez the Night Stalker. Or is it? Sentiment mining, vibology, and interest monitoring do indeed benefit the media industries, which have never been particularly hesitant about presenting the so-called "Death Row Romeo" as sex symbol. On the other hand, such sentiment mining also has to account for the exclamations of horror and disgust this content inevitably meets; it can certainly be argued that serial killer fandom is *less* co-optable, less profitable, and less automatically generative of revenue than mainstream forms of fan creativity.

Many scholars have raised the point that some forms of fan labor in convergence culture are, for better or worse, more incorporable than others (Scott 2019; Busse 2013, 2015). Suzanne Scott has done significant work on the typically gendered nature of this divide, noting that forms of fan work that are typically gendered masculine, such as modding and collecting, are often more valued, more visible, and more economically rewarded than those gendered feminine, such as writing slash. Scott (2019) coined the term "convergence culture industry" to describe the prioritization, appropriation, reward, and revaluation of fanwork that is typically gendered masculine. Consider the creation of wikis, the demonstration of and collation of encyclopedic knowledge, the creation of video game spinoffs via modification and streaming channels—even the occasional promotion of fanboy to industry-insider blogger or game developer. These shifts have been enabled by the cultural and economic revaluation of geek culture, and as Scott's 2019 work *Fake Geek Girls* encapsulates, girls and women are very often perceived as inauthentic outsiders here. To be clear, Scott isn't suggesting that the solution is to incorporate, repackage, and appropriate GIFs, fanvids, and fanfiction too. She is merely applying a critical lens to the celebration of convergence culture, asking whom it benefits, in what ways, and whom and what it excludes. I wonder, though, if the reappropriation of more fanwork gendered feminine is, in fact, where convergence culture is headed. This has not happened on any large scale yet—but it might be starting. Witness the *Fifty Shades of Grey* machine. The day when some form of slash fic reworked for traditional publication secures its film deal may well be on the horizon (by the time this book is published, it may have happened). Serial killer fanfiction, by and large, is not publishable in any traditional sense, and not recuperable by the convergence culture industry except as fodder for clickbait articles. Thus it returns us to the textual poaching lens of early scholarship.

Finally, I myself have developed the lenses of convergence culture and textual poaching in a rather different direction. In my 2020 book *Emo: How Fans Defined a Subculture,* I argued that we need to look beyond the idea of fans "taking" and "re-adapting" from industry. Emo, or emotional hardcore, is a music genre that I demonstrated had developed a coherent mainstream definition in the late 2010s—because fandom made one for it. "Emo" meant many things to many people for decades—but now, it has a relatively stable set of reference points that fans invented during the expansion of home broadband, which was then taken up by the music industry and resold. This occurs through the operations of discourse theory—the active, definitional properties of language to construct objects and positions (as opposed to "reflecting" something that already exists in reality). Since I first began applying discourse analysis to fanwork (Fathallah 2017), I have made the point that discursive analysis needs to take account of the reaction to and reception of statements. Statements can be rejected, silenced, and banned—or applauded, repeated, and elevated, and thus gain more definitional impact. That is why I take account of comments, views, and responses to fanwork in my samples (see below). The relevance of these insights here is that I will investigate to what degree serial killer fans define their own object of fandom, as opposed to poaching it in what is ultimately still a top-down model. What is the "Richard Ramirez" or "Aileen Wuornos" that fans celebrate? To what degree is it a poached and reappropriated object? To what degree is it a collective fannish invention? The key difference here to my former work is that when I looked at emo, for example, I had years' worth of archived, solidified, and curated material to explore—and these acts of archivism and collection are a kind of discursive consolidation. Serial killer fandom is rarely archived. Its materials vanish. Creators take it down after receiving backlash. Sites ban it. Its constructions are altogether a more fleeting and ephemeral phenomena. Yet it persists, and it has a cultural memory—several times, in this sample work, I found authors and creators claiming to have returned after being banned, creating a new account and identity, and continuing their discursive constructions.

I made the survey for this chapter across a selection of websites that host fannish content, informed by my preliminary reading on serial killer fandom and its venues. I began the search for fanfiction at the Archive of Our Own (AO3), then moved on to Wattpad, a less popular site overall but more popular within this niche. I then turned to YouTube and Tumblr for visual data, before venturing into relatively new territory as I explored TikTok. I will explain my exact methods and findings as I treat the sites in turn, and discuss how the lenses of textual poaching, convergence culture, and discursive construction have illuminated my findings. All the searches for this analysis were performed in January and February of 2022.

AO3 is a project of the Organization for Transformative Works, a nonprofit organization devoted to encouraging, promoting, preserving, and defending fanworks. It thus has something of a semi-official presence within many fan cultures (a fact which not all fans have been comfortable with). "Serial killers: fandom" and "serial killers—fandom" are both functional tags on AO3 (meaning that users have applied these as tags using a freeform system), though they have not been marked as common. I searched using both these tags, then excluded stories that were explicitly based on fictional portrayals and franchises. I noted the number of hits, comments, and kudos,[1] as well the completion status, on each story, and listed the results in table 1.[2] The table items are arranged by number of kudos in descending order.

---

[1] Kudos on AO3 are akin to "Likes."

[2] The only item on the list that I did not find by tag is the "Book One" entry, which was

Three points stand out at once: firstly, that self-proclaimed serial killer fanfic is not popular on this site. There are only twenty-two entries here, and the AO3 hosts over seven million fanworks in over forty thousand fandoms. Secondly, that several of the stories are unfinished, which may suggest a lack of audience engagement. This impression is confirmed by an exchange (2021) between author sunhealer24 and a reviewer in discussion of continuing the story "Safe and Sound":

> I am aware that I write for a very niche community, especially since my writing often tends to cross the line into taboo subjects that no one wants to think too hard about. I also understand that my writing is far from the best out there. (sunhealer24 2021)
>
> > It's been a while since I checked on this tag on ao3 (i admit i have obsessed over true crime for months, particularly Bundy's case) so when i read your fic I was immediately hooked [. . .] I'm a fan of this story of yours and if you ever need a beta reader, or heck just someone to talk to and exchange ideas with, I would be delighted to be there for you. (crowbar_p1per 2021)

The author also refers to her interest in "true crime," showing that for this reader and author, there is no distinction between "true crime" and the serial killer fandom with which the fic is tagged. Finally, note the dominance of three specific serial killers in the text: Ramirez, Bundy, and Dahmer. Wuornos features in just one, and then only briefly, as a throwaway side character. The media celebrification of certain male serial killers is thus amplified here. The relatively small sample on AO3 meant that I was able to inductively code every story thematically. The key themes I found are as follows:

A. Historical metalepsis

Metalepsis, a kind of self-conscious interplay between fiction and reality, is frequently discussed by scholars of digital fiction. I have written elsewhere that it is particularly applicable to Real Person Fiction (RPF),[3] because the "hypertextual, multimodal context of digital fiction allows for specific forms of metalepsis, which [. . .] we see at work in RPF in genre-specific ways" (Fathallah 2018a, 569). Here I was referring to the integration of real-world

---

linked directly from "Book Two." For all fan texts, titles and author names are stylized and capitalized as on the site quoted. Fan texts, reviews, comments, and responses are all *sic*, with minimal corrections/insertions to avoid confusion.

[3] I.e., fanfiction featuring real people, living or dead.

images and video into fictional text, which I did not find on AO3, but did on Wattpad (see below). The historical metalepsis I found on AO3 comprised a form of textual poaching based on a communal body of knowledge: knowledge of the serial killer's life, times, and certain key texts about him or her.

B. Fix-it/redemption arcs

"Fix-it fics" are a staple in many fandoms, serving to correct perceived injustices, failings, or tragedies in plotlines (or indeed, historical events). These stories tend to explain or rationalize a murderer's behavior as caused by trauma, mental illness, or adverse life events, and provide redemption narratives assisted by original characters/authorial insertions.

C. Self-referential comment on serial killer fandom

When a discursive construction is sufficiently developed, it begins to produce statements about itself and its norms. I found this less with regard to the killers as personas, but significantly so with regard to their fandom, as fans interrogated their own fascination with and affection for serial killers.

D. Sex

The explicit sexualization of serial killers was another theme. In the cases of Richard Ramirez and Ted Bundy, this theme is easily poached from mainstream media and adapted to the author's purposes.

E. Romanticization/cute-ification

These stories were less focused on explicit sex, more on discursively constructing the character as otherwise appealing/likeable. There is less "poachable" media content here, relying more on fan construction (though, cf. the relatively sympathetic portrayals of Dahmer and Wuornos considered in the previous chapter).

As table 1 shows, "A Handsome Face with a Monster Inside" by nevermoreflesh (2018) was the single most popular story tagged "serial killer fanfic/fandom," as measured by kudos. This story tells of a fictional meeting between Jeffrey Dahmer and Ted Bundy, whom the summary introduces as "perfect for each other, but not in the way you might expect." Metalepsis is established by reference to "canon":

> Note: The year is 1988, canonically Ted is 40 and Jeff is 28. He's also living at his grandmother's house at this time, though in this AU Jeff has started to work at Ambrosia and just killed his second victim. [. . .] Bundy escaped from Aspen to Florida, and was never caught again due to not attempting to kidnap Carole Deronch (hopefully That's how you spell it). (nevermoreflesh 2018)

"Canon" in fictional fandoms is a (disputed) body of works considered as authorized, and/or to have come from the official creators and owners of a text. (Multimedia franchise fandoms often dispute which materials "count" as canon, such as spinoff novels, prequels, or post-hoc comments from directors and writers.) The story explicitly flits between fact and fiction, positing fiction as an "AU," or "alternative universe" in fandom speak. Other Real Person fandoms also utilize this term to deviate from the real-life circumstances of their characters. The author states that it should be "pretty obvious I don't condone, because this story isn't romantic at all," thus implying that other serial killer fanfics—more romantic ones—might actually be written by authors who condone the killer's actions.

The story goes some way towards humanizing Bundy, attributing to him the "non-violent, non-sadistic pleasure" of enjoying socks (an invented quirk), but utilizes a particular imagistic trope that several real-life witnesses and acquaintances attributed to Bundy: his chameleon-like qualities. From Dahmer's point of view, "Ted's eyes were brown or black, but as the sun came over them he realized that they were in fact, blue. It was inhuman- extremely strange. It felt like looking at a whole different man" (nevermoreflesh 2018). This statement solidifies the construction of Bundy popularized by such media as *The Bundy Tapes*, wherein witnesses and law enforcement officials testify that Bundy seemed to change before them, including that particular quality of his eyes (episode 2). This statement ultimately ties into the conservative impetus of true crime media: It is not that law enforcement missed opportunities, but that the killer has some special ability to evade them. *The Bundy Tapes* thus provides a textual touchstone of which the community is presumed to be aware, similar to the way that key texts provided touchstones for Jenkins's communities of interpretation. Indeed, a commenter on a different Bundy fanfic acknowledges, "I just saw the tapes. Amazing" (JiKook_Namjin_taegiseok 2019), to which the author agrees: "So interesting right?!" (michaelsmistress 2019a). Acknowledged textual touchstones tie these stories together as poached within the same structure.

Table 1. Serial Killer Fanfic from AO3

Title	Author	Year
A Handsome Face with a Monster Inside	nevermoreflesh	2018
Life's Too Short to Match Your Socks	michaelsmistress	2019
A Second Chance	Upset	2020
Baby, I'm an Animal (But You Can Have a Taste)	orphan account	2020
Safe and Sound	Sunhealer24	2021
The One Where True Crime Meets High-school	orphan account	2018
Candy Necklace	Yolandi	2019
Blood Moon Rising	HauntedAttic	2021
Philocaly: My Love. My Beauty	orphan account	2017
We Don't Need to Be Friends	orphan account	2020
Flesh without Blooo	lovetoomanythings	2021
In This Together	jdimh7	2022
We Can See the Stars ... And They Don't Burn Anymore ...	2Lady4Mental6Hospital9	2020
Minutes of Joy	2Lady4Mental6Hospital9	2020
The Most Beautiful Happiness for Lizzie and Ted	2tady4Mental6Hospital8	2020
The Love of My Life-ls You, My Dear Lizzie	2Lady4Mental6Hospital8	2020
A Collection of Poems about Jeffrey Dahmer and the Original Female Character	2Lady4Mental6Hospital9	2020
Spinning Wheel	orphan account	2020
Don't Let Be This Eno in the Name of Love	2Lady4Mental6Hospital9	2020
Breaking and Entering	LittleMinxxx	2022
Book One-Jeffrey Lionel Dahmer	cheeto_twat	2021
Book Two-Theodore Robert Cowell [Ted Bundy]	cheeto_twat	2021

Table 1. Serial Killer Fanfic from AO3 (continued)

Characters	Hits	Comments	Kudos	Words	Cmplt
Ted Bundy,Jeffrey Dahmer	4,544	17	121	4,544	y
Ted Bundy	4081	7	105	10,699	y
Jeffrey Dahmer	2956	45	100	18,220	n
Richard Ramirez	1778	3	63	941	y
Ted Bundy	1527	32	61	2,710	n
Wuornos, Bundy, Ramirez, Gacy	2714	34	51	4,452	n
Richard Ramirez	1231	3	35	1,654	y
Ted Bundy, Jeffrey Dahmer	449	9	30	6,380	n
Jeffrey Dahmer	564	4	27	538	y
Richard Ramirez	318	6	24	1,938	y
Richard Ramirez	928	4	24	5,053	n
Jeffrey Dahmer	688	6	18	30,042	y
Ted Bundy	239	0	17	1,534	y
Ted Bundy	99	0	15	435	y
Ted Bundy	175	2	13	2,762	y
Ted Bundy	144	0	13	2,467	y
Jeffrey Dahmer	194	2	10	1,151	n
Jeffrey Dahmer	262	0	9	14,383	n
Ted Bundy	101	0	7	1,628	y
Richard Ramirez	177	0	7	3,093	y
Jeffrey Dahmer	64	0	2	538	y
Ted Bundy	192	0	3	725	y
Total	**23,425**	**174**	**755**	**115,887**	
Average	**1,065**	**8**	**34**	**5,268**	

"A Handsome Face" concludes with a fantasy scenario: The killers meet, and agree to go home together, each believing he is going to murder the other. The reader is left to imagine which, if either, would succeed. As reader, I was left with the impression of a short, fantastical horror story, rather like the untold number written about Jack the Ripper.

"Spinning Wheel" is similarly billed as:

> a novel of explicit and psychotic nature. With Jeffrey Dahmer as the main protagonist, the novel works around other killings in the same era with knowledge while including Dahmer as It's hitching post. The book is written under numerous points of view, as well as, the use of partial and impartial AU. Also, speaks on the secrets that Dahmer himself may have taken to the grave. (orphan_account 1 2020)

Look again at the interplay between avowed fiction, speculation, and history. The story is meticulously researched, creating a fictionalized "backstage" for a real period in Dahmer's life when he was stationed as a soldier in Germany. Several unsolved murders that took place in the area at that time were reinvestigated after Dahmer's apprehension, and in this story, of course, he is responsible. The author adds these historical circumstances, complete with quotations (which are correctly attributed but not sourced as they would be in an official document) as notes to the end of the piece. The story makes use of multiple points of view, notably those of Dahmer's fellow soldiers and associates, for whom the author has created fictionalized identities, informing us that "[the character] Andrew is actually Billy Capshaw (who is still alive til this day and don't wish to use his name for this reason)" (orphan_account 1 2020). This statement is interesting. The textual poaching utilized for this historical metalepsis seems to have a moral limit: Real, living people are off limits. This moral limit certainly does not apply to other kinds of Real Person Fiction.

"In This Together" and "A Second Chance," two other AO3 stories, are key examples of fix-it fics, thematically speaking. I consider them as a form of discursive construction, as authorial self-insertions and original characters are both utilized to assist in the character's redemption arcs, though traditional textual poaching is also in evidence. In "In This Together,"

> Amelia is a shy, lonely, friendless teen who can relate to America's most notorious serial killer, Jeffrey Dahmer, on why he did his crimes. She decides to help him when

> no one else did. She uses a small time machine to travel back in time and make this come true. (jdimh7 2022a)

Again, though the piece is explicitly tagged as a fanfic, the author professes not to "condone what he did" and wishes "may everyone rest in peace, and I mean EVERYONE who died. I don't condone what he did but I feel like he could've been helped. Like I really do" (jdimh7 2022a). "EVERYONE" then, includes Dahmer. Again, this sympathetic perspective is not unique to fanfic but poachable from mainstream media. John Backderf, for example, is the author of the very successful graphic novel *My Friend Dahmer*, later made into a film (Backderf 2012; Meyers 2017). Though Backderf professes to lose sympathy for Dahmer after his first kill, his regret for the damaged teenager he knew is explicit in his work. As an author profile in *The Independent* newspaper puts it:

> Backderf doesn't believe the course Dahmer's life took was inevitable, though, and his question has always been: where were the adults? Dahmer's behavior was bizarre, and his drinking was obvious to everyone, but no one in authority intervened.
>
> "They didn't care. They just pushed him along and figured, 'Well, next year he'll be somebody else's problem.' And of course he was somebody else's problem." (in Applebaum 2018)

"A Second Chance," in which the second-person narrator raises Dahmer from the dead in order to assist in his redemption arc, references *My Friend Dahmer* (2012) explicitly. The narrator has a copy of the graphic novel in her home, which the characters consult, and authorial notes explain their discussion with reference to the graphic novel. "In This Together" quotes Dahmer (again correctly, but without reference) in his more sympathetic moments:

> "It made it feel like they were apart of me." Those were the words Jeffrey Dahmer said to FBI agent and author, Robert Ressler, on why he ate his victims.
>
> A quote of Jeffrey is, "What worth is life if you can't be helpful to someone?", and I think that getting him involved with the community can make him feel worthy and that his life can be meaningful even if It's a little. (jdimh7 2022a)

The Amelia character assists the would-be killer in getting the proper diagnoses of mental illnesses, allowing him to "function in life." She does experience moments of fear, when she wonders if he will in fact attempt to kill her, and experiences a frightening dream where this happens. But she is ultimately "able to prevent Jeff from becoming this monster that we all know of." The author confesses in the notes that "JD is the serial killer [t] hat's most captivating to me," because she can "understand not having any friends and being lonely" (jdimh7 2022a). Despite her claims to absolutely not condone his acts, she agrees with a commenter that they are both "Jeffrey Dahmer supporter[s] all the way" (jdimh2 2022b).

"A Second Chance" is very similar thematically, with the notable difference that it is written in second person. The main character is "you." This is uncommon in fanfic, as in other forms of fiction, and prompts a degree of self-reflection in the reader. His or her deliberate choice to read this story is an involvement, perhaps an implication, in this fandom. Again, the redemption arc is explicit, indeed religious, as the notes instruct:

> You've been given the gift of resurrection, by God, who can say?
>
> However, you unknowingly bring back something much bigger and more dangerous than yourself, but you aren't so quick to give him up.
>
> Will you be able to keep the Milwaukee Monster under control and show him how to adapt to a much different society, one that he may very well thrive in? (Upset 2020)

The author once again states that she does not condone the killer's act, but bills the story as

> a psychological experiment based on a question I often asked myself regarding Jeffrey's early life and circumstances: could he have had a chance at a normal life in our current society, one that has come to accept homosexuality and views a fascination with paleontology as potential rather than freakish sickness?

Again, there is little here that seems particularly shocking or taboo. Speculation over whether a killer could have turned out differently in different social circumstances is commonplace. What perhaps renders this piece fannish is the focus on appealing aspects of Dahmer's physicality—his eyes described as "baby blue gutwrenchers." This is a fannish trope: Francesca Coppa (2006), for example, has written on the physicality of fanfic, the appropriation and arrangement of recognized bodies reminiscent to her of drama. It is the visual, voyeuristic aspect of these fanfics that is picked out as particularly, inappropriately fannish by some commenters, cited as "proof that God left this Earth, after he saw delusional women lusting after an actual serial killer and cannibal because they have this delusion they could change him" (Whoneedsanameforthissite 2020).

Sometimes, the tendency to sexualization prompts the theme of self-reflection in these stories. This is a fan-specific inflection of the discourse which does not fit so easily into the poaching/convergence model. In "Life's Too Short to Match Your Socks" (michaelsmistress 2019b), the main character (again: "you") is both the unwitting girlfriend of Ted Bundy and the lead detective responsible for apprehending the serial killer. The plot thus relies on dramatic irony, complicated by the suspension of knowledge required to enter the you-character. When the killer is revealed, the you-character confronts accusing newspaper headlines: "BLINDED BY LOVE: BUNDY'S GIRL IS LEAD DETECTIVE WHO FAILED TO CATCH HIM!" Being "blinded by love" is, in essence, what girls in the serial killer fandom are typically accused of. The you-character reads on:

> "In her statement, she said Bundy had demonstrated aggression towards her multiple times" "Upon hearing about the discovery of bodies Bundy apparently turned 'ghostly pale' is it any wonder he was disturbed by the fact his play things had been discovered?" "Bundy tensed up and appeared visibly shaken when being told one of his victims had come forward, how stupid is this detective?" (michaelsmistress 2019b)

Bundy himself comments in this story that "women are always so easy to lure to their deaths. A smile, a kind word, and they melt" (michaelsmistress 2019b). The story climaxes with the armed you-character and Bundy in their bedroom, surrounded by police, as she struggles with her conflicting feelings. The you-character pulls the trigger in the last line, but the reader is left not knowing if the bullet lands. The story reads as highly self-reflexive on serial killer fanfic as a whole, a question as to how far the entire construct is delusional: There is little evidence of textual poaching in this story. It is primarily a self-reflexive statement on the discourse of serial killer fandom, and fairly subversive of patriarchal ideas of romance.

On the other hand, I cannot ignore the presence of more straightforwardly sexual and romantic short pieces. "Baby, I'm an Animal (But You Can Have a Taste)" simply relates a sexual encounter between Richard Ramirez, described as "more interesting than most of the guys around here," and a second-person narrator who is described as uninterested in nice men (orphan_account 2

2020). In addition, or as an alternative to prompting self-reflection, the unusual prevalence of second-person narration in this marginalized fandom suggests a sort of conspiracy between reader and author, an understanding of a shared interest in this taboo genre. In "In This Together," Amelia ends up in a loving sexual relationship with Dahmer, despite his homosexuality. "A Collection of Poems about Jeffrey Dahmer and the Original Female Character . . ." (2Lady4Mental6Hospital8 2020) is exactly that. This is especially notable because fandom is generally thought of as a pro-queer space: Queering straight characters in fanfic is commonplace, but I believe this is the first time I have seen a queer individual straightened.

The short stories by user Lady4Mental6Hospital8, meanwhile, comprise romantic interludes between Ted Bundy and his real-life girlfriend Elizabeth Kloepfer (often called Elizabeth Kendall). In the fiction, they are expecting an imaginary child. Lest the reader be mistaken, the stories are tagged as "Cutesy" and "Out of Character." Similarly, the story "Candy Necklace" is a Richard Ramirez fic written specifically to fulfill a request from Tumblr:

> Please can you write a Richard fic where he and the reader are kind of chilling in a graveyard somewhere and he tells her that he loves her and they cuddle and stuff? Fluff pls. (Yolandi 2019, quoting a deleted Tumblr post)

"Fluff" is a fannish term for a light, silly, sweet story. The author likewise acknowledges that the responding story is "O[ut] O[f] C[haracter] in some ways but I think anyone who likes Richard will like this little break from reality" (Yolandi 2019). These are self-conscious acts of discursive construction. The authors and intended readers of romanticized fic know they are not writing in a way that reflects any pre-extant reality pertinent to the killers in question, much as RPF writers know they are writing about a media construct rather than a real person. Commenter Matt chastises:

> This is really gross. Ted Bundy was a real person and he hurt of lot of REAL people. Please don't romanticize him. Even if this is based on the plot of a movie, even if Elizabeth for one moment actually cared for him, please don't call what they had "true love" He was a misogynist, a murderer, and a monster.
>
> And if he were alive today he'd be happy at this kind of romanticized attention he's getting. (Matt 2020)

A user who has simply filled in the name form with "Fuckyou" responds:

> Dude, this is yust a fiction, obviously this never happen, and ted never loved her, but that is the point of made fanfiction, have fun, stop being gringe. (2021)

"Gringe" presumably means "cringe," implying that the concerned commenter is responding inappropriately, failing to appreciate the communal codes of understanding that sanction this as pure fantasy. This communal code suggests a reading through the lens of discursive construction, though the theory of community interpretation from *Textual Poachers* stands. But, as I explored in *Emo* (2020), the point of fannish discursive constructions is that, in an increasingly converged media culture, they rarely stay contained. That is how fandom defined emo as a genre—via reuptake and re-articulation by the mainstream media. Serial killer fandom is of course a much more closed, secretive community. Ted Bundy is not alive today—and fanfic of him doting over a fictionalized pregnancy is not recuperable for industry profit in the way fannish genre construction is. Nonetheless, Matt's comment seems to be hinting at a kind of unease that the fannish romanticization of serial killers has consequences outside of the community of understanding.

Finally, the two short fics titled "Serial Killers: Book One" and "Book Two" (cheeto_twat 2021a, 2021b) are essentially short biographies. It is questionable what characterizes them as fanfiction, save for the tags. In a sense, they are textual poaching, as the author inserts her opinions, for example, on Dahmer's parents, but there is little to qualify them as stories. Nonetheless, I have included them in the sample as per the methodology, because they described themselves as serial killer fanfiction and occupy a space in a self-declared fannish archive. Moreover, I did see this tendency to documentation picked up in other forms of textual poaching, as I will demonstrate below.

There are numerous positive reviews across the range of these stories, where the reader seems to have received them in accordance with communal norms: a hot fantasy, a psychological experiment, or a pseudo-historical exercise. Unlike most fanfiction on AO3 (Fathallah 2017), they also attract plenty of censure:

> So there's fan fictions of murders now? It's shit like this that makes me believe in abortion. (Lokisnotdead 2018)

> lmao not to be rude but don't fetishize serial killers ;^) (Tortellini 2019)

The authors, typically, do not care:

> Not to be rude or anything like that, but I truly don't care what your moral standpoint on it is. You read the tags and you still clicked on it, don't click on things you don't like. (orphan_account 3 2019)

This assertion of the reader's implication relates to the reflexivity I observed in the tendency to second-person narration. Unlike the romanticizing indulgences of films like *Extremely Wicked, Shockingly Evil and Vile* (Berlinger 2019b), to which one critic responded with the headline, "The Ted Bundy Movie Starring Zac Efron Sure Does Love Ted Bundy" (Wilkinson 2019), there is no way to engage with these stories without knowing at the outset what they are.

We turn now to the next set of findings, gathered from the platform Wattpad, an online social reading and writing platform founded in 2006. The site has a closer relationship with traditional publishing than AO3, as popular Wattpad authors of original stories are both approached by major publishing houses and connected to them via a Wattpad service. Nonetheless, it is now a popular site for fanfic, and, if anything, has a reputation for fanfic of lower quality and (perhaps unfairly) a younger, less experienced userbase than AO3. At the time of data collection, "serial killer fandom" and "serial killer fanfic" were not searchable tags. I found that stories tagged "serial killer(s)" turned up a multitude of unrelated (fictional or fiction-based) content. Therefore, I searched one-by-one for the names of the sample of serial killers mentioned in chapter 1 (Jack the Ripper, Holmes, Bundy, Ramirez, Dahmer, Wuornos), documenting the stories that also included the tag "fanfic" or "fanfiction." Recall that these were selected as a sample of killers with a high degree of celebrity, spanning a wide swath of history, whose fame has been inflected by their differing genders and sexualities. Wattpad does not offer wordcounts, but an estimated reading time in minutes, which reflects the length of each piece. I noted these, plus the number of reads, votes (again, akin to likes), and comments on each story. Comments are not recorded by Wattpad, but I counted them manually. The results are presented in table 2, arranged by descending vote count.

Again, some initial observations are clear from the data. Firstly, most of the stories are short, with an average reading time just over sixteen minutes. While this might, at first glance, look like more material than AO3 provided us, it was actually less, because many of these were simply short opening snippets that offered little for analysis. Very few of the stories are actually finished, despite a slightly higher average of comment numbers than on AO3. The most popular serial killer to utilize as a character is Richard Ramirez, and unlike on AO3, Jack the Ripper is represented here. H. H. Holmes did not produce any relevant results, nor did Aileen Wuornos. I think it fair to state, then, that serial killer fanfiction is sparser for Dahmer and much sparser for Wuornos than it is for Bundy and Ramirez, mirroring (rather than critiquing) the media's intense glamorization of the latter two killers and gender-based pathologization of the former.

Unlike AO3, Wattpad authors frequently integrate images into their title pages and headers. (It is technically possible to integrate images on AO3, but not much practiced as a site norm.) This practice is an illustration of textual poaching via multimedia convergence culture, as well as another form of multimodality. For example, see figure 2 for the header on richies-shadesofgrey's "Richard Ramirez: One Shots" (2022).

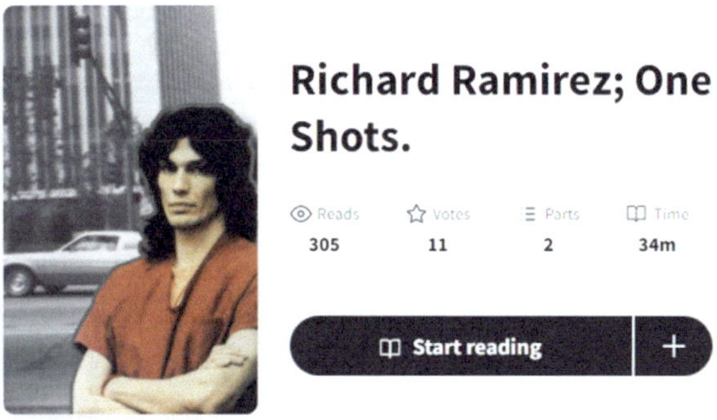

Figure 2. Wattpad story header by richiesshadesofgrey.

Here a full-color image of Ramirez in prison attire is superimposed over a black-and-white shot of a city, as the story has an urban setting, picking out his persona as the most important aspect. While this kind of metalepsis was more common on Wattpad, due to the site's norms of utilizing images, the stories here contained far less historical metalepsis within the text. Certainly, iconic locations are mentioned that played key roles in the serial killers' lives, and famous quotations are used, but there was nothing like the in-depth engagement and documentation observed in, for example, "Spinning Wheel." Sexuality, romanticization, and the self-referentiality of serial killer fandom persisted as themes, as did the presence of the "fix-it"

Table 2. Serial Killer Fanfic from Wattpad

Title	Author
Just Another Lost Angel: Richard Ramirez	rrebelyell
Bloody Paths-Richard Ramirez/Reader	rottenfuck
The Night Stalker	shesdanny
Richard Ramirez Imagines	RICHIES ANGEL
The Night I Met the Perfect Man: Richard Ramirez	FfionDunne
My Secret Killer Boyfriend	CourtneyBal£ombe
Carl Azuz x Ted Bundy	rxbbitlOser
His Evil Grin	RichardRxmirez
Richard Ramirez: One Shots	richiesshadesofgrey
Devoted Love/!Richard Ramirez	iijazzyxx
The American Dream	princessdaey
Midnight Dreamer	richie ramir3z
When I Met Him ...	whatisthisapp666
Blinded by Love	slutfeitan
Clifford's Big Red Cumshot	deadmayo
Serial Killer Oneshots	jeffreydchmer
Stockholm Syndrome	stopidontknow
The Untold Story of Jack the Ripper	stickstuckstack
Jack and His Paramore	FullMooners
Friendship Goes a Long Way	axolotlcore
Ted Bundy x Reader	Governorvera
Sleeping with My Demon	pureteen ger
Jack the Ripper	SarahSkarsgard
Jack the Ripper	Kaylabeeear
Jack	XianTan99
The Viper in the Glass	X_Paranomal_X

Table 2. Serial Killer Fanfic from Wattpad (continued)

Killer	Votes	Reads	Mins	Comments
Richard Ramirez	168	4,300	157	10
Richard Ramirez	40	1,200	21	2
Richard Ramirez	34	1,500	5	11
Richard Ramirez	27	1,000	5	25
Richard Ramirez	24	881	9	42
Bundy, Dahmer, Albert Fish	17	267	21	0
Ted Bundy	17	1,300	5	20
Richard Ramirez	13	1,200	5	0
Richard Ramirez	8	187	34	16
Richard Ramirez	7	164	15	2
Ted Bundy	6	176	5	6
Richard Ramirez	6	151	5	1
Ted Bundy	5	187	5	10
Bundy, Dahmer, Albert Fish	4	71	8	0
Ted Bundy	4	200	6	4
Ted Bundy, Jeffrey Dahmer	4	634	5	4
Richard Ramirez	2	7	6	1
JTR	1	99	9	0
JTR	1	22	8	0
Richard Ramirez, Jeffrey Dahmer	1	262	5	10
Bundy, Dahmer, Albert Fish	1	605	5	16
Richard R-amirez	1	95	5	0
JTR	0	18	5	1
JTR	0	17	5	0
JTR	0	10	15	0
Ted Bundy			50	0
Total			**424**	**181**
Average			**16**	**7**

trope. But the Wattpad stories also offered two new categories: explanation for the serial killer's actions *without* the redemption of the fix-it trope, and explicit and absurdist troll fics. In fitting with Paul Booth (2015) and Phillips and Milner's (2017) observations of internet culture, a stance of irony, humor, and mockery is common to online youth culture in general and new generations of fandom in particular.

The reader may have noted that one story in the table above is titled "Clifford's Big Red Cumshot." Clifford the Big Red Dog is a children's cartoon character, whose image the story utilizes as an icon. It is tagged "Ted Bundy" and "fanfiction" presumably as a prank on serial killer fandom, in order to attract readers looking for that content. The actual story is not about Ted Bundy at all. It opens on an evening wherein Clifford "goes to sleep happy knowing he won the Guinness World Record for biggest tip," unaware that "all this was about to come crashing down" (deadmayo 2022). This demonstrates how ironic use of tags inserts intentionally disruptive, absurdist statements into the discursive formation. On one hand, this tactic might be read as mocking the existence of a serial killer fandom—on the other, it is hardly issued from a position of moral high ground. It is more akin to carnivalesque absurdism, a kind of leveling humor in which the joker and the joke are implicated equally. Most of the troll stories, though, do feature the serial killers as characters.

As noted, historical metalepsis is present but brief and summary. I saw no examples of notes or references as observed on AO3, perhaps reflecting AO3's more academic norms. In the Wattpad stories featuring Ramirez, the Cecil Hotel is frequently mentioned. (The Cecil is the notorious site of numerous murders, and Ramirez lodged there during his killing spree.) The presence of sex was a much more prominent theme in the Ramirez stories, often featuring sadomasochistic fantasies of submission:

> She loved how he choked her, his big hand around her neck. She bit her lip suppressing a moan and nodded
>
> "I-I do, I love y-your cock, daddy." She whined out, feeling out of breath. (rrebelyell 2022)

Commenters appreciate the text as sexually arousing. Sex scenes often feature elements of romanticization:

> he was breathtaking but very sinister[.] [A]t the same time she just hoped that he would never be caught by the police, if he was that it would be the end of the relationship

> physically for her and she couldn't do that she loved him way too much[.] She loved spending all this months with him even if he was a so-called "Monster." She didn't care about that because she knew he had a heart underneath all the coldness that he showed towards of a human beings and her at some points in the relationship. (richiesshadesofgrey 2022)

Again, this might be unsettling, but it certainly isn't new. This romanticization dates to Ramirez's trial and the surrounding media circus, as solidified and reiterated in contemporary media. Remember the comments on Ramirez made by observers in the *Night Stalker* documentary: intense, charismatic, full of sex appeal. To an extent, this is textual poaching, just not in the ideologically progressive way Jenkins imagined it. The softening and romanticization are the author's additions to the sexualized celebrity of Ramirez, allowing the writer and reader to share the sadomasochistic fantasy in a relatively safe arena. As observed on AO3, some stories also comment self-reflexively on this tendency to fantasy. In "Just Another Lost Angel," the main character and narrative focalizer Naomi is explicitly described as naïve and sheltered. She is given lines that cannot but ring with dramatic irony, as another character asks, "'You got in a car with someone that you didn't even know? What's his name?'" and she replies, "'Richard. He's okay, don't worry!'" (rrebelyell 2022). She is later forced to confront her naïveté when her crush displays his violent tendencies, hurting and threatening to kill her: "'Why would I be gentle?' he demands: 'You're not special. [. . .] You're delusional. [. . .] And delusional whores have to be punished'" (rrebelyell 2022). Despite the sexually sadomasochistic overtones of "punishment," one can detect the same echoes of standard criticisms leveled at serial killer fans that were observed on AO3: that such fans are deluded in imagining that they could fix or change a killer who would simply murder them.

Fix-it fics remained a theme on Wattpad but overlapped substantially with a new theme I tagged "explanations." In short, these snippets and stories offered no redemption of the killer, but inferred explanation for their behavior based in trauma and mental ill-health. The childhood abuse suffered by Ramirez was frequently invoked, and interestingly, the short speculative stories concerning Jack the Ripper also hypothesized childhood trauma for the unknown killer. XianTan99's "Jack" imagines the young Ripper as a "boy who had lost those precious to him goes out seeking bloody revenge," and relates the murder of his parents:

> "No! Don't take mom! No!" Jack shouted in desperation.
>
> His father spoke weakly, "Son . . ."
>
> "Dad! "
>
> "I'm fine—" He smiled as he coughed out blood, knowing he doesn't have much time left.
>
> "Dad—" (XianTan99 2021)

"Mom" is an Americanism, evidencing the discursive construction of this imagined killer in (presumably) the writer's national idiom. The snippet is too short—and unfinished—to judge how this would develop or if any redemption would be offered, but the invocation of childhood trauma is also common to stories that do offer it. In RICHIES_ANGEL's "Richard Ramirez Imagines" (2021a), a chapter called "Teenage Richie" is illustrated with a real image of an innocent-looking Ramirez as a young teen. (In fandom, "imagine" used as a noun means a short, imagined scenario.) This piece is billed as a "short, cute fluff imagine were richie and the reader are teenagers and his going through depression and she comforts him." Once again, the you-pronoun is utilized as a narrative focalizer: "It was always your weekly routine to visit him because you knew his dad and uncle didn't really treat him well. You always wanted to make sure his [*sic*] okay because face it you love him" (RICHIES_ANGEL 2021a). Commenters stress the potentially redemptive nature of such a relationship, calling it "ADORABLE ● [I] r[ea]lly wish he had someone like this in his life besides his sister" (yourboyfriendsbimbo2 2021). To this the writer replies: "I[ ]k[now] r[ight]. He could of changed ● ●♥" (RICHIES_ANGEL 2021b). The commenter's response is "Possibly ●" (yourboyfriendsbimbo2 2021). The unsure, unhappy-face emoji stresses the uncertainty of the proposition.

Rrebelyell's long, developed story "Just Another Lost Angel" has Ramirez report in detail on the abuse he suffered as a child, before the focalizer character meets his family. His mother confesses to her that she is "glad" they are together, acknowledging that "My son was always, you know, complicated. But I hope that you're changing him for the best" (rrebelyell 2022). Of course, these statements are inflected rather ironically by the violence attributed to Ramirez in the story, his threats to the reader, and the reflection on delusions quoted from the same story above. More of the romanticization on Wattpad tends towards "cuteness," crossing over with some of the fix-it/explanatory theme (witness the Ramirez "fluff"). "The Viper in the Glass" appears to be a wish-fulfillment narrative in which "Ted Bundy saves Y/N from her abusive relationship that she hopes it will turn out of what she was hoping for" (X_Paranormal_X 2021). "Y/N" is an abbreviation of "your name," inviting the reader to insert herself into the family. It is not a particularly developed piece, but has time for such savior tropes as Bundy promising to protect the reader from her ex, taking her in after the death of her parents, and avowing that while he did, indeed, commit the past murders, he is now a changed man and "not that bad person anymore" (X_Paranormal_X 2021).

Finally, I must explore the presence of explicit troll/joke fic on Wattpad. I noted above the story that utilized Bundy as a tag purely for bait, luring the reader seeking serial killer fanfic to a story regarding Clifford the Big Red Dog and his "Big Red STDs" (deadmayo 2022). Another troll fic pairs Bundy in a relationship with the popular American news anchor Carl Azuz, who features regularly in comedic memes across the internet. The author creates an icon poaching the images of Bundy and Azuz, placing them together and superimposing red hearts around them. The fic is pure absurdism, utilizing ridiculous sexual scenarios, deliberate misspellings, and malapropisms. The protagonists enter a sexual relationship (for unknown reasons), until

> Carl's mother bursts in with garlic bread from her room. Her mom tall and Brunnet with beautiful brown eyes. They fastly get off each other with a quick moan. She gasps and winks at Ted. Ted feels uncomfortable with this but he feels a weird way about her soft warm flowing brown hair. He immediately leaves with no hesitation. (rxbbitlOser 2019)

His intention is of course to murder her, as Bundy's real victims tended to have long brown hair, an act which Azuz is initially upset by, but "as the time went on Carl had almost completely forgot about his dead mother." Readers are entirely privy to this joke, leaving comments replete with emojis that mimic the deliberate misspellings, like "mor sexie secen plez ●" (malscat 2019).

"Friendship Goes a Long Way" is of a similar type, concerning a love triangle between "Ricshart Ramirez," "Jeffrey Dumber" and Bundy. It likewise utilizes bad-taste humor such as the moment Dahmer opens his refrigerator to get food but "couldn't decide if he should grab Ben or Jerry!!? He grabbed Jeremy instead. Chomp!! He ate Jeremy cutely. 'Yum yum!'" (axolotlcore 2021). The fic concludes "69 years later" as "Ricshart, Ted,,,,,, and Jeffrey all went to bed and died from intense cancer and trees," prompting the police to arrive and hold an impromptu "funral." The commingling of humor and murder is, again, not unique to fan culture. These "fanfics" could hardly be said to glamorize the killers. A long discussion on the Reddit True Crime forum r/truecrime concerned the appropriateness (or otherwise) of comedy true crime podcasts, with frequent reference to *My Favorite Murder* (Reddit 2021). Many commenters felt that all such commixture was disrespectful; others pointed out that humans have always laughed about horror and tragedy, and that so long as the jokes were on the killers rather than their victims, they felt no discomfort.

Thus I observe that the key themes of the serial killer fanfic across AO3 and Wattpad were broadly similar, as were their protagonists. Romanticization and sexualization were certainly present, but so were self-reflexivity, and attempts to explain serial killer psyche and other more mainstream intersections from broader true crime culture. Particularly interesting was the lack of (any serious) exploration of queer sexuality, given its prominence in the mainstream media surrounding Dahmer and Wuornos. With the exception of troll fic (which is, I suppose, fairly queer in a variety of ways), fandom if anything has had a straightening effect via its poaching habits and discursive constructions of the killers. This *is* textual poaching, in its basic form, but it is not particularly progressive or resistant to mainstream media ideologies. If anything, it reinforces them: Serial killers are special people, and heterosexual romance is more important than queer lives. Perhaps the fics that differed the most from mainstream source texts were the troll fics, which are not exactly resistant, but exist in an ambivalent relationship to their sources (see chapter 5). I turn now to some sites hosting different sorts of fan media, to observe what the lenses of textual poaching, converged media culture, and discursive fan construction can illuminate.

Tumblr is a microblogging site founded in 2007, and a major locus of online fan cultures. Here users post and recirculate text, images, video, and other media via an online dashboard, and can follow other users or tags to receive more of their selected content. As Tumblr depends so heavily on reblogging, the reader should not assume that the blogs cited are the originators of each post attributed to them, but that if not, they have integrated it into their personal blog by recirculation. Tumblr is like a scrapbook. One might expect to see imagistic and GIF-based textual poaching here, as Jessica Hautsch (2018) did for the *Supernatural* fandom. One might expect, likewise, to see the multimedia affordances of convergence culture more heavily utilized. Actually, searching for hashtags like "serial killer fandom" and "serial killer fan" produced primarily exclamations of disgust and horror regarding the existence of such a phenomenon. However, entering "serial killer" and clicking the names of sample killers as hashtags did also locate some material that falls on the pathologized side of that constructed binary between legitimate interest and stigmatized fandom I noted in chapter 1: romanticization, professions of love, serial killer roleplay, fanvids, and expressions of sexual desire. Again, I am aware that the divide I am drawing here regarding the material to analyze is contestable, particularly as Tumblr users are less likely to use the term "fan" than fanfic authors. Nonetheless, Tumblr users draw quite discernible discursive lines separating what is considered to be fannish content from "proper" and normal interest in serial killers. Let us return to the lines drawn by Tumblr user v1ntage-p3psi1, neatly summarizing the boundaries that the True Crime Community seeks to uphold:

> What is okay:
>
> Being interested in true crime
>
> Wanting to find more about the killers
>
> Liking the killers but not excusing what they did
>
> Not idolizing or humanizing them
>
> What isn't okay:
>
> Literally wanting to suck off a serial killer
>
> Idolizing them
>
> Drawing fan art of them and making it all cute
>
> Shipping. The. Fucking. Killers. [. . .]
>
> Saying shit like: "omg the victims are dead they're not gonna care," they have families you uncultured swine. (2020)

Variations on this post are all over the true crime hashtags on Tumblr, mostly along the same lines, though "liking" is disputed. Searching the serial killer hashtags and names of the serial killers in my sample did produce a spread of content that fell on the "bad" side of the binary, and is received as such by other Tumblr users. Expressions of horror, disgust, and condemnation from the broader true crime community were common on the blogs I sampled, as was the direct injunction that the respective blog owner "kys" (kill yourself). My sample, taken at the end of January and beginning of February 2022, produced the following results as "top" rated according to the opaque Tumblr algorithm:

- https://nightst4lkerxx.tumblr.com/
- https://the-real-ricardo-ramirez.tumblr.com/
- https://angelrose-666.tumblr.com/
- https://sick-girl-666.tumblr.com/
- https://casdied.tumblr.com/
- https://gunsnkillers.tumblr.com/
- https://richardramirezx.tumblr.com/
- https://richardramirezricardo.tumblr.com/
- https://yourickie-x.tumblr.com/
- https://stalkersdisneyland.tumblr.com/
- https://the-real-dahmer.tumblr.com/
- https://datingdahmer-blog.tumblr.com
- https://nightst4lkerxx.tumblr.com/
- https://aileenwuornos-blog.tumblr.com/
- https://teddyshellclub.tumblr.com/

The blog owners understand which side of the binary they fall upon. The header on https://datingdahmer-blog.tumblr.com reads "Jeffrey Dahmer Fangirl. In my free time I write fan fiction, search for new pictures of Jeff and obsess over how much I love him❤" as of 2022. Tumblr is notoriously unstable, and I fully expect these blogs to have been deleted and/or banned by the time this work is published, but I saved the key images and posts for reference as I worked. Once again, I observed that Ramirez was the most popular killer, and this time Bundy less so. Wuornos and Dahmer received more attention on Tumblr than on AO3 and Wattpad. Searching for their names also revealed fannish content on blogs not specifically devoted to them, which I included in the sample. Tumblr supports all types of media, and posts were comprised of the following types:

A. GIFs, with and without sound or superimposed text

B. Images, edited and unedited

C. Music

D. Song lyrics

E. Fanvids

F. Written quotations from serial killers and those who knew them

G. Other text posts

Some of the key themes are echoed from the study of fanfiction, especially romanticization, sexualization, trolling, and explanation/sympathy for the serial killer's behavior. Tumblr does not support the kind of long-form text content that would make a narrative "fix-it" arc possible. There was an additional theme of historical documentation without additional fictional elements or metalepsis, and Tumblr also introduced the themes of radical feminism and queer sexuality with regard to Wuornos and Dahmer. These themes were continued and elaborated on TikTok. Again, this is interesting, because while Tumblr and TikTok are certainly thought of as queer spaces, they are not necessarily considered *more queer* than AO3. In this study, however, they proved to be so.

Documentation of the serial killers' lives takes the form of real photographs and quotations from official media. Some of this is romanticizing via selection, e.g., the reproduction of certain romantic letters Ramirez sent from prison to his admirers, replete with doodled hearts and expressions of love (richardramirezx 2021). Yet side by side with these are notes on Ramirez's more physically repulsive features, such as his rotten teeth. There are extensive quotations from official biographies (credited, but without page numbers), and reproductions of famous images from television. The image of Aileen Wuornos raising her middle finger to the judge at her sentencing, inscribed with the caption "You fucking motherfucker," is recirculated often in her tag. It could be argued that the lack of comment on these GIFs allows Wuornos's rage to rearticulate itself, particularly if one is aware of the context of her accusations—that she was set up by the world; that the judge and jury will burn in hell for sending a raped woman to her death—but it is hard to describe these actions as textual poaching. They are more like what fan scholars, after fan obsession_inc (2009), call "affirmational fandom": affirming, amplifying, and promoting the object of one's fandom rather than transforming it. In *Playing Fans* (2015), Booth referred to this sort of content as fan pastiche, a collection and documentation of texts of interest that does not subvert or contradict their meaning.

Some reuse of media, however, is explicitly sexualized and romanticized and fits better into the textual poaching model. Short videos of both Bundy and Ramirez speaking are set to songs by Lana Del Rey, an artist who is frequently criticized for glamorization of violence against women, with lines like "he hit me and it felt like a kiss," from her 2014 song "Ultraviolence." The Del Rey lyric "If he's as bad as they say then I guess I'm cursed looking into his eyes," from her 2019 song "Happiness Is a Butterfly" is frequently reposted. "I'm sorry for this," posts the owner of the blog *nightst4lkerxx*, followed by a red-faced, panting emoji, and the imposition of the words "Is this love, daddy?" in red on black over a series of Ramirez shots (nights4lkerxx 2014). Dahmer too receives a handful of "sexy edits," though Wuornos does not; her edits are dealt with below, in the section on radical feminism. This is notable. The sexuality of a gay man is apparently more appreciated than that of a lesbian, although lesbian rage is given space.

Tumblr presented the most explicit examples of "cuteifying" I had encountered so far. Chibi-style fanart featuring killers circulates among the blogs, such as these examples of Richard Ramirez and Jeffrey Dahmer (figures 3 and 4). There is much to unpack here. Though both images contain elements loosely poached and adapted from popular media narratives—figure 3 apparently depicts Ramirez at the Cecil Hotel, where he stayed during his killing spree, and figure 4 appropriates Dahmer's explanations that he killed out of loneliness—I would consider these more as fannish discursive constructions. They are deliberately slightly absurd, pairing kawaii-style aesthetics derived from Japanese animation with images of violence, inhabiting a semi-ironic, deliberately evasive tone that Whitney Phillips and Ryan Milner attribute to online youth culture in *The Ambivalent Internet* (2017). Irony seems present, yet it's difficult to pin down and define. The emblematic phrase of this tone might be the statement "Ha ha just kidding . . . unless?" One might call this cutefying theme "pastiche" in the sense of "blank parody" (Jameson 1991). It *seems* parodic, yet what exactly *is* being parodied evades us. The killers? Their fan culture? "Normal" interest in serial killing? Anime and chibi art, which can itself combine violent and kitchily cute images in all manner of publications? All of the above?

Explanation for and understanding of the serial killer's actions is also a key theme on Tumblr. Sometimes it appears in text form:

> Some not so fun facts about Richard Ramirez
>
> His family had a history of anger issues, a trait him and all his siblings inherited from his father. Once while fixing a sink his father got so angry over not being able to get a drainpipe to fit that he beat himself in the head with a hammer to the point that he had blood dripping down his face. Richard, and a couple of his siblings saw all of this. (sick-girl-666 2021a)

Compare:

> Jeffrey Dahmer was quoted saying that killing them was his least favorite part, though, and that all he ever wanted was a living "zombie." Maybe if his father wouldn't have forced him to get rid of the mannequin that he'd been keeping, none of this would've happened to begin with. (datingdahmer-blog 2017b)

Some users post images or edited videos of the killers as innocent-looking children, reflecting on the possibility of a life without the trauma that they claim led them to kill. One video, reposted from TikTok, utilizes Ramirez's real explanations of how abuse can damage a developing person to the point that "one day . . . he explodes" as a voice-over to fictional images depicting his childhood, then merges these into real court footage (nightst4lkerxx 2021b). The song "The Night We Met" by Lord Huron (2015) plays in the background. This minor folk rock piece was also featured in the American television series *13 Reasons Why*, thus creating an intertextual link with a text that explores the social causes for suicide and violence. This is classic textual poaching in quite a sophisticated form, and though it utilizes the affordances of media convergence, I consider the poaching model to fit it better because sympathetic interpretations of Ramirez are not common in mainstream media. Without making any statements on how far childhood abuse and head injuries determine future life choices, I would say that, certainly, the complexity of these pieces gives the lie to patronizing nonsense like "I worry about those kids" as a dismissal of serial killer fandom.

Images and video of Wuornos are also heavily poached to express empathy, identification—and here, feminist anger. "I cry every time I read about

Figure 3. Ramirez fanart (nightst4lkerxx 2021a).

Figure 4. Dahmer fanart (datingdahmer-blog 2017a).

Aileen Wuornos" is superimposed in block text over an image of Aileen taking an oath in court: "I really don't think she deserved the death penalty" (aileenwuornos-blog 2011). Nor do I, nor does Nick Broomfield, nor does Phyllis Chesler. Indeed, while it is anti-conservative and anti-patriarchal, I would consider this perspective to be mainstream enough that these posts seem more like an illustration of convergence culture than textual poaching. The post utilizes readily available text to make a political point that, while disputed, is still within the realms of mainstream discourse.

More notable, perhaps, are the posts and edits actively celebrating and endorsing Wuornos's actions. A now-deleted post from user smokinfeds briefly showed an image of Wuornos with a halo of purple hearts, and the inscription "kill your johns" over her body. The post was annotated "starting a radfem y[ou]t[ube] stream [. . .] and I made aileen fanart to use as the next background" (2022). The background of this blog was a repeated image of the symbol for "female," where an assault rifle forms the t-cross. A short video whose origin has been lost was briefly circulated with the annotation "touch me without consent . . . I dare you." In the clip, a young woman is lying on a bed with her back to the camera, turns around as though touched unaware, and morphs into an image of Wuornos.

Other posts tagged with Aileen Wuornos generally express the sentiment that women have every right to kill abusive men—that it is indeed a "net positive" (male-to-catgirl 2021)—or remark, "I hate when men talk about female serial killers . . . like first of all . . . you're already worse than them just be existing as a male, so don't push it" (its-jilleus 2021). Though the phrasing is somewhat facetious, I would call these more radical statements an explicitly political kind of textual poaching, the poaching of a media narrative for radical feminist purposes. It does seem, so far, that Wuornos fandom is qualitatively different than that of male serial killers. It is fandom of an idea as much as of a person: The idea that if a few men need to die in order for men as a group to stop killing and raping women with such casual regularity, so be it. If they happen to be the type of men that use destitute lesbian sex workers, so much the better. This would be serial killer fandom at its most political, its most subversive, textual poaching in the ideological sense Jenkins imagined it (though he certainly didn't imagine this ideology in particular).

Explicit trolling and joking was the final major theme on Tumblr. Similar to the tagging practice observed on Wattpad, there were blogs that utilized the names of serial killers simply for attention and/or shock value. A blog

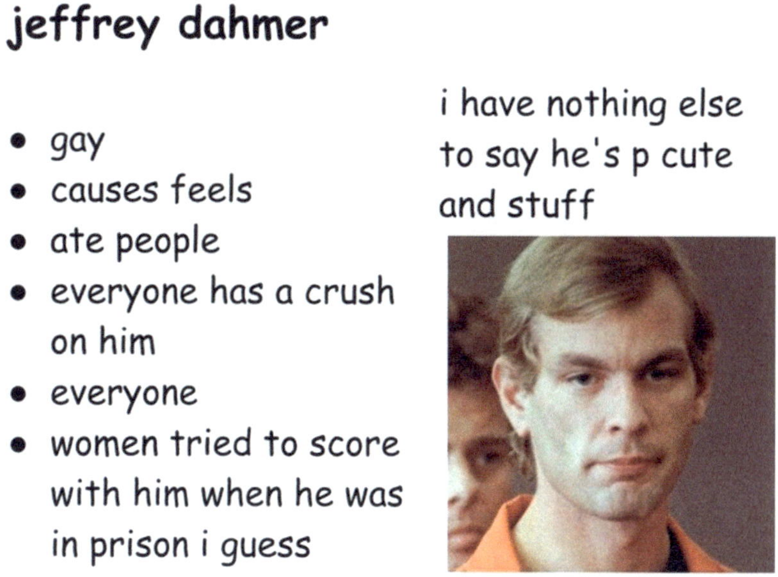

Figure 5. Jeffrey Dahmer "identification card" (datingdahmer-blog 2017c).

with the URL slug "ted-bundy-is-my-sugar-daddy" contained nothing related to Ted Bundy, just a range of images from films with a bleak aesthetic and jokes about depression. The troll/joke category plays up the absurdity broached in the cuteifying theme more explicitly, with more obvious irony and cynical humor. One example is the circulation of some sort of killer "identification cards," as in figure 5. The juxtaposition of "causes feels" and "ate people" is obviously humorous (although—it should be noted—objectively true). This again perhaps says more about media culture than it does about killer fandom specifically. Impositions of cartoon characters and puns over serial killers are commonplace. Bundy pontificating in court is captioned: "Not only do I feel ya—I *necrophilia"* (sick-girl-666 2021b); and a news story on a typo that briefly legalized cannibalism instead of cannabis in Ottawa is juxtaposed with an image of Dahmer edited with glowing laser eyes, a meme convention to convey intense interest and enthusiasm (sick-girl-666 2021c). Atrocity and tragedy humor is fairly widespread; these texts are rendered fannish primarily by their inclusion in fannish blogs and by the expressions of affection contained within the jokes. For this reason, I would still consider them an act of textual poaching, intended for circulation by and within a community of alternative interpretations, but enabled via the affordances of convergence culture. They should also be considered through the lens of fandom as play, to which I will return in chapter 4.

YouTube, a Google property, is a hugely popular video sharing website. Though not a fannish platform as such, it is another site where image, sound, and text are combined in the production of fanvids. Searching "Serial killer fanvid(s)" mostly produced fanvids explicitly based on fictional texts. So, again, I searched the names of the killers sampled above, plus the term "fanvid(s)." This produced a wealth of data. I selected the top ten results based on number of likes for each killer in the sample and recorded the results as below. Tables 3 to 6 shows the overall results, with totals and average comments, views and likes and dates, in order that the reader may compare the differences in average responses.

There were no fact-based matches for "Jack the Ripper" and "H.H. Holmes" with "fanvid"; Jack the Ripper defaulted to fiction, while Holmes produced no matches. In a sense, then, I am relying on the YouTube algorithm to define fanvid in this context—but the algorithm is informed by the ways users interact with the site, demonstrating how discursive boundaries are produced via human-technology interaction. The site judges these to be fanvids, as opposed to documentary clips, and that judgment is based on their content, keywords, tags, and the way viewers respond to them. Look at how often the creators utilize the serial killers' names in their username. Other usernames are more obscure: "Peek-a-boo" is the infamous final statement of shooter Eric Harris to his victim Cassie Bernall during the Columbine massacre, made directly before he murdered her. Again, I observe that Ramirez is the most influential figure, by some distance, with Bundy in second place, Dahmer third, and Wuornos the least—more replication of the mainstream media hierarchization by gender and sexuality. I use "influential" deliberately here, as opposed to "popular." Many of the comments on these videos expressed disgust and horror, which is to be expected on a mainstream site. On the other hand, many were supportive, and this must be accounted for when examining the discursive construction.

At the level of content, the videos were much like those observed on Tumblr: a mélange of televisual footage, popular music, captions, and editing, although they are often longer. Both the videos and the comments responding to them reinforced some of the previous themes and introduced some new material. Romanticization, sex, and explaining or empathizing with the killer all remained, as did trolling. But these videos also produced an intense self-conscious discussion of both fanvids of work as art, typically horror art, and of textual poaching. I already observed self-consciousness with regard to serial killer fandom in some of the fanfic, but here I found a tendency for commenters to police what may or may not be textually poached for these sorts of videos, as I will explore below. The fact that YouTube is a relatively open platform, making these videos easy for outsiders to stumble across, no doubt contributes to the broader range of statements I discovered here.

Regarding romanticization, the videos did not reveal significant new insights as compared to the Tumblr set. For example, "Ted Bundy Footage | Lana Del Rey—Summertime Sadness" (Белый Русский 2020) is, just as it sounds, real footage of Bundy after his arrest, set to the 2012 Lana Del Rey song "Summertime Sadness," a pop/trip-hop ballad concerning suicide. The most interesting point is the selection of Bundy footage; it tends toward captures of his least performative, less upbeat, less charismatic moments. He is frequently shown smiling and smirking, but this video focuses on those moments when Bundy seems perhaps not as in control of his circus-trial as he sometimes was. He is shown limping, returned to his cell after his second jailbreak, having lost a great deal of weight to escape through a ceiling hatch. Sometimes the viewer glimpses moments of what might be fear, as though the proceedings weren't going in the way he thought they would. Thus a certain depth is attributed to him, via combination with the song. Viewers are aware of how the poaching process inflects media: "Don't confuse the feelings by playing a beautiful song" says Jessica Pazo: "Make no mistake, he was evil" (2021). While the reader may take issue with religious terminology like "evil," Bundy was indeed a diagnosed psychopath. Thus the "inner life" and depth of feeling attributed to him by this piece of textual poaching is unlikely in historical fact, and a demonstration of how textual poaching works to create new meaning. Some viewers dislike the creator's choices of texts to poach:

> Please keep lana [Del Ray] out of your weird romanticization of homicide. (gabi mejia 2022)
>
> leave lana del rey out of this. (C.M.B. 2021, on "Ted Bundy: Sweet Serial Killer," featuring another Del Rey song)

I tagged these comments as "poaching police": It seemed to be important kind of boundary work for media fans in general. Textual poaching is a fine and acknowledged process, but the wrong sort of poaching is an offense. "Did

Table 3. Serial Killer Fanvids from YouTube (Bundy)

Title	YouTuber	Views	Comments	Likes
Ted Bundy Footage | Lana Oel Rey—Summertime Sadness	Ланселот	88,729	336	1,400
Ted Bundy Edit—Criminal	Mad Villain 29x24	78,986	781	1,400
Ted Bundy: Sweet Serial Killer	Theodora	53,080	460	971
Ted Bundy: She's Gone Away	Kiefer89	53,881	156	752
Ted Bundy—In the End—Music Tribute	My Head	25,629	69	406
Ted Bundy: The Unknown	Kiefer89	23,453	56	386
Ted Bundy | Edit | Dark Paradise	serial killer edits	12,012	19	209
Ted Bundy | Edit | Bang Bang Bang Bang	serial killer edits	8,840	20	187
Ted Bundy—SMELLS LIKETEEN SPIRIT	Buttercup	144	0	9
Average		**38,306**	**211**	**636**

Table 4. Serial Killer Fanvids from YouTube (Ramirez)

Title	**YouTuber**	**Views**	**Comments**	**Likes**
Richard Ramirez—Dirty Mind	Kelly Lambert	401,341	2,459	6,600
Richard Ramirez (Devil Eyes—Hippie Sabotage)	Queen Bee	191,217	986	3,800
Richard Ramirez | | Careless Whisper	Angeles Ramirez	90,686	571	1,900
Richard Ramirez—The Night Stalker	Angeles Ramirez	56,181	219	1,500
Richard Ramirez "Fell with the Devil"	Dew Ddtz	43,156	247	1,100
Richard Ramirez—Gangsters Paradise	theuncombe-done	22,914	74	1,100
Richard Ramirez—Heaven	theuncombe-done	23,252	102	741
SMELLSLIKETEENSPIRIT | Richard Ramirez Edit	Nighthunter	12,647	41	529
Richard Ramirez—Dark Para-dise	PEEK-A-BOO	5,451	28	194
Richard Ramirez—Animal (Glitch Remix)	PEEK-A-BOO	3,961	6	87
Average		**85,081**	**473**	**1,755**

Table 5. Serial Killer Fanvids from YouTube (Dahmer)

Title	YouTuber	Views	Comments	Likes
Jeffrey Dahmer-Creep (Tribute)	Luke Skywalker	36,437	280	770
Richard Chase, Ted Bundy, and Jeffrey Dahmer—The Devil within	Samantha Trecazzi	46,188	223	593
Jeffrey Dahmer Edit	Mad Villain 29x24	25,542	210	495
Jeffrey Dahmer Fan Edit [looped]	eleanor dahmer ▯ï▯	11,030	0	484
Jeffrey Dahmer: Love You Like I Do	Kiefer89	15,525	151	309
Summertime Sadness [Jeffrey Dahmer]	Poems of Plupp	7,402	40	235
Serial Killers Edit Richard Ramirez Ted Bundy Jeffrey Dahmer-Bad Guy Billie Eilish	STALKER ON YOUTUBE	5,690	34	182
Jeffrey Dahmer: Nothing's Gonna Hurt You Baby	Kiefer89	4,232	47	120
Jeffrey Dahmer | Edit | Maneater (lyrics)	serial killer edits	3,638	25	106
Jeffrey Dahmer Edit	Richard Ramirez	2,746	15	94
Average		**15,843**	**103**	**339**

Table 6. Serial Killer Fanvids from YouTube (Wuornos)

Title	YouTuber	Views	Comments	Likes
× Aileen Wuornos × Edit ×	Honey Bee	11,981	432	51
Aileen Wuornos: Sweet Dreams (Are Made of This)	Kiefer89	122,051	903	214
Aileen Wuornos Memorial Edit	serial.multi.fandom	5,507	268	23
▯ Aileen Wuornos—Edit	Mr. Bundy	2,688	136	9
Aileen Wuornos Edit—freaks	Monike Leyva Munoz Ramirez	810	39	3
Aileen Wuornos Edit—Billie Jean	Monike Leyva Munoz Ramirez	556	21	2
Aileen Wuornos Edit—I Was Made for Lovin You	Monike Leyva Munoz Ramirez	348	29	1
Aileen Wuornos Edit—Intro (Her Version and 3 Version)	Monike Leyva Munoz Ramirez	407	24	0
Aileen Wuornos Edit—Maneater	Monike Leyva Munoz Ramirez	663	34	0
Aileen Wuornos Edit—Bloody Mary	Monike Leyva Munoz Ramirez	585	29	0
Average		**14,560**	**193**	**30**

you really do Queen Brittney like that?" asks Haze Dante on a video pairing a Britney Spears song with Bundy footage (2021). Music, and the ability to edit clips to a beat, seems to be an impactful means of romanticization: "Ted Bundy was like a movie star. I think even now he's more popular than any film star," says Manoj Krishna on the same video (2021). Commenters make similar observations on videos utilizing clips of Ramirez in court, cut to songs such as "I Fell in Love with the Devil" by Avril Lavigne (2019), and, again, commenters are aware of how the poaching process works: "He does have a certain appeal in these clips with the music and all. But can you imagine sitting in that trial hearing all about his gruesome acts. I think that infatuation would quickly dissolve into contempt" (Mandy Monroe 2021).

So romanticization is both a common theme and a criticized one. Sex is likewise. Footage of Ramirez in court is quite often set to rock music or sexual music. The Julia Michaels song "Heaven" (2018) utilized in "Richard Ramirez—Heaven" (theuncombedone 2021) is known from the film franchise *Fifty Shades of Grey*, creating an intertextual link with BDSM practices. "Richard Ramirez—Animal (Glitch Remix)" (PEEK-A-BOO 2021) uses the 2014 song of that name by Maroon 5, which speaks of hunting down prey, eating one's lover alive, and other such violently sexual acts over a hard bass line and dramatic octave leaps. Ramirez is shown smirking, snarling, flicking his eyes, and performing to his followers in court, sometimes wearing dark sunglasses. "Richard Ramirez—Dirty Mind" (Kelly Lambert 2016) imposes the highly sexual, 2006 hard trance track by Hyper over very similar clips, but in black and white. Commenters, even on this open platform, are surprisingly receptive to the sex theme:

> I know he did horrible shit but you can't help but not look at him. (Nathan 2021)
>
> ikr,,even a guy like you cant deny that. (muan muan 2021)
>
> They called it "animalistic magnetism" and "greatest sex appeal" in Netflix documentary.●● It is what it is, uncontrollable.● (lovemusicmusa 2021)

These videos are more explicit in their tone than the discussion of Ramirez's sexuality in mainstream media, but the difference is one of degree rather than kind, and commenters are aware of this. What makes these "fanvids" rather than documentary footage is: a) the work of textual poaching, and b) the amateur-media, narrowcast context.

Empathy and sympathy were another key theme that endured here, primarily around Dahmer and Wuornos. As the title suggests, "Summertime Sadness [Jeffrey Dahmer]" (Poems of Plupp 2021) utilizes the same Del Rey song, but this time an instrumental version, over black and white footage of Dahmer as an innocent-looking child. These are intercut with his adult explanations of his violent compulsions, his knowledge that his behavior was wrong, and his methods for desensitizing himself to his actions. He typically appears devastated. Old scenes from Disney films are also intercut: Pinocchio pressing his hands to his mouth to stop himself from speaking (and presumably, lying); Mickey Mouse attempting to escape from a skeleton as Dahmer speaks on his desperation to keep his lovers with him. The suicide of an anime character and images from the 2019 *Joker* film are likewise spliced, creating a complex and questioning commentary on blame, guilt, innocence, mental illness, and culpability. The creator's note states, "Whether my Dahmer videos are a tribute to Jeffrey Dahmer or a mockery of his entire existence is completely determined by the viewer, just as beauty and art are in the eyes of the beholder. Peace" (Poems of Plupp 2021). Yet I would argue that the invitation to sympathy—especially through the use of childhood images—is fairly clear. The victims are absent from the video, though the creator does pin a comment listing their names and wishing that they rest in peace. A similar video pairs childhood images of Dahmer cuddling a dog and playing with firecrackers with Radiohead's mournful, self-excoriating alt-rock ballad "Creep" (1992), and his moving apology speech in court. Most of the comments express sympathy for his mental illness, and some commend the song choice.

On the other hand, the video titled "Jeffrey Dahmer: Love You Like I do" (Kiefer89 2015) actually shows images of his victims: their faces, ages, dates of death, real and fictional footage of the crime scenes. It also shows fictional footage of Dahmer caressing and preserving their skulls, his own death date is shown as a bell tolls, and an image represents his deceased body after his murder. This image may or may not be real: Such images were released to the press, but the damage to Dahmer's skull and head was heavily censored, making comparison difficult. The overall impression, as confirmed by the commenters' reception, is still of sympathy, but a sympathy complicated by an acknowledgment of his actions.

The Wuornos videos are similar, showing her crying, intercutting clips of her as a child, but also include her more aggressive moments, such as that often-circulated image of her raising her middle finger to the judge.

The fanvid "Aileen Wuornos: Sweet Dreams (Are Made of This)" (Kiefer89 2014a), which is a cover by Emily Browning of the Eurythmics song of that name, is essentially a short biography. This version of the song is from the 2011 film *Sucker Punch,* a story of the personal and institutionalized abuse of a young girl by powerful men, and her flights into fantasy to escape it. Feminist sympathy, then, is a sub-theme of empathy once again. (Though I only found one comment specifically referring to Wuornos as a feminist, remember that Wuornos videos attract the least attention in general.) The parallels with Wuornos's life are only recognizable to those who either know of or look up the version of the song, demonstrating the role of communal interpretation within a set of viewers sympathetic to Wuornos. The fanvid recounts the trauma of Wuornos's childhood through captions, utilizing clips poached from news media and documentaries, and inserting the creator's own additions of sky, an open road, and police headlights. Her victims are briefly shown. The music pauses and the audio of their "deaths" is supplied by the soundtrack to the 2003 film *Monster*. In the film clips, some of her victims are heard crying and pleading for their lives, but this does not prevent some commenters from siding entirely with Wuornos, declaring, "I'm a fan of hers" (Connie 2017) or "I think she was pretty kool. she sure did give those men what they deserved. they We're Weirdos" (Amber Bell 2018). Again, this is textual poaching in opposition to both patriarchy and conservativism. One might also interpret it is as a fannish discursive construction that is a political point first, and a comment on a real person's life second.

Others take a more even-handed view, complimenting the video's creator on their editing choices:

> This song really fits Aileen, she was very abused since the age of 13 she was sleeping in the snow banks of Michigan. And everyone even her so call Friend used her up.
>
> You know if you beat a dog or a Horse. They will turn on you. Aileen was set up by the system for Failure, Rest In Peace Aileen No one can hurt you now. (zClosurez 2019)

YouTube was also the first platform on which I observed something akin to romanticization of Wuornos, with commenters expressing "Love her soooo much. 💕💕💕💕💕💕💕💕💕" (Miss Noir in the shadow 2020) and "I was made for loving her" (Paula Moyano 2022). It will only be on TikTok, however, that I observe these empathetic-to-romantic statements merge into explicit sexualization, demonstrating that lesbianism remains a marginalized category even within this already-marginalized space.

Oddly enough, the fanvid "Richard Ramirez (Devil Eyes—Hippie Sabotage)" (Queen Bee 2017) plays Jeffrey Dahmer's apology speech for his actions over images of Ramirez, implying that the words are his. Though some commenters are sympathetic to Ramirez's abusive childhood, citing him as a "victim of circumstance," they are quick to "correct" the creator on this implied misattribution:

> So to clear things up the last part wasn't Richard it was Jeffrey dahmer. (Soo Soo 2021)
>
> At the end it is not RICHARD's Voice . . . he never apologize. (Valentina Flores 2021)

Thus, while textual poaching is understood and appreciated, commenters in this space seem to dislike the use of creative license to fictionalize "accurate" representations of the serial killers. This isn't unique to killer fandom or indeed to RPF—some fans object to fanfic where their favored fictional characters behave "out of character," after all—but I did see more permissiveness of this tendency on the fanfiction sites, where the "fluff" fics, for instance, were explicitly tagged as such. It seems then that the themes of empathy and sympathy attach mainly to the queer killers, an adaptation of the "tragic queer" trope.

Some of the fanvids mimic the aesthetic of a straightforward horror story, utilizing strong images of violence, and hard, heavy, sinister music. These tend to be presented and received as artworks. Kiefer89s "Ted Bundy: The Unknown" (2014b) merges real images of Bundy with fictional depictions of his violence, cut to the beat of the 2004 song of that name by Crossfade 2004. The minor guitar melody over a choppy, syncopated beat creates an eerie effect, not at all dissimilar to the many professional documentaries on Bundy (or Ramirez): more like a skillful piece of affirmational fanwork than a transformative one. Whether the affirmation is of Bundy or of serial killer media is left to the viewer's interpretation. Comments are primarily praise for the creator's skill, both as a textual poacher and as a well-known fanvidder with their own distinctive style:

> Absolutely stunning! This video, as always, has a great quality to it. I mean, it flows with effortless grace. Stunning. Thank you, Kiefer89. :-) (kkg108 2019)
>
> I haven't seen some of this old Bundy footage ever before. Thanks for being so thorough in your research, Kiefer89. (Garden Dormouse 2019)

> I remember your reply to my comment about how you wanted to remake some of your old videos and, while I don't think it was necessary, I must admit I've been anticipating the new products. I must also admit that when you said you were going to remake Ted Bundy-- The Unknown I was a bit saddened due to my love for the original, but with you I always have high expectations and was certain the new one would be just as good if not better ● (MKManiac 2019)

It seems that Kiefer89 is something of a celebrity-fan within this tiny fandom, as their videos are among the most accomplished and appreciated. I'll return to this idea in chapter 4.

Finally, some of the fanvids and comments seemed to fall into the category of trolling and joking, such as the imposition of the 2016 song "Maneater" by Nelly Furtado over clips of Dahmer both in court and in his private life, with the subject pronoun changed in the imposed captions from "she" to "he'[s] a maneater" (serial killer edits 2021). The song is a light-hearted R&B pop track concerning a woman who is so attractive she causes men to spend all their money on her, and regret they "ever met her at all." A single image of Dahmer passing his hand over his hair as he walks, surrounded by law enforcement, into a court room, is repeated many times, in a way that, when combined with the lyrics, suggests sexualized preening. It wasn't: Dahmer was no Ramirez and, on the contrary, was generally self-conscious, highly awkward, and walked with a stoop. The clip is explicitly poached and reconfigured here for humor, a fannish discursive construction. "Lol this is perfect" (your-little-edit-witch 2021) reads a comment that has been pinned and liked by the creator, further situating the video as a joke. The top comment, also pinned by the creator, is "He's so handsome ●●" (Bumi 2021). To which the response is: "yasss jeffrey! SLAY😈" (A B 2021). This statement utilizes the discourse of queer culture in a rarely seen acknowledgment that Dahmer was entirely homosexual. So far there has been surprisingly little acknowledgement of this fact in the supposedly queer-friendly spaces of fan culture (see the fics where he falls in love with the reader's female stand-in). Another sort of joking and trolling coalesced around commenters with male usernames expressing flat admiration for the "work" of serial killers:

> Your a good man Ted Bundy lots of respect to you a good job well done. (mark quish 2021)

> Overpopulation is a problem. Thanks for doing what you had to do Richard. Rest easy legend. (Sherminator 2021)

A clear illustration of internet ambivalence, the level of irony can be hard to judge here. But the juxtaposition of an official-sounding, polysyllabic term like "overpopulation" with the implied solution of killing people does suggest black humor.

Other comments utilize the discourse of online misogyny and right-wing culture, purporting to read the sexualized videos as such:

> I'm just in awe of this dark triad mogger, Im Richard Ramirezmaxxing as we speak. (Antonio Salviano 2021)
>
> ramirezpill is indeed brutal. (Keith Grenier 2021)

These statements take some unpacking. Firstly, the "dark triad" refers to a psychological term for the traits of narcissism, Machiavellianism, and psychopathy, which in combination are a high predictor for criminal behavior.[4] "Mogger" is a verbification of the acronym AMOG (Alpha Male of the Group), a term originating in incel subcultures. A "mogger," then, is one who regularly dominates others—who regularly takes actions worthy of such an "alpha." "Ramirezmaxxing," one must assume, is an invented term to describe being overcome with emotion due to the mediated presence of Ramirez. "Ramirezpill" is a variation of Blackpill, itself a variation of Redpill. To be "redpilled," a term originating in the 1999 film *The Matrix*, is used in far-right circles to denote an act of awakening, to see the world as it "truly" is for the first time (according to far-right, misogynistic, nationalist ideologies, or sometimes according to related conspiracies). To be "blackpilled" means, for a heterosexual male, to give up all hope of attracting a mate and resigning oneself to celibacy, due to the realization that women are impossibly shallow and literally only care about physical appearance. To realize that Ramirez has female admirers, then, is the Ramirezpill: the ultimate illustration and "proof" of this sentiment. Via this process of reflexive discursive construction, serial killer fandom becomes the manifestation of what has gone terribly wrong with both society and gender relations . . . if it is taken seriously. As I will further explore in the chapter on digital play, the ever-ambivalent internet resists easy definitions, yet never quite allows us to dismiss these statements as only jokes.

The relatively new platform TikTok offered numerous search results for serial killer fandom. TikTok became increasingly popular during the

---

[4] An unavoidable use of the term here, as that is unfortunately how it's used in the psychology texts.

COVID-19 pandemic, becoming one of the world's primary platforms for short user-created. It specifically targets teenagers and preteens in its marketing. Like Tumblr, TikTok attracts a fair amount of concern regarding teen sexuality, bullying, supposedly deleterious effects on the developing attention span, and other vague consternation around teenagers doing things on the internet. Again, there was a large amount of content here; I think it is fair to say that serial killer fandom tends more towards the visual/audio/hybrid modes than strictly written forms of production. As this chapter is primarily focused on texts rather than community, I analyzed the content of the most popular account result for #serialkiller and #fandom, along with the most popular fan accounts for the celebrity serial killers I have been using as a sample set, using the search term #[name] and #fandom and/or #fan. Connections between these accounts, and the utilization of hashtags around community, will be considered in the next chapter, as they will for Tumblr. Table 7 presents the name, featured killer, and number of videos for these accounts. It also shows the total number of plays those videos have received, the average number of plays per video, the total number of comments received per account, the average number of comments per video, the total number of likes received per account, and the average number of likes per video. This data was recorded in the second half of February 2022.

Once again, Jack the Ripper and H. H. Holmes offered no relevant results. The tag #JacktheRipper only offered material from explicitly fictional franchises. H. H. Holmes had no results hashtagged with fandom, though plenty of TikToks were available on him under "interesting/creepy/historical fact" genres, and he was featured on the general "famous serial killers" account. Ramirez is the most popular subject based on amount of content. For the first time, Wuornos is more popular than Dahmer at the level of content, though not in terms of impact on the discursive formation as measured by reception. Note that Dahmer content still has the higher share of plays, likes, and comments. Note as well that the account name "aileenswife" is a specific reference to an appreciation of her lesbian sexuality—a point I will return to under the theme of sex.

Despite the fact that the videos were shorter, the thematic analysis revealed very similar patterns to those found on YouTube, with the exception of the "famous serial killers" general account. This was composed of documentary-like footage, with information in captions presented over black and white or color photographs of historical serial killers, some lesser known. These videos, again, are a product of convergence culture, but lack the ideological impetus implicit to textual poaching, simply meshing documentary footage and photographs with information. Booth would call them fan pastiche (2015). Commenters received them as informational works, being generally concerned with the correctness (or not) of the captions displayed:

> Indiana and Illinois [are] two different states. (*Daddy* 🐱💕2020)
>
> [Holmes's] "Hotel" was at 63rd and Halsted it was torn down in the late 90s early 2000s[.] Read "The Devil in the White City." (user9361478211356 2020)

Commenters were also concerned with correctness on other, more traditionally fannish accounts, but the tone is more aggressive and mocking. On a video showing letters purported to be from Ramirez, one viewer objects:

> BAHAHA he did not right that [. . .]
>
> That's a fucking joke and the worst fakes I've seen😂😂(Amyna_summer 2021)

Because @richard_ramirez62 produces explicitly sexualized, romanticized videos, lacking the pose of distance and objectivity implied by documentary-like footage, responses tend to be more heated and imbued with emotion. It is unclear whether these specific objections are to the misattribution of the letter, or simply to the fact that a Ramirez fan account exists. (And there was plenty of objection in the comments.)

The key themes documented on TikTok, then, were again a self-reflexive strand of discussion on textual poaching and fanwork as art; explicit sexualization; explanation and sympathy; and trolling. The reflexive discussion on textual poaching included, again, policing of the creator's choice of content. User theodorerobertbundy imposes the frenetic beats and distorted vocals of the 2009 Insane Clown Posse song "Chop Chop Slide" over images of Bundy in court, an effect that seemed to me somewhat humorous or trollish. Commenters, however, took issue, advising the creator:

> Any member of icp would beat the shit out of you and they should. (Ken 2021)
>
> don't ever use an insane clown posse sound their entire thing is hating bad people. (deleted user 2021)

One user utilizes the comment section to advertise her own song about Bundy, linking to her YouTube account. Makayla Singleton's "Ted Bundy"

Table 7. Serial Killer Fan Accounts from TikTok

Account name	Featured killer	No. videos	Total plays
famous_serial_killers	Assorted	14	14,9220
_theodorerobertbundy	Ted Bundy	6	20,385
richard_ramirez62	Richard Ramirez	88	957,761
jeffrey_dahmer17	Jeffrey Dahmer	2	978,146
Aileenswife	Aileen Wuornos	8	11,004

(2021a) uses vocal autotune to eerie effect over a minor synthesizer melody, telling a first-person story of abduction by Bundy, intercut with samples of Bundy speaking. The video features an image of a bloodied Volkswagon Bug. Viewers reacted:

> Great tune for the spooky season. It reminds me of the soundtrack for a scary movie. (Jeff Hilton 2021)

And the creator replied:

> thank you. thought it would be good for Halloween. (Makayla Singleton 2021b)

The TikTok user's account, then, is incorporated via links into a presentation of textual poaching as an art form, regardless of the fandom's marginalized identity.

As mentioned, a large amount of content on the Ramirez account is explicitly sexual. A typical example shows the creator lip-syncing the spoken introduction to the 1993 song "Whatta Man" by Salt-N-Peppa (featuring En-Vogue), that is: "You're so crazy, I think I wanna have your baby." It then cuts to a montage of Ramirez preening in court as the song plays. Most of the content is quite similar: images and montages of Ramirez cut to explicitly sexual music, and/or the account creator responding to his images by performing sexual arousal. The comments are a fairly even mixture of appreciation and claims to share in her attraction for him; and condemnation, expressions of disgust, and demands that Ramirez's fans acknowledge the names of his victims.

Table 7. Serial Killer Fan Accounts from TikTok (continued)

Average plays	Total comments	Avg. comments	Total Likes average	Likes
10,659	60	4	1,281	92
3,397.5	230	39	1,991	332
10,884	4,060	46.14	6,7451	766.5
11,000	129	65	998	499
1,376	115	14	2,463	308

What is interesting about the theme of sex on TikTok is its ventures into queerness. I have already noted that the account name "aileenswife" acknowledges both Wuornos's sexuality and queer attraction to her: There was a slight acknowledgement of this on YouTube in the professions of love for her from commenters with feminine-coded names, but TikTok reveals more. There is little sexually coded material for the creator to poach here: Wuornos did not present herself as a sexual or charismatically attractive being in court, and the media certainly did not present her as one. Instead, the creator relies on music to inflect the material selected, such as imposing a song about oral sex over clips that show Wuornos's tongue as she speaks. Commenters admire "her body" (V 2022a) and observe "She fine fine" (JaŻ 2022). Wuornos as sex symbol is a fannish construct, which exists in stark contrast to her treatment by the mainstream media.

Conversely, the Dahmer videos were not constructed as sexual (see the section on empathy below). When female commenters discuss their attraction to him, the response is:

> first off: He's a murderer. second of all: he was gay he would not want you. (Jude the Dude 2021)
>
>> I've been thinking about this for the past few days thank you for saying this. (🔪🔪 2021)
>>
>> seriously It's like even if he wasn't fckin evil to an indescribable degree they're denying and disrespecting a real person's sexuality. (Jude the Dude 2021)
>>
>> He would have been a gay icon surgeon but no he had to kill innocent men. Ppl need to accept the fact that he was a gay man. (🔪🔪 2021)

These statements inflect the discursive construction of Dahmer in a corrective way. His queerness has thus far been massively pathologized by official media and positioned as the cause of his actions, then elided and ignored by his fandom. TikTok produces the first statements reinforcing Dahmer's queerness yet denying it as a source of his pathology, acknowledging his potential, indeed, to become a "gay icon surgeon" (presumably because of his obsession with internal anatomy).

Trolling and joking remained a key theme on TikTok—meaning that AO3 was the only site where it wasn't. This may reflect the fact that AO3 has a more traditional and in some ways more "academic" reputation than the other fansites. This is not to say that AO3 does not host fan humor: It hosts plenty. But serial killer fan humor is a little beyond its site norms. Here on TikTok, I have already mentioned the Bundy video cut to Insane Clown Posse's "Chop Chop Slide," a short clip that edits rapid-cuts of Bundy smirking in court to the frenetic beat and lyric refrain "alright, pull your hatchets out," a visual joke in the same vein as the cannibalism puns. Jeffery_dahmer17 (2020) offers a video with the caption "here are some cursed photos of me" ("me" implying that the creator assumes the role of Dahmer, as in the account name). "Cursed" is quite difficult to explain as online slang: It can mean distorted, ugly, absurd, stupid, or simply discomfiting, and is usually applied to images and/or comments. "Distorted" is the meaning that applies to the audio, titled "Rhythm Thief but Cursed—TikTok": that is to say, an audio clip circulating on Tumblr that distorts the soundtrack from the computer game *Rhythm Thief & the Emperor's Treasure*. None of the photographs in the montage seem particularly "cursed" (except perhaps for the clip of a teenage Dahmer beside a giant bong built entirely of snow). But the caption plays into the ambiguity and irony inherent in the descriptor, asking, "Should I do the mugshot trend next? (jeffrey_dahmer17 2020). Once again, one senses parody, yet it is hard to say what is being parodied, exactly. Viewers, likewise, experience this sense of ambivalence: On a clip which photoshops the Ramirez channel's creator into Ramirez's actual wedding pictures, one user with the account name "richardramirezsbadbreath" writes: "CONGRATS " (2021), while another user, with username ".", complains: "i cant tell if these comments are satire or not" (2021). I'll return to this theme in chapter 5.

Empathy and sympathy are present in these videos, though this is a weaker theme than on YouTube. I have noted irony in the presentation of the jeffrey_dahmer17 account, yet the content of at least one (of two) videos is quite sympathetic to him, relying again on those clips of his childhood, depicting him as innocent, intercut with clips from the film adaptation of *My Friend Dahmer* (Meyer 2017). These show him being bullied at school and suffering various humiliations, and are edited to the R&B ballad "POV" by Ariana Grande (2020), a song about wishing to appreciate and love oneself as a lover sees one. Most of the comments are actually condemnatory, with users accusing the creator of being sick, appealing that they "please for the love of god get help" (izzy 2021), and asking if the creator is aware of the details of Dahmer's crimes.

Empathy and sympathy are more validated on the Wuornos videos: "She looks soft or idk," writes user V on a video showing Wuornos in a feminine cream blouse (2022b): "I wanna hug her." Viewers claim to be on "her side always" (✪ [username] 2021), to understand and support her, and to empathize with her. The creator roundly endorses these comments. Expressions of sympathy for Ramirez are present in the comments, too, though not really as a theme in the videos, which as noted are almost purely sexual. Where sympathy is expressed for him, it tends to be scorned and denied.

I have found, then, that the older lens of textual poaching is sometimes an appropriate tool to analyze serial killer fandom. These texts depend on communal interpretation from within a relatively marginalized culture, and attract a huge amount of censure on more open platforms like YouTube. Media convergence is more like a pathway which allows for textual poaching, but texts may also be utilized through convergence in a way that lacks the transformative impulse of textual poaching. This fannish pastiche, which Booth would call "coloring inside the lines" (2015, 2), will be returned to in chapter 5. The most explicitly political poaching concerned the reclamation of Wuornos as feminist icon, justifying violence against men as retaliation for male violence. Multimodal fanwork seems more popular than fanfiction utilizing written text alone.

Self-conscious discursive formation is also at work, such as when fanfic authors tag their fic as "out of character." The sexualization of Wuornos is a fannish invention. Fannish discursive invention accounted for a relatively small amount of the total data and is unlikely to be reincorporated by the media industry. I also observed some ways in which fanwork reinforces the discursive constructions of mainstream media: the primacy of male (and straight) serial killers over female and queer ones, and the heterosexual sexualization of their personas.

At the level of thematics, there was surprising continuity across the sites, though with differing emphasis. Sex and romanticization persisted everywhere, though it was only on TikTok and to a lesser extent YouTube that queer sexuality was allowed space. Explanation for and identification with the serial killers was another theme, and radical feminism was a sub-theme of this category on Tumblr only. Tumblr and TikTok, taken together, have proved both queerer and more feminist-identified that the traditional fanfic platforms, which is a notable finding considering that the marginalization of female and queer identities was a key political impetus in early fan studies. Perhaps the most complex theme, and the one most evasive of the textual poaching model, is the one I have tagged joking/trolling: This theme will be further investigated and better accounted for in chapter 5, on fandom as digital play. One can easily read parody though a textual poaching lens, but parody is not quite the right term for the material I have thus far discovered. Its object of satire is too difficult to pin down, infused with an invasive irony and ambivalence that elides easy definition.

This chapter has focused on fantexts. In the next, I turn to a theoretical model through which interfan relations have been traditionally addressed—that of affective community.

CHAPTER 3

Affect, Bonding, Boundaries

Is There a Serial Killer Fan Community?

Conceptions of fandom as a community, like those of fans as textual poachers, originate in the efforts of early fan scholars to redeem fandom as social, healthy, and productive. Henry Jenkins (1992, 280) described fan gatherings as an "alternative social community" where other (better) practices were valued than those of the workaday world of capitalism. Camille Bacon-Smith (1992) was concerned with fandom specifically as a women's culture, wherein feminine and feminized readings and experiences could be valued in spaces evasive of (if not resistant to) patriarchal oppression. The common and unproblematic theme is that many if not most fans seek out others who share their interest, hobbies, and favored topics of discussion: One might hesitate to generalize as strongly as Clerc that "the most primal instinct of a fan is to talk to other fans about their common interest" (1996, 74), but this is certainly a strong desire for many, especially when that interest is stigmatized, as early forms of fandom were and as serial killer fandom is today.

In this chapter, I'll review some key ideas of "community" as applied to online cultures and fandom in particular. The foundational work of Rhiannon Bury and Nancy Baym on online fan community still holds merit, and provides some grounding theory for this chapter. However, I believe that the term "community" is now over-used and under-defined, applied too freely to the kind of brief interactions and acknowledgements that are better served by the term "networked individualism," which Baym later preferred in many contexts (2007, 2010). Thus I will begin this chapter by recapping some of the attempts to define what online community is or can be, specifically as applied to fandom and the sites that host it, before turning to the data for evidence or lack thereof. I'll briefly expand on the idea of a fandom gift economy. I'll then survey evidence for serial killer fan community on Tumblr and TikTok, sites which are generally quite permissive with regard to content and thus the potential growth of stigmatized fandoms, before turning to Reddit, a site more suited to analysis of online "community" in traditional terms. I discovered that, contrary to my expectation, the traditional architectures of Reddit did *not* support killer fan community more consistently than those of Tumblr and TikTok. Pathologization and stigmatization by outsiders was a stronger factor in the formation of communal bonds than site architecture. However, the forms of community I discovered were not particularly strong on any of the sites: Typically, users demonstrated weak ties of affiliation and affection, partly due to the instability and frequent deletion of the materials they created.

Any study of a community where participants don't interact face-to-face is ultimately indebted to Benedict Anderson's (1983) conception of "imagined community." Anderson demonstrated how mass print assists in forming a conception of a "nation" as community, via the production of a national consciousness and set of (supposed) common values, despite the fact that the vast majority of the populace will never meet each other face-to-face. When fan scholars turned to the internet, they were concerned to establish online fan communities as real forms of sociality. When Nancy Baym and Rhiannon Bury wrote their influential works *Tune In, Log On* (2000) and *Cyberspaces of their Own* (2005), respectively, they were working within an academic culture that was only just beginning to consider that online community might not be an oxymoron, after Harold Rheingold's now-classic study of early home internet usage for social purposes (1993). As Ruth Deller wrote, those debates were archaic even in 2014, as "'community' [was by then] widely accepted as a description for groups of people gathering online and frequently used across web platforms" (2014, 239).

Michael Hammond observed that the term online community "has been used across a wide range of contexts, covering issues of attachment, emotion, community strength, motivation for participation, and relationship to technology" (2017, 1). This is true of the ways it has been used by fan scholars, from Baym (2000) and Bury (1998, 2005) onwards. Hammond's own threshold for online community definition is quite high, requiring both commitment and consequences for one's actions, in addition to the factors of "connection to others; reciprocity; interaction" and "agency" (2017, 1). But Hammond also recognizes that community comes in degrees, which he describes as weaker and stronger. I don't think an online community necessarily needs to fulfill a strict list of requirements to merit the name. The definition of online community (and community in general) is probably situational.

In *Tune in, Log On* (2000), Baym centered her argument for fan community on a Usenet mailing list of soap opera fans. She argued that the textual practices of the group constituted community in several ways. Firstly, through shared practices of interpretation and comparing perspectives on the soaps, such as relating storylines to their personal experiences. They also shared criticism of the text, often humorously, and established interpersonal relationships that went far beyond the programs, discussing and sharing good and bad experiences from their lives. The group had established norms of writing, notably the use of standard English and the performance of wit. Certain posters developed strong individual identities through their styles of posting and habitual signatures. The community, overall, was established by norms, practice, and self- and mutual recognition *as* a community, which was later threatened by an influx of new users unschooled in its norms. Bury's research (2001, 2005) shared many of the same themes, except that, as the title's allusion to Virginia Woolf suggests, it was concerned specifically with female fans and the spaces they create for themselves. Both Baym and Bury were concerned with groups established in the face of relative stigma: Soap fans are/were stigmatized for their choice of text, while Bury's fans were stigmatized for loving more culturally respectable texts *in the wrong way:* notably, sexual attraction to the actor David Duchovny from *The X-Files.* The "David Duchovny Estrogen Brigade," a tongue-in-cheek self-reference to the way male fans of *The X-Files* conceived of them, was a group of mailing lists set up by female fans in order that they could freely discuss their attractions without mockery, in addition to all sorts of other subjects.

Bury conceived of these female-dominated spaces as "heterotopias" (2005, 17), after Michel Foucault, or spaces operating according to a differing social order from mainstream culture, in which performances of female and feminine desire could be celebrated. This claim of heterotopia is less convincing than Bury's claim for community, because, while female-dominated, Bury's subjects upheld norms of standard English writing, politeness, and reasoned debate. Indeed, both Baym and Bury's early books belong to the phase of academia that was concerned to present fandom in its most culturally respectable light. Bury herself concedes that the expressions of attraction within the forums were fairly restrained, noting that "the pressure exerted by normative discourses of femininity to be 'ladylike,' which includes avoidance of sexually explicit language, cannot be discounted" (2001). For both Bury and Baym, however, fan community is ultimately established by the repetition and consolidation of specific textual practices within bounded online spaces. These focus on the shared celebration and interpretation of favored texts, but also include identity creation, mutual support, discussion and sharing of life events, and linguistic performances of intelligence and humor. Importantly, users professed to experience their participation as a community, citing strong ties with other list members and the ability to talk to them about all kinds of matters, even those they would not discuss with family and friends.

Baym and Bury's studies were focused on the traditional format of Usenet groups. As Bury went on to acknowledge, the nature of community is mediated by and dependent on online platforms (Bury et al. 2013; Bury 2017). Platforms such as Tumblr and TikTok, however, do not support community in the same way as threaded lists of comments and replies linked to a stable online identity. But Bury has "questions as to the ongoing centrality of online community in the late second media age" given that "the design and architecture of listservs, newsgroups and discussion forums," still used but no longer dominant, "plays an important role in enabling the kind of in-depth, sustained interactivity required for community formation and maintenance over the long-term" (2017, 627, 633). Bury found that Twitter and Tumblr users didn't see these platforms as supportive of fan community. As one of her interviewees put it:

> I think the problem with Tumblr is that it doesn't have threaded discussions or you are re-blogging everything. So I think if it did have threaded discussion I think it would be perfect for fandom and I think fandom probably would have jumped on it much faster. But as it is, like so much of fandom is discussion that it's just, I don't think it's ever going to be that ideal of a fit. (in Bury 2017, 639)

Bury considers that "online community will not disappear, but it may well become residual, to borrow a term from Raymond Williams (i.e., no longer the main or dominant mode of engagement)" (640). She claims that platforms like Twitter and Tumblr lend themselves, instead, to networked individualism, wherein the individual creates an online persona with multiple weak ties to other personas across multiple webspaces, but not to community in the bounded, truly reciprocal, committed sense. I thus hypothesized that the idea of fan community might be applicable to serial killer fandom in two forms: firstly, in the sense of making space for a stigmatized group interest that is relatively resistant to industrial co-optation; and secondly, on the more traditionally formatted platform of Reddit, which is divided into interest groups called "subreddits."

Some scholars do report finding evidence of online community on Tumblr. I have already noted Barnes on the "boundary work" of the self-professed "true crime community" of interest, wherein community is defined both by a common interest and by contrast to its Bad Other of killer fans (2019). One might posit that being defined as Bad Other offers serial killer fans a sense of self-definition, and definition as a community. Similarly, Jessica Kunert utilizes Tumblr as a site of study to continue in the theme of female sub-sections in male-dominated fandoms. Her article "The Footy Girls of Tumblr: How Women Found Their Niche in the Online Football Fandom" (2021) argues that female football fans create their own spaces on that platform for much the same reasons as Bury's *X-Files* fans did. Here women can talk freely about football without accusations that they are invested for the "wrong reasons," that they are attracted to the players rather than the game, that women can't be "real" football fans, and without male participants speaking over them. Kunert also sees textual-linguistic style as constitutive of a community of practice, including "creative endeavors, such as fan art and fiction, one's own jargon, and a celebrity discourse that resembles those in music or film fandom" (2021, 246). Fans translate and provide media for those in other countries that may not have access to the same texts, such as match reports. In short, this reads very like an updated, multimedia, more internationalized variation on Baym's work, though the focus is more on shared texts and communal interpretation than the creation and connection of individual personas.

Sneha Kumar (2021) also argues for community on Tumblr, contending that the online fandom of the lesbian vampire web series *Carmilla* "can be understood as a lesbian community of feeling based on the exchange of positive and negative affects" (1.1). Kumar understands affect as "emotions that have an energetic dimension to them" (1.4), or a kind of mobility, capable of moving back and forth with greater and lesser intensity. Affinity spaces, then, are social spaces demarcated by the flow of affect. Kumar argues that

> for *Carmilla* fans, Tumblr acts as both an affinity space and a participatory culture. Moreover, the act of reblogging intensifies affect across the site. [. . .] The intensity of affect builds on Tumblr though user practices of repetition—reblogging the same image at different points in time. [. . .] Tumblr users often reblog posts that resonate with them—a post about ***Carmilla*** fans storming into Shaftesbury, the company that produced the series, to demand more *Carmilla* content has been reblogged a total of 350 times, indicating a shared desire by many in the *Carmilla* fandom to see a sequel to *The Carmilla Movie.* (2.12–17)

In this way, Kumar argues, "positive affects are able to travel through Tumblr because of its encouragement of reblogging content that speaks to varied experiences and interests" (2.17). Again, in this definition of community, the individual persona-building that Bury and Baym stressed is secondary to the flow of affect and the sharing and shared interpretation of fannish material.

Serena Hillman et al. (2014a, 2014b) also found that their fan-participants conceived of Tumblr as a community—interestingly, as "the Tumblr community" (2014b, 287)–rather than a set of subcommunities. The constant access to Tumblr allowed by portable devices and the adoption of a "unique set of jargon and use of animated GIFs to match their desired fandom activities" (2014b, 285) are key parts of this experience. (The use of GIFs can cross fandoms on Tumblr in addition to being fandom-specific: Though the authors don't spell this out, the mobility and exchange of GIFs may be a factor in experiencing Tumblr as a community rather than as a set of subcommunities.) GIF and jargon use can be understood as the multimedia update of the in-group ways of typing Baym and Bury identified. Hillman et al. found that the concept of belonging to a specific fandom on Tumblr—rather than Tumblr as a whole—was "fuzzy" (2014b, 287). This makes sense, as the architectures of Tumblr don't subdivide users into groups from which one can be accepted or rejected, or voluntarily join and leave. As such, belonging to an individual fandom on Tumblr is entirely a subjective experience: Users "are part of the fandom when [they] feel [they] are" (187). Significantly, Hillman et al.'s subjects frequently felt more able to express their "authentic" selves on Tumblr, as its relative anonymity and lack of connections to offline friends and acquaintances allowed users a degree of freedom they did not feel, for example, on Facebook. This finding will be important for my test-case of a stigmatized fandom. Finally, Hillman et al. found that while the learning curve for Tumblr participation is steep, with many technological barriers to overcome for first-time users, this paradoxically works to strengthen community feeling. Casual enthusiasts or those who dip in and out of a fandom are likely to give up and find an easier platform to navigate, so that those who master Tumblr become a self-selecting group of highly interested, highly invested media fans (2014a). Shared experience between such participants afforded users "a sense of support, friendship, and community" (2014a, 781). Hillman and her co-authors do note, however, that Tumblr's "restrictive approach to private messaging [only to blogs one has followed for more than forty-eight hours] privileges content generation and communities of shared interest over the ability to focus on one-to-one relationships" (784). This legitimates my observation that the definition of community on Tumblr is primarily based on shared texts, shared feeling, and shared interpretation.

There is some prior research on the idea of "community" on TikTok, though not on fan community *per se*. Most prior English-language interest in this relatively new platform has been concerned with data management, user privacy, and its controversial or banned status in many countries (Kesling and Wells 2020; Wang 2020; Zeng et al. 2021). However, the TikTok Cultures Research Network and the Global TikTok Researchers network in the United Kingdom are uniting researchers taking a more sociocultural perspective, as evidenced by the publication of Trevor Boffone's edited volume *TikTok Cultures in the United States* in 2022. Several of its essays are concerned with community and how TikTok can enable or disable it to varying degrees (Divon and Ebbrecht-Hartmann 2022; Skinner 2022; Rochford and Palmer 2022). Boffone himself holds that it is "algorithmic personalization that enables identities, communities, and cultures to take shape on the platform" (Boffone 2022, 7; and cf. İnceoglu and Kaya 2021). Elle Rochford and Zachary Palmer consider the possibilities of trans community on TikTok via the output of trans creators, but ultimately conclude that the algorithm and affordances of the site facilitate trans *content* more than they do *community* (2022, 85–86). The majority of TikTok users are not trans, and the algorithm is always going to privilege and promote videos addressed and accessible to the majority rather than the minority, regardless of who the creator is. Moreover, the structures of the site are not particularly conducive to community-making:

> Conversations in the comments are often difficult to follow. Replies are nested but users may comment on responses starting new threads or reply to the wrong comment. Comments and replies are not presented by like or chronologically so users new to the comment section many respond to something that had already been resolved or misunderstand the comment they were responding to. Nuanced conversations are all but impossible. (88)

Similarly, Diana Zulli and David Zulli note that TikTok is unusual in that the "For You Page" does not immediately present the user with the videos of those they have followed or friended (2021, 1878). It is notable that users refer to being *on* a certain sub-section of TikTok (Lesbian TikTok, Fashion TikTok) rather than *in* it (1883). Zulli and Zulli do use the term "community" to describe these segments, but they place the term in double quotation marks. I am not convinced that the data they are describing really merits the term "community." I will thus return to Zulli and Zulli in chapter 5, on digital play, where I think their insights are more useful.

Overall, TikTok is a platform that privileges content, and a difficult one to study beyond that level. We know a little about how the TikTok system of video recommendation, i.e., the "For You Page," works: It bases its recommendations on videos the user has previously watched, suggesting similar content and re-used songs, but also uses weaker signals such as the user's location and type of device. It also deliberately diversifies the videos it offers (TikTok 2020). Its structures privilege spreading and replication, particularly of sound. TikTok has a "use that sound" feature, which allows users to create a new video set to an existing audio clip, often one that is in popular circulation. An automated system is supposed to identify and credit the sound's original creator. It is often wrong, meaning that some users have developed a sort of honor-system of attribution by tagging, but this is by no means universal (Kaye et al. 2021). D. Bondy Valdovinos Kaye et al. write that "the community thrives on the creative reuse of popular video, audio, or meme formats, and the platform promotes copying" (2021, 3197). At best, then, we might expect to observe some form of community akin to Kumar's affective community, where amplification by repetition of content enacts the flow of affect. I wonder, though, if we are stretching the meaning of "community" too far now.

Conversely, Alexa Hiebert and Kathy Kortes-Miller did find that TikTok served as an online community platform for gender and sexual minority youth throughout the COVID-19 pandemic. The authors write that "without commenting or producing content the researcher was able to feel a sense of connection and belonging within this community" (2021), simply by accessing the stream of content produced and hashtagged by gender and sexual minority youth. Relatedly, Ellen Simpson and Bryan Semaan (2021) document how LGBTQ+ youth manipulate the mysterious TikTok algorithm to the best of their ability, strategically liking and blocking posts, in order to receive a feed that feels more relevant both to their self-identity and their sense of an LGBTQ+ community, often against the direction they felt the algorithm had been pushing them. While not discounting this experience, I wonder if the term "community" can be used here in the same—fairly specific and rigorous—way that Baym and Bury have used it. The authors did document supportive comments made by participants to each other, specifically during difficult times in their lives, which is more in keeping with the theme of mutual support. TikTok users even offered offline support such as a place to stay for those at risk of homelessness. If we accept a minimal definition of community as consisting of mutual support and empathy between individuals sharing some identity factor, then this was community at work, but it may not live up to the more stringent definitions of Baym and Bury, which require developed individual online personas and consistent interactions over time. Michelle Zappavigna proposed the term "ambient affiliation" for a minimal, impermanent form of community bonded around topics of interest (2011): She was analyzing Twitter, but Melissa K. Avdeeff suggests the concept could apply to TikTok trends as well (2021).

Reddit is in many ways a more traditional community platform. Built on similar (if modernized) architectures of threaded comments, posts, and reply chains to the groups Baym and Bury originally studied, Reddit allows users to create enduring online identities through the consistency of their posting. Kelly Bergstrom and Nathaniel Poor call Reddit "a present-day embodiment of a message board system, evolved from earlier forms like Usenet and modem-based bulletin board systems" (2021, 4). There is nothing to stop a Reddit user from creating multiple identities, but many value the accumulation of "karma" via upvotes, awards for helpful, funny, or informative posts from other users, and the general creation of an online identity often dating back years. The site is divided into subforums by interest, known as subreddits. These range from the extremely general (r/news), to the incredibly specific (r/ronperlmancats, for pictures of cats that look like the actor Ron Perlman). Subreddits are moderated by user-volunteers. Kimery Lynch discusses how these relatively traditional, relatively hierarchical structures enable community gatekeeping. Taking a K-pop fan subreddit as a case study, she argues that "having moderators distinguishes Reddit as a platform from Twitter or Tumblr. Twitter and Tumblr by design have no official built-in central leadership for each community" (2022, 108). Moderators gatekeep the subreddit's feed by removing posts and comments that violate communal norms, which again are fairly traditional and relate back to Baym and Bury's analysis of politeness, civility, and reasonableness. Lynch quotes a user as expressing feelings that "they were 'raised right' as a new fan and 'guided' to be a model BTS fan" by the Reddit fan community, and "would not have the same 'perception, depth, and maturity' as a fan if they participated on any other social media platform" (Lynch 2022, 116). Other writers have studied Reddit gaming communities and demonstrated their importance as social support and friendship beyond users' initial attachment to the game (Bergstrom and Poor 2021).

In keeping with Bury's later work, it seems that while some definition of "community" could be argued for a variety of fannish platforms, how far and in what ways the term applies is highly contingent on the site's affordances and norms. Common themes in the definitions of fan community include interest and shared interpretations around key texts; the spread of affect; mutual support; in-group behavioral norms that may differ from other fan communities or the norms of the platform more broadly; and shared visual and textual languages. How far a user needs to construct a stable persona to participate in a community seems to be an open question. The question is particularly pertinent with regard to a stigmatized fandom like that of serial killers, which on one hand may be reinforced through pathologization by outsiders, but on the other, is subject to deletion and banning of materials across a range of sites.

One further note is needed before we turn to the material. Some academics have posited that fan communities are bound by a "gift economy" (Hellekson 2009), wherein fans gift their time, skill, and textual creations to other fans without expectation of direct return. This is based on a general understanding that gift-giving benefits the community as a whole, because, as a non-depletable resource, there are more creations for everyone to consume. Tisha Turk calls this "circular giving," which is rarely one-to-one. The default is one-to-many, as each created gift is available to all:

> Fandom's gift economy is therefore fundamentally asymmetrical: because a single gift can reach so many people, and especially because it can go on reaching people

> well after the initial moment of distribution, most fans receive far more gifts than we give. Even the most productive fans generally don't make as many vids as we watch, code as many sites as we use, moderate as many convention panels as we attend, or create as many links as we follow. This asymmetry is critical to fandom's functioning because it balances out the asymmetry in the other direction: not every gift recipient will reciprocate with "the gift of reaction" (Hellekson 2009, 116). (Turk 2014)

In a fandom that is both small and relatively taboo, one might assume that any gifts are created and shared with less expectation of communal return. Firstly, there are fewer members to create gifts. Further, one might imagine serial killer fandom to have a greater percentage of anonymous lurkers than active participants, reluctant to leave digital traces, consuming fan creations in silence. How will this affect the gift economy of serial killer fandom? Can it still be said to provide the bonding material of a community?

After a brief survey, the three sites I considered that hold the most potential for serial killer fan community were Tumblr, TikTok, and Reddit. The data analyzed in this chapter was gathered simultaneously, over a three-month period in spring 2022. Though the delineations of community may (or may not) be weaker on TikTok and Tumblr than on Reddit, these sites are among the most permissive with regard to content. For Tumblr and TikTok, I realized that a participant-ethnographic approach was the best way to approximate the experience of community, or lack thereof. Thus I created a Tumblr with a generic auto-generated name, and began by following the list of popular killer fan blogs already identified in the previous chapter. On Reddit, I found one subreddit devoted to self-declared fandom of Richard Ramirez. It was fairly small and did not afford much data, but I also identified the subreddit r/hybristophilia, which afforded much more. This was lucky: r/hybristophilia was deleted and banned just as the data collection period concluded. My analysis of the Tumblr and TikTok data is grounded in participant ethnography, due to the rapid turnover of posts and immersive experience created by the sites. The Reddit data, which is more textual in a traditional sense, was inductively coded by theme.

To recap, the Tumblr blogs that I initially followed were:

- https://nightst4lkerxx.tumblr.com/
- https://the-real-ricardo-ramirez.tumblr.com/
- https://angelrose-666.tumblr.com/

- https://sick-girl-666.tumblr.com/
- https://casdied.tumblr.com/
- https://gunsnfilms.tumblr.com/
- https://richardramirezx.tumblr.com/
- https://richardramirezricardo.tumblr.com/
- https://yourickie-x.tumblr.com/
- https://stalkersdisneyland.tumblr.com/
- https://the-real-dahmer.tumblr.com/
- https://datingdahmer-blog.tumblr.com
- https://aileenwuornos-blog.tumblr.com/
- https://teddyshellclub.tumblr.com/

Having followed these, I returned to my newly created Tumblr dashboard to view their content as the algorithm presented it. The first thing I noted is that the blog richardramirezx had retained a GIF of Ramirez as its header but deleted all its posts. The only text on the blog was this header:

yuzuru hanyu

" supporting athletes.

don't repost!

—new account

The imperative not to repost suggests that the former blog had been deleted due to harassment, or reported to the site and issued with a takedown notice. Yuzuru Hanyu, Google informs me, is a Japanese figure skater, suggesting an entirely new direction for the blog despite the header. I observe immediately that if community exists here, it is insecure. Blogs vanish, respawn, change direction. Some, like this one, give no explanation. Others, such as sick-girl-666 (which had respawned since the data for the previous chapter was collected), used explanatory headers like:

> IM BACK!!!
>
> Someone report my blog and it was delete!!!
>
> FOR EVERYBODY : IF YOU DONT LIKE MY BLOG PLEASE LEAVE IT!!! DON'T REPORT MY BLOG!!! (sick-girl-666 2022)

To persist with serial killer fandom requires some evasion, some determination, and some luck. Like the LGBTQ+ users' experience of TikTok (Simpson and Semaan 2021), serial killer fan community has to be built in negotiation with and via manipulation of the algorithm, rather than relying on it. Attempting to curate my dashboard, I followed the tags "serialkillerfans," "serialkillerfanfic," and "serialkillerfanfiction," even though they hadn't been productive in the research for the previous chapter, just in case they turned up relevant content. But when I returned to my dashboard, with these new follows, I found it overwhelmed by posts relating to the Columbine massacre. Most of these were fannish and celebratory of the school shooters, but clearly if one wishes to partake in serial killer fandom specifically, one needs to do a lot of filtering. I unfollowed the blog "truecrimefiend," which hosted and reblogged the bulk of them, and followed instead the blogs from which my selected sample reblogged. My dashboard also offered me a list of new and related Tumblrs to follow, as well as more tags, but they were too generic to reveal much relevant material, attempting to push me towards more normative true crime content such as documentaries and informational posts. All this demonstrates Hillman et al.'s (2014a) points regarding the high barriers to entry and steep learning curve for entry into a Tumblr fandom. If there is serial killer fan community here, one must be quite committed and determined to find it.

Nonetheless, after much tweaking, I did end up with a dashboard stream of serial killer fan content, in addition to some irrelevant promoted posts and notifications from the Tumblr staff. These posts seem to be unavoidable. Very few of the serial killer fan posts had comments, and those that did weren't necessarily fannish interpretations. For example, cr0w-is-dummy commented on night-monster-666's image of Ted Bundy posing in court: "ugly-ass motherfucker who murdered innocent women bc he's a fucking monster" (cr0w-is-dummy 2022). Symphony-of-damage posts on an image of a "romantic" letter to a fan sent from Ramirez in prison: "why didn't this mf try and get girls by being sweet and passionate like he pretended to be to his penpals instead of fucking r@ping women and children huh"

(2021). The use of the @ symbol is to avoid site censorship, demonstrating that even those with a more traditional interest in true crime may resort to anti-censorship techniques when violence is concerned. It seems difficult to gatekeep or maintain boundaries for a killer fan community on Tumblr, as the platform's structure would predict. User deathrowrorry reblogged a series of photos that were removed by the site for breaking the terms of service, with the caption: "Crime scene photos are the most fascinating types of photos to look at. I find it surreal that Richard did that, he saw this, he made the rooms like that. These photos make me feel like I'm seeing in his perspective and it sets some sort of mood, a really distraught, devastating, surrealism type of mood" (2020). The post has 621 likes, but only three comments, the first of which is "Richard Ramirez is a lil bitch who don't even know how to draw a pentagram. Like fam, That's a pentacle" (somebodyhelpme 2020). Recall Kumar's suggestion that reblogging consolidates and transfers affect—which it does—but that affect can also be punctured by such scathing takedowns in the comments.

Some comments, however, are expressions of friendship, like "love your blog x" (truecrimefiend 2022) and "thank you s[o] m[uch] cutie" (your-rickie 2022). Other users made requests for information and more media on killers and cases, sometimes in multiple languages, akin to the knowledge community creation witnessed by Kunert (2021). "Can you tell me any weird/unusual facts about our boy Jeffrey Dahmer? Whenever I read facts or stuff online, it's mostly the same thing over and over again. I know the basics :)," asks an anonymous user on a fanblog (Anon. 1 2022). The possessive pronoun situates Dahmer and his life as the mediated text shared between the fans. Posters instruct each other quite specifically on where to find what they are looking for. Afacewithouteyes, for example, is seeking information on the Cecil Hotel room where Ramirez stayed during some of his murders. Dead-desert-star advises:

> @afacewithouteyes There's this guy named Jake on YouTube that makes funny videos and in one he goes to the Cecil and actually goes into the room he stayed in (1418 or 1419). Just type in Jake Webber/Cecil Hotel/Richard Ramirez and it should come up. His facial expressions in the video are hilarious and you get a good look at the room. (dead-desert-star 2021)
>
> > @dead-desert-star Thank you! My Google searches turned up nothing so this really helps ●. (afacewithouteyes 2021)

> @afacewithouteyes no problem! He's got a another video too where he opens a box of Richard"s stuff/memorabilia That's kind of funny. (dead-desert-star 2021)

Note the cordial address, the use of emojis, and the readiness to assist. Dead-desert-star's profile figure is of a woman's face, presumably herself or at least her online persona, suggesting a relatively stable online identity.

Posters share images of merchandise related to their favored killers and compliment each other's collections. They share fantasies and report dreams, and express appreciation for the upload of rare pictures, thanking each other directly. The use of emojis is commonplace, and posters tag each other directly for attention in conversations. Favored emojis are black hearts, smiley faces, and smiley faces with hearts in their eyes. In addition to the mutual investment in and interpretation of shared texts (as funny/informative, for example), these sorts of posts convince me of at least a minimal level of serial killer fan community on Tumblr. These mutually supportive posts are scattered across the landscape, though a large number of comments were removed. They may have been removed by the blog owner for abuse, or by Tumblr staff, but I suspect that in many cases the former is more likely, because I realized fairly quickly that many of these posts were not tagged, or at least not tagged in a way that reflects their real content. The way to find serial killer fan community is not by searching tags, but by the method I arrived at—by knowing which blogs to begin with, and working outwards from them. This contributes to the sense of an in-group: a knowledge community that is in some way dependent on already possessing knowledge. Camille Bacon-Smith underwent a similar process in attempting to access the inner circles of *Star Trek* fandom, such as those producing slash fiction (1992). If I did not know Tumblr housed serial killer fandom, I would never have located these posts—which might be something for the authors of moral-panic clickbait to consider in their rampant publicizing of it. Though I kept refreshing my dashboard daily, the posts—and the users—did not vary much. This again aligns with Hillman et al.'s argument that the architectures of Tumblr lend themselves to tighter and more exclusive communities with high barriers to entry (2014a).

Of course, outsiders do find these blogs, probably through the generic tags or being directed to them by other users. Again, the architectures of Tumblr don't lend themselves to the kind of offline, fairly secretive gatekeeping Bacon-Smith experienced, nor even the moderated communities of Reddit. User the-real-ricardo-ramirez, for example, operates an "askbox," wherein users may submit questions which are posted to the blog. These are often anonymously penned instructions to commit suicide, or advice that "your blog makes for free birth control" (xiigauge 2021). The site owner seems amused by this, and either responds with ironic expressions of love, or equanimous retorts:

> K[ill]y[our]s[elf] fat cunt (Anon. 2 2021)
>
> Only if you do it with me whore (the-real-ricardo-ramirez 2021a)

Users from within the killer fan community will often support the blog owner: "your response was everything" (jelicaalynn 2021); "lmao you're funny I like you" (ang3l-bitch 2021). They assure the blog owner that they are doing nothing to warrant death threats. In one retort to an accusation that "you and this sick blog are so disgusting" (Anon. 3 2021), the blog owner responds, "if you aren't gonna say it off of anonymous then fuck off" (the-real-ricardo-ramirez 2021b). This is notable. One of Hammond's (2017) definitions of community was that community entails some sort of accountability or consequences for one's statements. Anonymity is the easiest way to evade communal consequences for one's statements. The-real-ricardo-ramirez implies that, by choosing anonymity, the commenter loses the right to make judgments. To another insult, s/he responds: "tell me off anon then we'll settle this" (2021c), implying that consequences will follow from a revelation of the accuser's persona.

Some blogs take a less aggressive stance in their attempts at gatekeeping their fandom. They refer to those who despise them and their blogs as "antis," presumably from "anti-fans." An image set addressed to said "antis" was recirculated, laying out in multiple text boxes justifications for serial killer fanblogs, such as the humanity of serial killers and their families, the argument that punishment simply creates more crime, and that enjoyment in punishing criminals is primitive and brutal. A reasonable argument, overall: Though it doesn't actually justify serial killer *fandom*, it does flag the irony of asserting that serial killer fans should die or kill themselves. There are clearly repeated attempts to carve out some kind of space for these blogs on Tumblr—by re-registering when deleted, by aggressively confronting "antis," or by attempts to reason with them and requesting they simply leave blogs they dislike rather than report them.

As the usernames suggest, many of these blogs utilized an element of roleplay, a popular fan activity I will also address in the chapter on digital play. For the moment, I should note how roleplay enables interactivity between Tumblr users. I found accounts roleplaying (intermittently) as Richard Ramirez, Ted Bundy, Jeffrey Dahmer, and Aileen Wuornos, as well as a host of mass shooters and other criminals. There was even an account roleplaying as Darlie Routier, a woman convicted of murdering two of her children and awaiting execution in Texas. These commenters seem to assume her guilt.[1] Most of these blogs, of which the-real-ricardo-Ramirez's is one, dip in and out of the killer's voice, utilizing it to respond to commenters who address them in-role:

> I want you in these guts (Anon. 4 2018)
>
> > How about I slice you open and take your guts? (the-real-ricardo-ramirez 2018a)
> >
> > Are you the real Richard? (Anon. 5 2018)
> >
> > Yes, I came back from the dead using my lord Satan's help (the-real-richard-ramirez 2018b)

This last comment seems to be ironic, or at least a humorous acknowledgement that, no, of course this is not the real Richard Ramirez, who has been dead since 2013. As Nicolle Lamerichs (2011) and Ellen Kirkpatrick (2015) wrote of cosplay, fan roleplay is a liminal experience which involves the fan's self in dialogue with the mediated "role." Compare:

> omg r u the rEaL Ted Bundy????😱👀shook omg😳🔥. (Anon. 6 2018)
>
> > There's two Teds but I'm the original good one. (the-real-ted-bundy-blog 2018a)

The use of emoticons and random capitals suggest the asker is being ironic, performing excessive fan behavior upon "meeting" their favored celebrity. The acknowledgement that "There's two Teds" points up the fiction of the roleplay. The roleplay blogs make reference to a discord "group chat" in

---

[1] The case is very complex, and one of the most mystifying I have personally heard of in my years of true crime interest. The real Routier maintains her innocence.

which the "serial killer" personas are involved. Users attempt to persuade "the-real-ted-bundy-blog" to join them:

> Join the discord chat teddy boi all the killers are waiting for their King to arrive. (Anon. 7 2018)
>
> > As flattering as it is to be called king, I don't know what it is. (the-real-ted-bundy-blog 2018b)

Discord is a real-time chat network on which one must be invited to join groups, so this is obviously one way of gatekeeping the serial killer fan community space against antis. Once enlightened, the-real-ted-bundy appears to concede to join, after being assured there is "no drama" in the chat and any reports of such has been "lies" (Anon. 8 2018). It seems that the serial killer fan community is just as prone to infighting as other fan communities can be.

Sometimes it is difficult to tell whether the blog owner is speaking as themselves or as their character. Consider this complicated exchange, in which the users/roleplayers are confessing an attraction to either each other, their characters, something in between, or both:

> tell me. i wont judge to[o] hard (the-real-jazzy-richardson 2018)
>
> > OMG FINE ● Because you said [you love me] "In a friendly way (I GUESS)" so which means you really don't, you love me in more than a friend way but you don't want to admit it because I look like someone from one direction (the-real-ricardo-ramirez 2018c)
> >
> > u do look like someone from one direction. and i *guess* ur cute but u obviosuly dont want to date my edgy ass so………… (the-real-jazzy-richardson 2018)
> >
> > EDGY ASS???? Please. I totally would (the-real-ricardo-ramirez 2018c)
> >
> > so ur saying you would date me? thats surprising im a goth mop sitting in lonely corner depressed [. . .] im the worst person around here dude (the-real-jazzy-richardson 2018)
> >
> > Yes, yes I would. Oh please you aren't the worst person around here I've seen worse. You aren't even near worse anyways. So yes I would (the-real-ricardo-ramirez 2018c)

For context, Jasmine Richardson is a Canadian woman who, at the age of twelve, planned and committed the murder of her parents and brother in conjunction with her then twenty-three-year-old boyfriend. Obviously, the real Ramirez can no longer date anyone (nor did he particularly look like "someone from One Direction"). And where is "around here?" Tumblr? The serial killer fan community? Are the real users—the real community members—assuring each other of their likeability, or the likeability of their personas? I will delve deeper into this, and into roleplay in general, in chapter 5, but for now I will take it as evidence of some sort of community-based support and sociability, though obviously quite different to the sort based on stable online identities that cohere with an individual's offline self-conception. We might recall Hillman et al.'s participants stating that they felt more able to be their real selves on Tumblr than in the offline world (2014a). Perhaps rather than assuming a coherent alternate identity, we should take roleplay and flitting between personas as constitutive of this "real"ness. There are also more concrete offers of support and friendship that are clearly aimed at the user rather than to any persona, on non-roleplaying blogs. Friendly reminder [username] posts "stalkersdisneyland" under a cuteified cartoon of Ed Gein clutching a radio, "in case you need someone to talk and socialize with, I will always be available" (2022).

Fan communities are generally said to adhere around textual interpretations. At a very broad level, I would say that this one coheres around a sympathetic and/or sexualized interpretation of the mediated lives of popular serial killers. There is discussion and debate about their crimes, provision of sources and material, and the sharing and reception of support. Roleplay was a dominant form of engagement, and while this can offer support and friendship in some sense, it should also be addressed through the lens of digital play (chapter 5). The rapid deletion and replacement of blogs was a clear barrier to community on Tumblr, as was the difficulty of gatekeeping a killer fan community from outsiders. However, if one knows where to begin, by selecting the most popular serial killer fan blogs and working outwards via follows and reblogs, one can with effort discover at least a minimal level of community. This works primarily at the level of transferred affect—love emojis, expressions of support—and of practice, via reblogging and liking. I found little evidence of a specialized language or jargon beyond a basic level, such as the repetition of famous quotations and GIFs of favored serial killers, or the use of said quotations in headers. (Ramirez's laconic statement "See you in Disneyland," in response to receiving the death penalty, appeared with some frequency.) All Tumblr users use emojis, and an informal tone is the norm. I did observe that serial killer fans were far more polite and cordial to each other than they were to accusatory outsiders, but that is hardly surprising. Moreover, it seems that if one is prepared to engage significantly, one can be invited to more private spaces, such as Discord chats, away from the influence of "antis." This might be a sense in which being defined as the Bad Other of the true crime community contributes to communal boundaries: Killer fans remove themselves collectively to a different space to conduct their more private exchanges.

I employed a similar ethnographic technique in my approach to TikTok. First, I created an account and followed the accounts already sourced for the previous chapter. The account named @theodorerobertbundy was deleted as soon as I began to compile data. However, an account named @ted..bundy took its place as the top search result for #tedbundy and #fandom, and @aileenswife was replaced in the respective place by @aileenwu0rnos. These accounts appeared and disappeared with more frequency than on Tumblr, suggesting more active monitoring. This would accord with reports of TikTok's intense user surveillance, though not with the popularly held opinion that TikTok data-gathers for purposes of Chinese intelligence (Cuthberson 2019). Several accounts contained a header stating that their previous incarnation had been banned, and that they were returning with a similar username, such as "Old acc[ount]-rrmylover-got banned" (rrmyloverr [with an additional r] 2022a). I then returned to my newly created "For You Page," and found it absolutely irrelevant, both in terms of the videos it displayed and the accounts it suggested to follow. Whatever the proprietary algorithm does do, it was clearly not about to help me access a serial killer fan community so easily. I doubt this has anything to do with content censorship, but more to do with the promotion of profitable content, and it may have become more precise if I had reshared relevant videos rather than just liking them.

Throughout the data collection period, TikTok continually (and comedically) attempted to persuade me to follow such accounts as @edsheeran or @gordonramseyofficial, regardless of how many serial killer fan accounts I followed. I returned to the TikTok homepage and followed several more accounts tagged with #serialkiller and #fandom or #fandom and the names of my celebrity sample. Even searching for these turned up dozens of short videos condemning their existence. It soon became clear that "antis" from outside the community were using these hashtags strategically, tagging videos with "#Jeffreydahmerfans" in order to mock and insult them. These searches did, however, turn up more tags such as #tedbundystan and #hybristophilia. Hybristophilia is a paraphilia of attraction towards those who commit violent crimes, and seems to be used on TikTok almost exclusively for murderers. Every single one of these tags produced results designed to mock and express outrage at its existence—but they also produced results akin to the content analyzed in the prior chapter, such as brief fanvids and expressions of lust for killers with the accompanying supportive comments. The process of "favoriting" tags in order to follow them also made my "For You Page" slightly more relevant, though the videos displayed once again attempted to "nudge" me towards normative true crime content, which was informational/educational in tone. Moreover, as the days went on, I realized that I could refine the tags I followed and blocked to a certain degree in order to create more coherent communal boundaries. Obviously, tags like "ihaterichardramirezfans" were blocked, but with experience, I realized that while "tedbundyfans" (plural) was more likely to produce hate content, "tedbundyfan" (singular) was more likely to produce fan content. Still, the best and most coherent way to create a sense of community was not through tags, but by searching for popular accounts of the type I wanted and following them.

TikTok serial killer fans express support and love for each other more frequently than those on Tumblr, where posts typically had more reblogs and likes than comments. Many of the TikTok videos had long streams of comments, including some that self-reflexively constructed themselves *as* a community (cf. Bury 2005). User richardsleatherjacket, for instance, captions a video simply "I[ ]l[ove]y[ou] all" with a heart emoji. It opens with the onscreen text "Introducing the most hot, toxic and badass fandom" before flicking through rapid cuts of other Ramirez fan accounts (2021). "Toxic," in this context, seems to be a badge of honor, demonstrating that being cast as the Bad Other of the true crime community works as a definitional boundary. Among the responses are: "Richie stans are always beautiful (aleks_toddy 2021); "love you too 💓" (RichardLiItleDevil 2021), and "i love this fandom s[o]m[uch] (blee 2021.). One even professes to be "Proud of our fandom ⚫ love you bestiesss" (Victoria💕 2021); and while an apparently lost outsider does interject, "Mother help me I'm on Richard Ramirez fans tiktok" (Repent to kidzbopism 2021), they are clearly on alien territory and aware of it. Serial killer fans do have "space" on TikTok (heterotopic space, one supposes), and one of the ways they gatekeep is by limiting commenting ability to mutual friends.

Akin to Baym's discussion of how soap fans relate soap characters' experiences to their own lives, serial killer fans offer each other emotional support based around their interpretations of killers' lives and relation to their own. "I actually really relate to Ed [Gein]," says Dan●, "he is talking about his 'issues' so well. I hate that his mother didn't know any better than just treating him like trash" (2022). The account creator infers from this that the poster is having issues with their own life, and responds, "I really hope everything is going good♥my dm's are always open if you wanna vent/talk●I'm here to help and I agree his mother should've known better" (.213 [username] 2022). Dan● responds with gratitude. In parallel to the offers of offline support observed by Hiebert and Miller (2021), user Richard Ramirez♥writes over a video displaying her own face, "Anyone else just want to runaway and do the dumbest sh!t until they get caught or just me?" (2021). Several users respond that they are ready and willing, going so far as to ask for her location. This probably isn't literal, despite richardramirez9996's plea, "Pick me up pls ●●●●● I'm fucking serious pick me up idc where you live come get me ●●●●●●●" (2021), given that the users could feasibly live on different continents, but the performative bond is one means of establishing "imagined community" between individuals who will (probably) never meet each other. Other forms of communal support include the exchange of compliments on accounts and creating particular videos or edits at the request of a fellow fan, who is then tagged. The video may be created for or at the request of one fan in particular, but everyone can view and enjoy it in the public communal space, so overall, gifters receive more than they give. TikTok was the platform on which I found most evidence of Turk's (2014) circular gifting, suggesting that, in some ways, it might be more amenable to community than Tumblr, and even, surprisingly, Reddit. Participating in a gift economy did require the creation of profiles linked to a love of killers (to give and receive the gifts), but the nature of circular giving means that should the recipient's account vanish, the gift remained. There was still a certain expectation of return, but that return could simply be approving comments from the community in general.

As on Tumblr, fans recommended source media to each other (*My Friend Dahmer* in both book and film versions was popular). Some express relief at finding other serial killer fans with whom to socialize. jeffreydahmereditzz posts "my comfort people <3" (2022), on a Bundy fan video, expressing that they feel comfort in the presence of others who share their serial killer fandom. Interestingly, with regard to textual interpretation, I found that Wuornos fans were keenest to express and share their understanding of Wuornos's actions as justified with each other and with outsiders. "she's our queen bro," says one user (🕊 2022) on a video by aileenslvr, to which the creator responds, "yeah sis 🤜🤛💓" (2022). The abbreviations of "brother" and "sister" and the fist-bump emoji expresses solidarity with a political cause. Wuornos fans deliberately construct themselves as a radical feminist community, espousing the view that fatal violence against rapists is justified: "men be like: 'she killed innocent rapists whats wrong with you ●●'" (marimbasolo4 2022). These users are thus coordinating around a specific interpretation of the media texts surrounding Wuornos. It is not the dominant interpretation, for Wuornos was indeed executed, but not a particularly obscure one either. After the hoax declaration of a so-called "National Rape Day" on April 24, 2021 gained currency on TikTok, a spate of Wuornos GIFs accompanied by assertions that men in general should be purged appeared on the site, and remained un-banned as of the collection period.

I also observed community manifested in friendly competition. User Jeffreydahmeredittzz posted a sort of visual quiz wherein one must guess serial killers from context clues, with the caption "if you didn't get at least 3 points we can't be friends" (2022b). Ruby is eating my heart? [username] replies, "Got all right ● 👍" (2022), to which the creator replies, "Great, I wouldn't like to end our friendship ●" (2022c). The emojis demonstrate that the exchange is non-serious. The users have a friendship that will endure the mock-test regardless, but the post does show that being well-informed makes one a valuable community member. This is a form of identity construction akin to that which Baym observed in her soap fans, who would quickly recap episodes for each other. Some fans were competitive about their level of knowledge and enthusiasm for the subject. Jeffreydahmereditzz thanks .213 for help regarding some of the historical timeframes mentioned in a video, to which .213 replies, "(anytime, yk I know everything●)" and jeffreydahmereditzz agrees, "You really do BAHAHHA" (2022d).

Friendly (or unfriendly) competition over fan knowledge is commonplace across fandoms (see chapter 4 on subcultural capital), but competition over expressions of enthusiasm can be more complex, subject to policing for emotional/sexual excess or improperly fangirl-like conduct. This was not the case within serial killer fandom. User rrmyloverr posted a short clip of Ramirez in court showing off a pentacle drawn on his palm (whether or not he thought he was drawing a pentagram remains undetermined). Over the image is imposed:

> You're interested in the night stalker case but I stay up until 3am most nights to try to talk to Richie. I play every song that reminds me of him so many times that ik every detail about the songs. I have a whole wall filled with photos of Richie. [. . .] I've almost watched the night stalker 100 times [. . .] (rrmyloverr 2022b)

Some commenters attest to similar behaviors, but user りムノ丂リ♥ replies, "Cool, It's not a competition through♥❣" (2022). What is particularly interesting here, in terms of pathologization, is that in the music- and television-based subcultures I am used to studying, professions of "excessive" fandom are looked down upon as embarrassing, feminine, or *cringe* (Fathallah 2017, 2020). Their profession seems almost a contest in fangirl excess. Perhaps serial killer fandom's already-pathologized status drives some fans to simply embrace the Bad Other position: indeed, to double down on it in a space more heterotopic than the relatively restrained or "ladylike" spaces Bury observed (2001). The pseudo-concerned comments like "Are you doing okay like in life?" (● 2022) and

> I'm telling u these people are insane. (Cleo <3 2022)
>
> > Surely It's ironic (JoeLedeen 2022)
> >
> > Nope these people are ac[tually] f[or] r[eal]. (Cleo <3 2022)

seem almost to be invited by the post, as excess is performed for both community insiders and for those looking in via the permeable structures of the site. These serial killer fans, positioned as freaks by fandom in general, are performing to their pathologized name. Fan community on TikTok once again centered around affect, then—but I actually found more evidence of shared interpretation of the mediated texts, especially regarding Wuornos, than on Tumblr. I also found more explicit communal support, and arguably more persistent online identities. These converged around identification as a pathologized category, celebrating fangirl excess, and a taboo object.

Reddit had only one small, not very active community specifically labeling itself serial killer fandom, which was "r/RichardRamirezFans" (164 members). However, it also hosted r/hybristophilia (2,400 members). This larger and more active subreddit was significant enough to come to the attention of other Reddit communities like "r/cursedsubs," devoted to pointing out and discussing "the most vile and bizarre subs to ever plague Reddit" (r/cursedsubs 2022). The first comment on its acknowledgement in r/cursedsubs is "might as well call it TikTok" (FlaerZz 2022), evidencing my impression that TikTok is considered a contemporary hub for serial killer fandom. I studied the Ramirez fan subreddit first. Though it is tagged as suitable for users over eighteen only, there is no real way of keeping out anyone younger. A pinned post at the top of the forum is titled "r/RichardRamirezFans Lounge," and reads simply, "A place for members of r/RichardRamirezFans to chat with each other" (xkx09977 2022). This immediately sets up the space as communal, and the discussion that takes place under this post is fairly innocuous, mostly discussions of documentaries to watch and trivia such as Ramirez's smoking habits. Such discussion could be found on any true crime forum. Other posts included the sharing of fanwork, such as "The Tale of The Night Stalker, a mini documentary I made for y'all" (darknight8200 2022), a ten-minute recap of Ramirez's crimes that, though salacious and light-hearted, does not precisely endorse them. Commenters on YouTube inform the creator that they have come from Reddit to appreciate his video, demonstrating fan movement across platforms in search of community gifts and materials. There was also some indication of this on the other platforms, such as fans asking each other if they have a profile on another site or use Discord. Reddit fans also recommended Tumblr to each other as a good place to post fanwork:

> Hi I think you might put them on Tumblr, There's a lot of fan[s] of Richard like you, if want my Tumblr is @serialkillersyouth you might post what you did here :-) because as I can see There's not a lot of people here. (medeakid 2021)
>
> > Oh, That's a good idea! Mine is @acidburnsthings, I'll post them and you can find it there if you want! (_acidburns_ 2021)

Commenters were also keen to display their level of knowledge related to serial killer media, with comments like, "I find it interesting how I know exactly what references you used for every single one of these sketches lol" (Throwaway-num1 2021). These fans were typically supportive and complimentary of each other's knowledge displays. There was also some evidence of communal bonding beyond a shared interest in Ramirez. Here Princesss7 is describing El Paso, the city both she and Ramirez were born in:

> It's a decent sized city almost 1 million plus We're literally minutes away from Mexico We're right on the border:) lots of Hispanic culture :) unlike any other city in Texas. (Princesss7 2021)
>
> Yeah, Texas is pretty white. My mom was from Corpus Christi and they used make fun of her for being Chicana :(Are you Latina btw? Salvadoran-Italian (my mom grew up with Mexican culture but she was of Italian descent). (Felicino 2021)
>
> I'm also a salvi :). (Tiny_Cryptographer25 2021)

Thus I would argue for a minimal degree of community here, based on gift exchange, shared texts and knowledge, and affective bonding. Overall, though, the small size of the subreddit limited the insights available. The now-purged r/hybristophilia was more fruitful. The description read:

> Welcome!
>
> This is the place to post pictures, videos, interviews, or whatever hybristophilia-related content you like in a judgement free zone.
>
> This community is meant for those who have these unusual and conflicting feelings to be able to find camaraderie and insight, and for others to learn about hybristophilia from firsthand accounts. (2022)

Indeed, some users did feel internal conflict over their attraction to murderers (though by no means all did). This sets the subforum slightly apart from the reveling in Bad Fandom I observed above (though some of that was also present). Because the subreddit covers attraction to any and all violent criminals, I inductively coded all the posts and replies that featured the names of the killers in my sample. I was very lucky in the timing of my data collection, because the subreddit was banned and purged right at the end of the data collection period. I found that the posts came under four overlapping categories:

A. Sharing and bonding over fantasies

B. Gatekeeping against community outsiders

C. Making content recommendations

D. Sharing fanwork (circular giving)

Under the theme of sharing fantasies, posters describe their attractions. Sometimes attraction is explained in terms that psychologists have already explained as factors in hybristophilia (see Ramsland 2012):

> I've been into guys like Richard Ramirez, Jeffrey Dahmer, and Ted Bundy every [*sic*] since I was a teenager. And I don't like them because they're conventionally attractive, I like them because I know what they've done to people. That's what turns me on. I rewatch We Need to Talk about Kevin and season 1 of American Horror Story over, constantly. My biggest fantasy is trying to "change" or "save" a serial killer from whats wrong with them. I watch porn where the guy borderline abuses the woman. (Deleted user 2 2022)

A responder assures the poster, who seems to be female, that this fantasy "is not new or unheard of; there are so many different movies and shows of all sorts of genres that explore [. . .] that theme, and even I myself get this warm feeling at the thought of being the kryptonite for some crazed person" (Deleted user 3 2022). Others are less conflicted about their fantasies, and simply seek like-minded people with whom to share them. "Tell me some of your fantasies?" requests one user:

> Sometimes I imagine that I'm Ted Bundy and I'm friends with Jeffrey Dahmer. Jeff is in love with me and I know that so I exploit it for whatever reason basically playing with fire, but then one day Jeff gets tired of my games and decides to perform one of his sexy diy lobotomies on me and I'm like "Nooo Jeff!!" but It's too late, I pray it kills me but unlike all of the other victims my lucky ass survives, reduced to this helpless bumbling pet he takes care of who can never leave him. Its so humiliating, but I totally deserved it and I guess we live happily ever after or something.. or I dunno, Jeff is happy and maybe I become Stockholm syndromed over time. (bundysimp 2022)

Responses included being strangled by one's killer of choice, as well as more elaborate scenarios involving necrophiliac kinks. Apparently even before the mass deletion, though, users did not feel able to reveal their most extreme fantasies here, as partyhardcake remarked, "can't say, would make the mods narky lol" (2022). This resulted in requests that the user "message me now and spill the beans" (Thechildkiller 2022), meaning that the fantasy-based bonding could continue in a more private space. Not all the fantasies revolved around violence. "Anybody Feel the Same Way As Me?" one user asked:

> [I'm]not even that smitten by his or other serial killers looks, because I don't have to same attraction to Ted Bundy/Richard Ramirez on the same level as I do with Dahmer. Even though he was gay and selfish, I want to live out some sort of fantasy life with him, care for him and be there for him. Fix him, in a strange way. I don't want to be hurt or raped like other hybristophiles, I want to help him. (Deleted user 4 2022)

Another respondent professes to "understand this on a deep level," having been

> in love with Ted Bundy since the peak of my true crime obsession began, around my 12th birthday (I'm going on 33 now) [. . .] I guess he's like the ultimate bad boy and being able to "change" him would be the accomplishment to end all accomplishments. If you ever wanna chat about this kinda stuff, feel free to message me any time. P. S. Have you watched My Friend Dahmer yet? (Deleted user 5 2022)

Several of these conversations resulted in invitations to chat in more private spaces, including Discord. In this way, it seems that the subreddit was certainly a facilitator of communality, if not a community per se. Commenters expressed a specific desire to connect with others who share their infatuations. "[I'm] glad I'm not alone" (Deleted user 6 2021) was a commonly repeated sentiment, relating this community right back to the insights of Jenkins and Bacon-Smith. Some commenters expressed that they were gay, autistic, or belonged to other minorities, and related this in some sense to their pathologized hybristophilia.

The second category of posts consisted of gatekeeping, guarding the subreddit and its interests against outsiders. A deleted user opens a typical discussion on the experience of loving a killer then adds:

> Please no hate comments as they will be ignored because why tf are you even on a subreddit if you're going to be hateful? That's like going to a bar and complaining that There's alcohol there. Friendly discussion is fine tho[ugh] if you wish to understand more about this fetish. (Deleted user 7 2021)

Despite the architectures of Reddit allowing gatekeeping by moderation, outsiders did find their way to the subreddit, probably via attention from subreddits like r/cursedsubs. In response to accusations of being disgusting or "sick fucks" (MozzUpDown 2022), outsiders are typically informed that they are "on the wrong subreddit" (Deleted user 8 2022) or advised to simply leave. Their minority on the subreddit is pointed out: "I don't know if You've noticed this or not: You are one voice in a sub of 1,440 members. I don't know what your goal is here, but I can promise you that you aren't getting anywhere" (Throwaway-num1 2022). However, in response to a post expressing disgust with hatred for hybristophiles as expressed by "antis," a deleted user asks:

> Don't antis play their part in defining the community though? If there were no antis and if hybristophilia was more accepted by society, would there be as much of a sense of community on this sub and in the TCC? (Deleted user 9 2022)
>
>> That's a good point. The tight-knit community makes it strong. I guess I'm just sick of the bullying and close-mindedness of those who don't even try to understand. And tbh the fact that most "normal" people are so shocked by this just makes people wanna do it more. It's the big red button effect. (Deleted user 10 2022)

There are several points of note here, which lend support to some of my initial hypotheses. Firstly, at least some serial killer fans do consider themselves a community. Secondly, some consider their interest part of "the TCC." Thirdly, the hostility of outsiders causes some fans to lean in to their pathologization, or "the big red button effect" of temptation to provocation. Some admit that they reserve their "real" fandom for the Reddit space only, akin to Hillman et al.'s (2014a) Tumblr fans who only expressed their "real selves" on Tumblr. One user describes themself as "coming onto this subreddit to fantasize about Richard Ramirez after saying he's a disgusting excuse of a human being" (hyejooloveclub 2021a). Others recognize the sentiment:

> stop calling me and my fake serial killer hate page out 💀👍(Aggravating-Bag6986 2021)
>
>> LMAOOOO NAH F[or] R[eal] . . . I would be commenting on groupie"s tiktoks like "y"all need to get help" then go watch richard interviews and kick my bed with my feet (hyejooloveclIb 2021b)
>>
>> STOP BC LITERALLY ME i got caught complimenting a columbiner once and it almost ended my career (Aggravating-Bag6986 2021)
>>
>> ENDED YOUR CAREER ● stop this has gone on too far!!!! I've been caught lacking a few times . . . in 19372K ultra high definition. (hyejooloveclub 2021b)

To be "caught lacking" is slang originating in Chicago street culture, and initially meant to be caught by one's enemies without a gun. It has expanded to mean caught unprepared, or off guard, in any kind of situation. "19372K ultra high definition" is a hyperbolic exaggeration, meaning with great precision, or obviousness or undeniability: hyejooloveclub is empathizing with the fellow poster who accidentally revealed pathologized fandom in a space linked to their professional identity, with implications for their career. There are parallels here with fans who kept (and still keep) their affection for slash, or Real Person Fiction, or Real Person Slash secret and separate from their professional identities in times and places where those interests are pathologized. The subreddit functions as a heterotopic space where relative anonymity allowed these posters to express that side of themselves—or it did, until the end of May 2022. Posters also bonded with and supported each other over their discomfort with their fantasies, assuring each other that fantasies in themselves are harmless, and moreover, that feelings of empathy for a killer are a sign of one's humanity: that feelings of wishing to nurture the damaged are normal, humane, and even morally commendable. This demonstrates that not all serial killer fans lean into the position of pathologization—some are happier to rationalize their feelings in terms of normal psychology, akin to the early phases of fandom-redemption by academics.

The category of recommendations on what to watch and read was pretty standard, and not worth quoting in depth: Fans simply asked each other if they had yet seen a film or documentary, and indicated where it could be accessed. The sharing of fanwork produced some more interesting results. As well as the usual fanvids and fanart, one poster known as FandomVulture333 was a self-employed taxidermist, and posted photographs of such creations as "a Jeffrey Dahmer fan art [. . .] out of squirrels skulls and skeletons. It's a diorama of his shrine that he drew" (2022a). These creations were extremely impressive in their precision and attention to detail:

> I knew exactly what it was just from the spider lamp. I love it!!! Great job! (xscumfucx 2022)
>
> > ●●● Glad you love it. I strive to make accurate looking fan art. (FandomVulture333 2022b)

FandomVulture33 also provided information on their craft:

> So that website sells animals and animal parts that have been culled for population control or whatever reason and they get a lot of exotics from Africa and Asia as well as the US [. . .] I'm actually in the process of trying to find enough whitetail deer ribs to paint them black and then paint very finely little gold aviator glasses (Jeffrey Dahmer) on them. I plan to sell those. (2022b)

It turns out that FandomVulture33 is a self-declared member of the online "vulture culture," a subculture and practice of taxidermy utilizing the remains of animals that have died of natural causes. They direct other Redditors to their Instagram account, wherein they take commissions—the first example I have seen of a serial killer fan able to convert their fandom into economic capital. There is certainly an element of the gift economy here, as Fandom-Vulture33 allowed fans to view their creations for free, but the gift economy is not the only economy that serial killer fandom supports, as I'll observe in the next chapter, on cultural capital. It seems that, contrary to my hypothesis, the relative anonymity and small size of serial killer fandom does not create a significant barrier to the practice of circular giving. Enough fans respond, at least with praise, that certain fan-creators are sufficiently encouraged to gift their creations to the group.

It seems fair to argue, then, that serial killer fan community exists online in a weak sense. In favor of the concept of a fan community, I observed:

A. Social support and bonding

B. The circular gifting (and occasionally sale) of fannish work

C. Sympathy and empathy with a pathologized interestThe invitation to further discussions, and

D. The shared interpretations of media texts.

Mitigating against a stronger definition of community was the inherent instability of the platforms, the rapidity with which content was deleted both by choice and force, the relative lack of a specific in-group jargon, and the relative anonymity of most users. That said, I believe that in-group jargon is becoming progressively less confined to particular fandoms as fannish practices become more mainstreamed and overlap with digital culture more generally. Anonymity can work both ways. I observed on Reddit that some users felt this was the only place where they could express their true desires, akin to Hillman et al.'s Tumblr users. r/hybristophilia is now banned and purged, but it seems inevitable that some new subreddit will spring up in its place, just as new Tumblrs and new TikTok accounts are constantly created in response to deletion. Seeking out a serial killer fan community took some effort, especially on TikTok and Tumblr, but, as Hillman et al. showed, this can actually be a factor in consolidating a community online; compare this with the comments above on "antis." I was correct in my expectation that pathologizing would reinforce the self-definition of a community, but incorrect that the traditional architectures of Reddit would support community more consistently than those of Tumblr and TikTok. Indeed, it may well be that r/hybristophilia would not have been banned if it had been harder to find; the Reddit search algorithm means it was easy to stumble across when searching for anything true crime–related, or related to a specific case. I was also incorrect in thinking that anonymity and the small size of the fandom would inhibit the practice of circular giving.

I turn now to the next major lens through which fan cultures have been analyzed, that of (sub)cultural capital.

CHAPTER 4

Killer Fandom and (Sub)Cultural Capital

Theories of cultural capital based in the work of Pierre Bourdieu have been a major influence in the field of fan studies. A huge range of scholars have adapted them to analyze fandom and the workings of fan communities and spaces: see, just for example, Bacon-Smith (1992); Fiske (1992); Jenkins (1992); Thornton (1995); Baym (2000); Hills (2002, 2005); Thomas (2002); Shefrin (2004); Williamson (2005); Williams (2010); Bennett (2014); Milner (2011); Chin (2018); Wu (2019); and Balanzategui and Lynch (2022). For Bourdieu, all participation in culture is essentially strategic: In demonstrating "proper" appreciation and interpretation of the "correct" cultural works, we gain social position in relation to other people (1984, 1991, 1996, 1993). Even if our cultural engagement is experienced as pleasure, what pleases us is actually a matter of "playing the cultural game well, of playing on one's skill at playing, at cultivating a pleasure which 'cultivates'" (Bourdieu 1984, 498). Bourdieu wasn't writing about fan culture, or popular culture in general, but rather of "official" culture in the context of his native France: museums, traditional or avant-garde art, the "correct" kind of cinema, and so on. Correct appreciation of culture, the kind that gets rewarded with status, is intellectual and disinterested, rather than over-emotional or over-invested. Bourdieu famously wrote that "taste classifies, and it classifies the classifier" (1984, 6). When we express a judgment or display our knowledge "correctly," we gain cultural capital, as we are classified as an informed, rational, intellectual person of good taste, specifically in relation to other people.

Through this insight, academics have discussed how mainstream culture has historically derogated fandom through the stereotypes I have discussed (Jensen 1992). By expressing over-enthusiastic investment in cultural forms that have not historically been appreciated as "proper" culture, such as television or pop music, fans have been classified as lacking: lacking in proper taste, lacking in rationality, lacking in maturity. Yet scholars have also built on the cultural capital approach to understand how fans compete for distinction over the capital of particular subcultures (Thornton 1995; Hills 2002). Members of fan cultures, in this view, compete to be distinguished, to demonstrate the most knowledge, to be the best informed, the most connected, the most up-to-date compared to other fans. Their objects of enthusiasm are just different from those of official culture—or at least, they used to be. Some fan cultures are now so mainstream and disparate that the "subculture" label is tenuous. This chapter will detail some of the prior applications and adaptations of Bourdieu's work in the field of fan studies, then explore how and where it can be applied to serial killer fandom on Tumblr and TikTok before I enter a new sphere: I will turn to investigate websites for the buying and selling of murderabilia, items associated with serial killers, their lives, and their crimes. I have already established that Tumblr and TikTok are rich data sites, and that the collection of items/objects associated with fannish objects is a key means by which fans gather cultural capital (Geraghty 2014). However, murderabilia sale and collection is directly implicated in circuits of economic exchange, and thanks to the convergence of digital media and media industries, fan subcultural capital and economic capital are now in a closer relationship than they have ever been before.

For Bourdieu, cultural and economic capital were relatively distinct (Shefrin 2004). Yet cultural participation has an oddly economic rationale: "[A]ccording to Bourdieu and his followers, fans play in the sense that they tacitly recognize the 'rules' of their fan culture, attempting to build up different types of fan skill, knowledge and distinction" (Hills 2002, 20). They do this in order to gain position, vis-à-vis each other. Fan cultures are cut through by hierarchies, competition over such factors as knowledge, access or closeness to the fannish object, and social status. The term "BNF," or Big Name Fan, has been used as a not-entirely complimentary byword for the kind of fan who is well known within their community, who has a reputation for vast knowledge, and/or high quality fanwork, and/or being especially connected to other fans and perhaps the object of fandom. Cultural capital is by far the most discussed element of Bourdieu's work, but he actually discussed three kinds of capital: "social capital ('who you know'), cultural capital ('what you know') and symbolic capital, referred to as 'prestige, reputation, fame'" (quoted in Williams 2010, 281). Matt Hills suggested that in fan studies, social capital could be conceived of as "the network of fan friends and acquaintances that a fan possesses, as well as their access to media producers and professional personnel linked with the object of fandom," while symbolic capital could be, for instance, "those fans who are nominated as spokespeople for their fandom" (2002, 69). Obviously, being connected to an object of fandom is going to be more straightforward and evident in traditional media fandom than in my case study. (One cannot very easily tweet at a serial killer and hope they follow back. Particularly not a dead one.)[1] Nonetheless, I did find that being able to evidence a network of fan friends—or more specifically, "followers" on social media sites conferred distinct subcultural capital, while a degree of symbolic capital adhered to the proprietors of more official forms of fandom linked to economic capital: the owners of murderabilia websites.

Bourdieu no doubt over-generalized and exaggerated the applicability of his rather grand and abstract theories. Firstly, many academics would object to the idea that human involvement in any kind of cultural activity is entirely strategic (Hills 2002; Thomas 2010). Bourdieu does not account for any ludic dimension at all. He seems to overlook entirely the possibility that one might engage with cultural texts simply for fun. But I am not utilizing his ideas as a total explanation of fandom (which would be ridiculous for any theory)—merely as one lens among the other major lenses I am applying to serial killer fandom in this book.

Some of the first adaptations of Bourdieu that occurred within fan studies were based on the insights that he viewed "culture" too monolithically, failing to account for the workings of "popular cultural capital" (Fiske 1992) or "subcultural capital (Thornton 1995) and their applicability to the complex lives of individual social agents. In her work on clubbing cultures, Sarah Thornton wrote of the "hipness" of clubbers as "subcultural capital"

---

[1] Though the killers in my sample are dead, I wouldn't go so far as to say this is impossible in all cases. Some incarcerated persons do have intermittent access to social media in certain jurisdictions. William Noguero has been detained on death row in San Quentin, California, for over thirty years, for a murder committed in the course of a robbery. His artwork, books, and social media can be viewed from https://linktr.ee/William.noguera.art.

which "confers status on its owner in the eyes of the relevant beholder. [. . .] Just as books and paintings display cultural capital in the family home, so subcultural capital is objectified in the form of fashionable haircuts and well-assembled record collections" (1995, 26–27). Knowledge, information, and its interpretation are fundamental elements of popular or subcultural capital (Jenkins 1992, 2006; Milner 2011), as applied to different sorts of objects: popular media texts, popular music, and so on. Fiske held that "popular cultural capital, unlike official cultural capital, is not typically convertible into economic capital" (1992, 34). I'm not sure how true this was even twenty years ago. As early as 1995, Thornton was discussing how fan cultural capital could be converted into economic capital by writing for niche publications, citing "music and style journalists and various record industry professionals" as examples (1995, 12). As I write this, I would wager that Fiske's claim is obsolete: Some kinds of popular cultural capital are *highly* convertible into economic capital, and the kinds are expanding faster than this researcher can keep track of: Apparently, if you gain enough followers, you can monetize your TikTok now. Xianwei Wu (2019) presented an interesting case study of a forum wherein fans could literally buy subcultural capital in the form of "forum currency," using real money. This forum currency allowed them to use more of the site's affordances and access more material. They could also earn forum currency by "upload[ing] private resources that can be sold [. . .] In this way, real world economic capital is directly translated into online economic and cultural capital." On the interchange between fannish (in his work, nerdish) and economic capital, Benjamin Woo argues that

> what appears in lay and media discourse as the mainstreaming of nerd culture might be better understood as a revaluation of its specific capitals. Capital is convertible not only between forms but also between fields, and when the "exchange rate" of field-specific capitals change, making them more valuable in a greater range of social and cultural contexts, it follows that more people will "invest" in them. (2012, 670–71)

Some fan capital is doing very well on the exchange rate at the moment. Fans who have gathered enough subcultural capital via their appreciation of video games, for example, are making whole careers out of streaming. Fanfiction is translatable into blockbuster film series. Professional cosplaying is a viable career. Of course, these exchanges are not available to everyone, and dependent on a variety of socio-economic factors, but the point is that fan capital itself is potentially translatable to economic capital at a relatively high rate. Once again, it is a trait of serial killer fandom that fits better with more traditional fan studies lenses that, with the important and significant exception of murderabilia sales, its capital is less convertible.

For Thornton, key to subcultural capital in the clubbing world was the notion of authenticity. The "authentic" clubber must demonstrate distinction from the mainstream dance enthusiast, from the inauthentic masses lacking in taste and the "correct" knowledge of dance music (1995). One notable aspect of her work, which will become pertinent towards the end of this chapter, are her insights into the relation of subcultural capital and its circulation to the mainstream media. Negative responses from the media mainstream, such as the construction and promotion of moral panics, caused the subcultural capital of dance events and trends to rise, allowing them to play on their rebellious nature and opposition to the "cultural status quo" (1995, 129). I found that sites retailing murderabilia, an object-based form of fandom, likewise play on their notoriety and the status it confers.

Conversely, Milly Williamson (2005) objects to the idea that fandom operates in a subcultural space outside of mainstream culture—rightly pointing out that earlier writers, like Fiske and Thornton, have misread Bourdieu in the sense of positing one, monolithic mainstream culture. Rather, the struggle for cultural capital in Bourdieu's conception of culture operates between two poles, the dominant and the dominated—the dominant being the production of, say, art for profit and the economic valuation of that art (the heteronomous pole), the dominated being the conception of art for art's sake (the autonomous pole, populated by avant-garde artists). Both the dominant and dominated fractions are elements of the bourgeoisie, elements of the dominant culture. In her wide-ranging study of vampire fandom, Williamson argues that fandom operates in much same way: at one pole, the official, licensed arena of fanclubs and events, in a close relationship with economic capital, producers, and the media industry; at the other pole, unofficial, unlicensed forms of fandom that resist the involvement of money and distance themselves from the media industry. I think Williamson's point is well argued and well evidenced *in the particular fandom she is* studying—but note that the fans she studies aren't particularly lacking in official capital cultural in the first place. Rhiannon Bury (2001), likewise, collected data on fan fiction communities that guarded their boundaries according to traditional norms of "good" writing, Standard English, and taste. It seems to me that the distance of fan subcultural capital from official cultural capital is going to be largely fandom-dependent—vampires, after all, are almost respectable. Serial killer fandom is not.

Collection and the display of physical objects related to the object of fandom is one means of gaining fannish capital (Fiske 1992; Geraghty 2014). Ekaterina Kulinicheva, in an interesting application of this theory to the subculture of sneaker enthusiasts (or "sneakerheads"), argues that collecting is about both collecting knowledge on the subject of sneakers and collecting sneakers themselves (2021).[2] The materiality of sneakers, the story behind a design, and the cultural history of sneakers attracts sneakerheads to their shoes. A large collection of expensive sneakers does not confer capital by itself. Subcultural capital is built up by the demonstration of knowledge and understanding around the collection, especially with regard to sneaker history. Fiske argued that this fannish collecting

> tends to be inclusive rather than exclusive: the emphasis is not so much upon acquiring a few good (and thus expensive) objects as upon accumulating as many as possible. The individual objects are therefore often cheap, devalued by the official culture, and mass-produced. The distinctiveness lies in the extent of the collection rather than in their uniqueness or authenticity as cultural objects. (1992, 44)

In gathering the data for this chapter, I found the opposite. When it comes to the collection of murderabilia, authenticity (expensive authenticity) is the primary measure of subcultural capital. There was a definite parallel here with Thornton's observations that "the distance between a record's production and its consumption is relevant to the cultural value bestowed upon it," and that "the environment in which a record is produced contributes to its authenticity" (1995, 106), which I explore below. Finally, Hills (2015) has argued for a newer kind of subcultural capital based in nostalgia, and the distinction conferred on certain fans for having been physically, bodily at certain types of events which are believed to belong to the past. His case study is cult cinema, which of course is no longer restricted to physical cinema buildings. He argues that the emergence of

> a "mainstreaming" discourse has become prevalent in scholar-fan responses to technological changes surrounding cult "cinema," most especially torrenting and allegedly "easy" contemporary online access to previously obscure, hard-to-find cult texts. (2015, 118)

2 For my fellow non-Americans: sneakers are trainers, the sports shoe.

Too much accessibility, too easy replication, has devalued the subcultural capital associated with simply having seen, or having owned a copy of said texts. However, this tendency

> can be countered by considering how fans who were "there" for earlier 1970s and 1980s forms of cult (midnight movies, the Scala, and video nasties) can now perform a particular mode of retroactive subcultural capital, where the very historical inaccessibility of past cult lends it exclusivity and authenticity. (118)

Lincoln Geraghty has a related argument in his book *Cult Collectors: Nostalgia, Fandom and Collecting Popular Culture* (2014). He writes that the collection of authentic props and artifacts from cinematic and television history takes on special importance, as we don't "own" films in any physical sense: We own copies, which lack the aura of authenticity and originality. Ultimately, this line of thinking can be traced to Walter Benjamin ([1936] 2005), and his argument that a work of art loses its "aura" as it is reproduced by copying technology. For Hills specifically, however, capital attaches to the fan's physical body. This was also accounted for by Thornton, though she was concerned with the appropriate style of dress, movement, and haircut rather than the retrospective accumulations of subcultural capital across time.

This phenomenon, of fannish nostalgia capital, is not limited to cult cinema or clubbing. When I was conducting the research for *Emo: How Fans Defined a Subculture* (2020), the iconic emo-rock band My Chemical Romance was assumed to have permanently broken up. (Beyond the fondest hopes of emo kids of every generation, they re-formed in 2019.) Many, many younger fans expressed their envy to me that I had "been there" for the emo wave of the early-mid 2000s, that I had seen MCR "live," been physically present as a fifteen-year-old in the relatively smaller clubs and venues that the bands they loved were playing at the time, rather than the distant arena tours they tended towards by the late 2010s. They assumed that they would *never* "be there," bodily, for an MCR show: This distinction retrospectively accrued to the bodies of those of us who were. In serial killer fandom, no one has "been there" (hopefully). But what *have* "been there" are objects: objects that have physically touched the bodies of iconic serial killers, which have tended to attract the most subcultural and economic capital on the murderabilia sites. Moreover, I observed in the introduction how the quality of "authenticity" is attributed to serial killers in their general celebrification: the authenticity of the outlaw, the man or woman who lives entirely according to their desires.

There is not a great deal of work on how subcultural capital operates on platforms such as Tumblr. Bertha Chin, discussing social capital specifically, writes that, at a superficial level, fans' migration to social media platforms seems to signal a move toward "nonhierarchical, rhizomatic" forms of engagement, which Chin argues is only true "on a structural level (i.e., the ways these platforms function and operate)" (2018, 244). But as Chin goes on to argue, fannish interactions and statements on these platforms indicate that the theory of subcultural capital should not be dismissed. Dispensing with the concept would elide "the importance fans still place on the notions of reputation in their interaction with each other in their respective fandoms" (244). Chin argues that "fandom is still driven by the notions of presence and influence, demonstrated through the number of likes, retweets, reblogs, and shares" (244). This point is evidenced by a post I found by user svarvasoks in the middle of my data collection for this chapter. It read: "It's strange when I have thousands of followers but I only get a handful of notes. I feel like a ceo of a failing company hahah" (szarvasoks 2022). The CEO of a company is someone one would *expect* to have high social and cultural capital (e.g., a high follower count), but as the company is failing, they actually do not (the low engagement). Simply *having* followers is a weaker indication of both capitals than their engagement with a post. In Chin's study, social capital can also be gathered as "social media platforms now enable these fans to interact with celebrities and content producers" (244). This is not particularly applicable in my study except for in one very specific instance, discussed below.

Briony Hannell suggests that within the *Game of Thrones* fandom on Tumblr, screencapping and annotating GIFs of female characters with feminist-inspired commentary was a means of building subcultural capital (2017). I wouldn't particularly call this subcultural capital, but rather an illustration of Williamson's principle that fan capital isn't as distinct from some imagined discrete official culture as some theorists suggest, when discussing mainstream fandoms.

There is very little extant work regarding cultural capital on TikTok: Theorists are really just beginning to identify how and in what ways the dynamic operates. Jon Stratton has documented a trend for TikTok users to appropriate songs from previous eras, which are "part of the cultural capital of Generation X" (2021, 412), and rework them with new lyrics appropriate to the COVID-19 pandemic. He states that "the proliferation of these popular culture references in the coronavirus song lyrics can be understood in the terms of vernacular creativity and shared popular cultural capital"

(425), but it isn't particularly clear how he is using the term, and it doesn't bear much resemblance to its usual use. It essentially seems to be a synonym for "understanding." Michelle Phan (2020) argues that the appropriation of Black cultural capital by police officers on TikTok, in the forms of music, humor, and styles of speech, for example, effaces structural violence against Black people and exploits Black labor and creativity. I would not disagree, but Phan's article is really more about surveillance, racism, and power than (sub)cultural capital on TikTok per se. Finally, Gabby Unipan (2021) suggests that the deployment of lesbian-queer cultural capital within the immaterial space of TikTok defines and marks out parts of it as a community space in the absence of those physical spaces that were inaccessible during the pandemic. Again, the article is convincing so far as its premise goes, but all that is really established so far is the fact that (sub)cultural capital is gathered, deployed, and exhibited on TikTok. None of the studies are particularly detailed as to how.

When it comes to serial killer fandom, one might assume that capital is more genuinely subcultural than it is in mainstream fandoms, operating within a more restricted sphere. This would be another example of how serial killer fandom is better served through older fan studies lenses, those which treat fan cultures as relatively discrete, self-contained entities. Often, this was true: Mainstream condemnation was frequently converted into subcultural capital in the findings below, as it was for Thornton's subculturalists. However, there were exceptions. On Tumblr particularly, the display of knowledge from more normative true crime content earned subcultural capital. Moreover, I found that tagging Aileen Wuornos content with radical feminist ideology was a means of capital building: specifically, a form of radical feminism which endorses retaliatry violence against men. Again, this is not a "mainstream" idea, but the endorsement of violence on behalf of the oppressed against the oppressor is definitely a recognizable political position. It is also a demonstration that cultural capital crosses between social spheres and connected online spaces in complex ways. When it came to the study of murderabilia, subcultural capital enters a relationship of exchange with economic capital, once again demonstrating the permeabaility of fields. I also found that Bourdieu's concepts and Thornton's refinements require some tweaking to account for the relative anonymity of serial killer fandom on Tumblr and TikTok: The accumulation of subcultural capital was more applicable to posts and blogs than to users, who generally do not have a stable, long-lasting online presence.

The data for this chapter was gathered between June and September 2022. I began with a return to Tumblr, and the accounts I had previously identified as the most popular (see above). Only two (your-rickiex and angelrose666) were still active, but I kept following those, and then began searches for the most popular content again. I followed the top ten results for the hashtags "serial killer" plus "fan," "fans," and "fandom," as well as the top ten results for the name of each killer in my sample with the fan hashtags listed above addended. Again, there were no relevant matches for Jack the Ripper, though there was one for H. H. Holmes. Some of the results were on the borderline as to whether they should really be included under "fannish" or non-fannish content, so I naturally had to exercise some discretion, and some were repeats, so that the total number of blogs followed was forty-one.

For each blog, I analyzed the most popular postings based on number of "notes" (i.e., likes, reblogs, and comments), and also conducted a daily inspection of my dashboard for posts with an unusually high number of notes. The first thing one should note here is that, due to the unstable and semi-anonymous nature of Tumblr, posters don't really "build up" capital to a stable identity and position themselves against each other by utilizing it. Particular blogs gather subcultural capital, thus turn up at the top of the search results, and so do particular posts which go on to high recirculation. Moreover, there was a distinct pattern to the type of posts that gained traction, and this spawned trends of imitation. Clearly, users want their blogs to attract subcultural capital, and they learn particular strategies, consciously or not, to gain it.

The types of posts that gathered the highest number of notes were inductively coded into the following categories:

A. High-effort informational posts

B. High-effort aesthetic posts

C. The photographic display of collectible objects, including murderabilia and original documentation related to killers and their crimes

D. Jokes and humor

E. The espousal of radical feminism, in the case of Wuornos

At first glance, it seems that knowledge remains a key means to build subcultural capital within this fandom, just as it does with most. But the findings were actually a little more complex than this. Posting long, detailed informational posts about lesser-known serial killers and their crimes could be well-rewarded with notes regardless of the lack of celebrity attached to their subject. In these cases, the quantity of knowledge itself is the important factor. But when it comes to celebrity killers, more obscure information that gives the impression of being reliably sourced is the most effective means to gain a higher number of notes. So in both cases, "rare" information is rewarded, and this can be either by virtue of its subject *or* by virtue of the information itself. Posting well-known facts about well-known killers is not well-rewarded with many notes. The following post, apparently a quotation from a book, had 2,143 notes at the time of data collection:

> As befits a man who himself became the subject of many gruesome jokes, Dahmer would sometimes try to break the monotony by kidding around with guards and inmates. "I bite," he would warn. Once he even reportedly posted a sign on the prison bulletin board for a "Cannibals Anonymous" meeting; it was swiftly removed. He was temporarily fired from his job after impersonating a staff member on the telephone. "He had a very interesting sense of humor," says Wisconsin prison system spokesman Joseph Scislowic. (bluudstainbarbie 2021, originally posted by jeffreysdahmer)

Googling the quotation doesn't actually reveal a source beyond Tumblr. But I would still class it as a high-effort post, because if the original poster did not source it from a non-indexed book or elsewhere, he/she wrote it, with some skill. Note that the degree of effort attaches subcultural capital to the original posts, just as their *recirculation* attaches subcultural capital to blogs. In this case, the blog is a very popular result for "#Jeffrey Dahmer" paired with "#fandom." The blog attracts enough subcultural capital to appear prominently in the search results, primarily by *recirculating* high-effort informational (or "informational") posts, functioning essentially as a broker in a network. This is not in line with how Bourdieu envisaged social agents gathering capital, but recirculating content is still a means of utilizing it to gain popularity and thus subcultural reward.

Another example of a high-effort post, recirculated by one of the highest-ranking Richard Ramirez fanblogs, is a detailed account of correspondence with the killer that claims to be "translated from the French book, *Richard Ramirez: Le fils du diable* (*The Son of Evil*) by Nicolas Castelaux" (deathrowrorry 2021, 743 notes). This is a real book, but again, I find no source for the translation outside Tumblr. If a Tumblr user translated it, that would certainly count as high-effort. By contrast, posting and recirculating well-known quotations from Ramirez, such as the ubiquitous "we are all evil," attracts very few notes. One of the most-rewarded posts of all, with 4,581 notes, was a detailed pie chart showing the method of body disposal, by percentage, for a sample of 151 serial killers, complete with a written explanation for how the figures were arrived at (serialkillersandstuff 2013). The chart appears to have been created by the Tumblr user in a program such as Microsoft Excel, while charts simply copied from mainstream news or academic reports received far fewer notes (usually 20 to 30). Interestingly, then, it seems that effort is actually being rewarded over and above reliability, though the *impression* of reliability is appreciated. It is also worth noting that subcultural capital accrues over time, and that this post has been circulating since 2013.

Annotating photographs or providing information widely known to be false will attract a correction from commenters. Could this be an attempt to construct an impression of respectability for serial killer fandom, to demonstrate its similarity to the more "respectable" aspects of other fandoms—indeed to academia (cf. Hills 2002)? If so, this would be quite anomalous with my findings so far. I think, more likely, that it is a demonstration of the capital of a related arena—i.e., more normative true crime content—crossing over into the sub-domain of serial killer fandom, rather than capital being restricted to specific fields or arenas, for the other types of content that get rewarded are less "respectable" in traditional cultural terms.

Subcultural capital also accrues to high-effort aesthetic or creative posts. Well-made GIFs, edits, and photographs of popular serial killers such as Ramirez or Bundy receive high note numbers, though I also found an interesting counterexample. One blog, *your-rickie*, posts highly filtered and edited pictures of Ramirez to the point of erasing lines and creases in the skin, perfecting teeth, and giving a generally unnatural, uncanny valley–like appearance. These would require some editing skill to make but were not well received. One reason, as in Thornton's seminal work, authenticity is a valued quality. Ramirez did not really look like these pictures (some of them barely look human). The difference between these and edited photographs that say, juxtapose Wuornos with a statue of the Virgin Mary, is that those are *supposed* to be read metaphorically, whereas the "corrected" photographs of Ramirez are more in line with those of Instagram users who edit their skin to suggest an unnatural degree of smoothness and uniformity as "real." The Virgin Mary post is self-consciously an "art" post, and high-quality fanart is rewarded. As I have discussed the content of fanart, such as GIF-edits and edited images, at length in previous chapters, it is not necessary to repeat it here: There was no significant variation from the previous findings.

Jokes, humor, and puns about serial killers, including image-based comedy, could receive hundreds of notes. Bear in mind that any post receiving thousands of notes was unusual; Tumblr doesn't offer any means to calculate statistics, but based on what now amounts to several months of immersion in serial killer fan Tumblr, I would estimate that any post receiving over 300 notes is high capital. Over 1,000 is very high; multiple thousands are the exception rather than the rule. A post with 388 notes superimposes famous images of Ramirez onto mocked-up Valentine's Day cards, amending his well-known sayings to refer to both killing people and sexual intercourse with the reader. Another post, voicing amusement and cracking jokes regarding appeals from Netflix for viewers to stop expressing attraction to Bundy, circulating shortly after the *Extremely Wicked* film premiered, had over 2,000 notes. This supports Thornton's observation that subcultures revel in condemnation by the mainstream media, gaining subcultural capital via their opposition and notoriety. This is another illustration of where serial killer fandom fits better into older fan studies models than newer ones based around media convergence.

Not all the jokes land. Some may even be too grim for the approval and reward of this subculture, and these, it seems, are jokes made at the direct expense of victims. While I was in the middle of the data collection, an image of a prone woman in a nightdress appeared on my dashboard as an original posting by a user with Bundy's image as their profile, with the caption "What does an orgasm and a pulse have in common? I don't care if she has either" (murder-mystery-theatre 2022a). Only one person had liked it two months later, and no-one reblogged it. When the same blog posts jokes where the killers are the butt of the joke, they do better. An image of Dahmer's face superimposed over that of a man eating a hamburger, with the caption "I don't think There's Five Guys in this," received almost thirty notes within two days of posting (2022b).[3] The pursuit of subcultural capital is prone to errors and missteps, and users can misjudge the boundaries.

The display of objects and documentation related to serial killers was another means by which posts accrued subcultural capital. Again, I say posts and not users, because the posts were often recirculated and thus the poster was usually not in possession of the object photographed. Some of the

[3] Five Guys is an American burger franchise.

photographs have watermarks from auction sites, and this does not prevent their appreciation and reward on Tumblr. Posting letters that Ramirez wrote from prison gains a popular Ramirez fanblog hundreds of notes, despite the fact that they tend to be superimposed with "Supernaught" or the name of another auction website (see below). In the pursuit of subcultural capital on Tumblr, curation, annotation, and display matters, as does possession, which is unsurprising given the scrapbook-like structures of a microblogging platform. Contra Thornton on the necessity of restricting access to subcultural media (1995, 161), the subcultural capital gathered by these posts is not based on exclusivity, and sharing them does not apparently dilute it. An anonymous user submitted a question to *TrueCrimeStuff:* "This might be kinda stupid but where do you find the photos from the crime scenes? Or autopsies?" (Anon. 9 2021). The blog owner replied that they primarily use Reddit, and publicly provided the URLs for several relevant forums. Such posts on this blog tend to gather hundreds to low-thousands of notes, in appreciation of the effort in finding and cataloguing authentic photographs and reports. That said, possession of the object *can* act as a trump card. The letter-image with the most notes that I found (1,600) did not have a watermark, and the original poster claimed to own it. User eliasblas writes:

> I wasn't gonna share this on here but I knew there'd be people who might appreciate seeing this.
>
> It's beyond surreal to have a letter written by Richard Ramirez in my possession. I can't quite explain how strange it felt to touch something he did. (eliasblas 2017)

The importance of "touch" in murderabilia collection is explained in *Murderabilia* (Damon and Fiennes 2019, episode 1) as a kind of "contagion theory": a superstitious belief common to most humans that could be summarized as "once in contact, always in contact." It is essentially a mystical belief, whether or not the toucher would actually endorse it with their rational mind: the idea, or at least the "feeling," that in touching something which has been in contact with X, some "property" of X is transferred to us via the object. This belief is related to Hills (2015) and Thornton (1995) on how subcultural capital can accrue to the subculturalist's body, except that in the case of murderabilia, said capital must be transferred by an intermediary object. The belief is also related to the attribution of authenticity to serial killers, as special individuals who exist outside any human-made laws or norms. I will discuss this in greater detail in the section below on auction websites.

Images of contemporary newspaper reports on the crimes of famous killers are highly rewarded. A lot of these "primary source" posts were originally created by the user Morbidology, a professional true crime writer and podcaster. It would be somewhat dubious to categorize Morbidology as a serial killer fan: She is rather too official and professionalized for that. If this were a more mainstream fandom, she would be—a perfect example of one of those fans who have gathered enough subcultural capital to exchange it for professional economic and social capital. Yet Morbidology could never actually express affection or enthusiasm for serial killers themselves (which would ruin her brand, for one thing), and some of her Tumblr is devoted to advertising her work or upcoming appearances at true crime conferences. These do not get recirculated in the fan space, but her posts of original source material do, accruing high numbers of notes. Again, subcultural capital circulates with posts rather than affixing to users. I do not think this is fan social capital of the sort gained by association with respected figures. It isn't the association with Morbidology that matters. Perhaps in the space of more conventional true crime fandom, it would be: She might qualify as something of a subcultural celebrity. But anyone can follow her Tumblr, and for serial killer fandom, it is the selection, arrangement, and reproduction of relevant posts that enables the circulation of subcultural capital, whether displaying physical objects such as gravestones or weapons, or documents such as mugshots and newspaper reports.

Combining relatively obscure information with authentic photographs enacts two strategies of subcultural capital-accumulation at once: The only popular blog dedicated to H. H. Holmes, for example, hosts a blueprint plan of the so-called "murder castle" in which Holmes committed his crimes, a photograph of the actual building, and some information on the photographs. Primary sources get far more notes than posting, for example, merchandise such as bobble-heads of serial killers or jewelry constructed from their photographs. This is contrary to Fiske's observation that, in other fan cultures, the expansiveness of one's collection matters more than the specific objects within. Possessing a single letter that Ramirez has touched is more valued than any range of mass-produced "Night Stalker" merchandise. (One can find examples of this sort of merchandise at sites like psychokillerbobbleheads.com.)

Via the affordances of Tumblr, these primary sources are reblogged into a distinctly fannish space, carrying with them the capital of authenticity and authority. But once there, they are differently inflected with meaning.

One standard piece of historical documentation that circulates on Tumblr (and had gathered 1,679 notes at the time of data collection) is a high school yearbook photograph featuring a teenage Dahmer, his face blacked out with ink. As the original poster explained in a caption (quotation marks in original, unattributed):

> "As a high school student, future serial killer **Jeffrey Dahmer** would try to sneak into as many club yearbook pictures as possible. After a teacher found out about his prank, she smudged his face out with a permanent marker. Here, he is pictured in the top center." (dahmerfordayz-blog 2018, originally posted by ted-bundie)

A distinctly fannish user comments, "i wanna see the smug lil dahmer face so bad" (queertcc 2018), and another supplies the unedited photograph with the comment, "HERE HE IS DJKSKFJSJ" (jeffreydrunk 2018). The random string of letters approximates the user smashing the keyboard, and is commonly used in fan cultures to express excitement and glee (see Hillman et al. 2014a). A relatively solemn, factual accounting is inflected with emotion and appreciation in the fannish space; describing the young Dahmer as "lil," an abbreviation of "little," implies cuteness and affection.

Posts about Wuornos accrue fewer notes than any of the other killers, in keeping with the general pattern found in this study. But those that gather the highest are those that tap into the cultural capital of a distinct kind of radical feminism, and indeed, profess to do so. "Radical feminism is the only hope for women," reads the tagline of one of the top results for "#Aileen Wuornos" plus "#fandom." The user radykalny-feminizm advertises herself as an unapologetic "misandrist." The most popular posts include a GIF taken from the Broomfield documentaries of Wuornos leaving court, raising her middle finger to the judge, and exclaiming, "Putting someone who was raped to death? You motherfucker!" (1,181 notes). Another (1,032 notes) has the caption "Too many women called evil for what is honestly a net positive," beneath an image of Bugs Bunny in a tuxedo. Inside the image are the words "I wish all women who kill abusers & rapists a very pleasant evening." From the different font styles, it is apparent that words have been added over the original text (figure 6).

Figure 6. Death justified for abusive men (radykalny-feminizm 2022, originally posted by male-to-catgirl).

Though not explicitly tagged with Wuornos, this post circulates in her fan blogs and is clearly a reference to her. Here is another example of how capital recirculates on Tumblr rather than accruing to particular users. As it circulates, its meaning is inflected, and capital from one field can be "translated" into another. I prefer to use the term "translated," rather than, say, "exchanged," because this is not a one-to-one relation: The informational posts carry weight over from more traditional true crime fandom, but become inflected by fannish affects. Statements on the necessity of retaliatory violence against men cross over from radical feminism, and become inflected with particular fannish appreciation for a woman who killed violent men. Thus I would argue that the theory of subcultural capital can be usefully applied to serial killer fandom on Tumblr—to an extent. It needs to be quite radically modified to account for the relative anonymity of users and the practices of circulation and recirculation that accrue capital to posts more readily than to users (though, as the ranking of search results shows, whole blogs can gain it in some sense). The theory also needs to be modified to account for those instances where capital moved between and across fields, and the practice of curation and documentation of primary objects in addition to possessing or touching them as a means of subcultural capital building.

As noted above, when it came to analysis of TikTok through the lens of cultural capital, there was very little precedent for me in terms of where to begin. On TikTok, user identity is even more unstable than it is on Tumblr, at least in this fandom, due to the rapid turnover of deletions and remade blogs. Thus, once again, it is more accurate to speak of subcultural capital accruing to and moving through a network of videos, which can be adapted as the basis for new videos due to TikTok's affordances. Users can, for example, utilize the "duet feature" to create a new video by splitting the screen of another user's video and inserting their own content on the other half. They can reuse the sound of one video to create another. Users can also attempt to consolidate a following via the "respond to comment" feature, wherein they provide, for example, a cropped or edited version of a previous clip at a follower's request. Moreover, TikTok users are *aware* of the potential for capital accrual both within and across subcultures, and attempt to boost their own and each other's videos to recognition by the TikTok algorithm—thus increasing their chances of appearing on "For You Pages" and feeds. As previously discussed, the fine details of the algorithm are quite mysterious, but many users attempt to boost their videos by tagging them with as many hashtags as possible, including "fyp" or "For You Page." It is a persistent myth on TikTok that this hashtag catches the algorithm's attention. This practice suggests that the serial killer fandom on TikTok is more concerned with gaining subcultural capital—which might come in the form of censure from mainstream TikTok as much as it might from praise—than with staying hidden. Users attempt to assist their favored videos, sometimes commenting in capital letters, expressing the belief this will enhance their visibility to the algorithm.

Generally, subcultural capital on TikTok is measured by the popularity of the account in terms of search results, and by likes and comments on individual videos. I did not consider that "plays" were a strong indicator of subcultural capital accrual (though they might be a weak one), because a play can be recorded for multiple reasons and users know this.

In addition to the accounts I was already following from the past data gathering cycles, I re-performed the hashtag searches as described above, then followed the top ten results for each search. Some of these had changed from the last data collection period, and other accounts had been deleted. Some of the results were overlapping, meaning that in total I was following eighty accounts. The number of videos per account was relatively small, often just one or two, and thus I was able to supplement my impressions with some statistical analysis. In addition to monitoring my dashboard daily for high-capital content, I identified the most popular video in each account by comments and likes to make up the sample. The average number of comments on a video in the sample was 126. Comments, of course, could be negative, but again, negative attention can actually operate as a measure of subcultural capital in this space. The average number of likes was 4,069. However, these are pulled upwards by two videos with an extraordinary number of comments and likes. The median and mode average for both categories was zero, meaning that any video with over approximately one hundred likes ought to be considered relatively high in subcultural capital within the serial killer fandom. The two videos with extraordinarily high subcultural capital were:

A. A GIF from the Broomfield documentary Life and Death (2003), wherein Wuornos exclaims, "You are lost, Nick!" objecting to Broomfield's attempts to reason with her in her paranoid state (6,843 comments, 102,200 likes)

B. A well-made compilation of Ramirez news reports, splicing them with sexualized pulsating music and dramatic images of the killer (2,308 comments, 206,200 likes).

The comments on these videos are almost uniformly approving and supportive.

When inductively coded, the most well-received videos in the sample fell into somewhat differing categories to the Tumblr posts, though there were also overlaps. These categories were:

A. High-quality fannish edits

B. Comedy

C. Roleplay

D. The defense of Wuornos

A few points of note: Firstly, information and knowledge were *not* a particularly reliable means of gaining subcultural capital. Those videos belonged quite distinctly to the sphere of "true crime TikTok," which was more clearly delineated here than on Tumblr. My "For You Page" continuously attempted to nudge me towards this more normative content, probably because it receives more views and likes overall, and thus more promotion. But the capital of these videos did *not* transfer or translate into the fannish sphere. Serial killer fans on TikTok have other interests—notably, roleplay. On TikTok, however, it gathered more subcultural capital generally. The defense of Wuornos was less specifically grounded in feminist capital on TikTok than on Tumblr, relying more on emotional expressions of love and admiration than the justification of retaliatory violence against men.

By "high-quality fannish edits," I mean video edits of the type explored earlier—splicing footage of killers with effects and other media, usually to a popular song—that displayed a high degree of technical competency. Many of these had a slightly "trollish," or deliberately provocative, quality, that will be further explored in the next chapter, on digital play. For example, user ._tedbundy edits a video of herself dancing sexually (while laughing) to the song "Woman," by Doja Cat (2021), surrounded by images of Bundy and superimposed with cartoon hearts (._tedbundy 2021). The video received 300 likes and 62 comments. Many of the comments were condemnatory, such as listing the names of Bundy's victims, presumably to induce guilt or at least reflection in the creator. Yet, as it was with Thornton's subculturalists and their desire to shock the mainstream, this is still a form of subcultural capital, because condemnation is exactly what the video is inviting.

A Dahmer video, likewise, cut to the song "POV" by Ariana Grande (jeffrey_dahmer17 2020, 89 comments, 585 likes), has a comedic element in its juxtaposition of Dahmer, in odd poses and flat facial expressions, with the romantic song. Some are more straightforwardly sexual: The most popular Ramirez accounts post upbeat, sexy songs to Ramirez posing in court or jealously romantic tracks against images of him with a girl. These typically gained hundreds of comments and over a thousand likes, including one of two exceptional cases that pulled up the averages of likes and comments. An edit of Bundy images over the song "Pumped Up Kicks" by Foster the People (2011)—a somewhat odd choice, as the song concerns a school shooting—received 174 comments and 9,324 likes (tedbundy_r 2022). The distinct effort and skill involved here is that the creator has provided subtitles in Spanish. Effort and skill is rewarded, and conversely, when a creator is perceived as having exaggerated the skill and effort that has gone into making a video, they are criticized. One video by thenightstalker1960s appears to show a portrait of Ramirez created out of black and white dice. "You didnt built that, its an app," objects a commenter (s 2021). "I like using that edit app It's good for me to use ●," the creator confirms (thenightstalker1960s 2021). This seems almost an admission, the emoji suggesting bashfulness—a failed bid for subcultural capital that has been called out as inauthentic.

Comedy is probably even more rewarded on TikTok than on Tumblr, and much of it concerns Dahmer. Perhaps the nature of his crimes influences this—cannibalism being a subject of much comedy horror—or perhaps his media-constructed status as queer tragic monster prevents him being taken quite as seriously as Ramirez or Bundy. Some accounts engage in joking roleplay, claiming to be Dahmer himself and confessing such crimes as having eaten their own hamster. One user films herself reacting with expressions of appreciation to the 1995 song "Dahmer Is Dead" by the Violent Femmes (jeffreydahmerlover 2017). For the uninitiated, this is a short, banjo-heavy mock folk song built around the refrain "Dahmer is dead / Dahmer is dead / A broomstick bashed him upside his head."

Some of the Ramirez and Bundy vids are comedic too, but the object of the comedy is rarely the serial killer himself. Such videos are more likely to be self-reflexive, with the fan laughing at herself as she performs an excess of emotional investment in the killer, as with the fan who dances to the "let me be your woman" refrain by Doja Cat. Another video shows the creator pretending to scream to images of Ramirez to the recirculated sound known on TikTok as "Simp Scream." The scream is one of adoration—a simp, in popular cultural terms, is one who is hopelessly and ridiculously devoted to their object of their affection, who is either using them or does not acknowledge them at all. This tendency to self-mockery is complicated. Excess emotional investment is traditionally looked down on, both in cultural and subcultural spheres. It tends to deplete capital. Yet here, just as the fan attracts subcultural capital via notoriety in enjoyment of an "improper" fannish object, she also attracts it via the performance of "improper" fandom. It is these types of videos, after all, that attract the most censure and thus the most subcultural capital-via-notoriety: the lists of victims' names, the injunctions to seek help, the accusations that the creator is sick or disgusting.

Roleplay as a serial killer was a means of gathering subcultural capital that seemed to be unique to TikTok. It was not the most popular one—that would be the well-crafted edits and the display of technological skill inherent therein—but it did appear several times in the results. Roleplay on Tumblr tended to be largely ignored, or responded to only by a very small and selected cross-section of fellow roleplayers. On serial killer TikTok, a roleplay is usually constructed by posting a video of the killer one is playing, using either their name or some variation as an account name. The videos were captioned with invitations to their "fans" or "groupies" to interact with them. One playing as Bundy, for instance, received 242 likes and 52 comments, some of which were censure, but most of which were actual engagement by self-proclaimed fans. A similar Ramirez example gathered 21 comments and 178 likes. Hashtagged "groupies," an image of Ramirez is captioned "hey my loves. Talk to me[.] Tell me about yourself" (real.ramirez 2021), to which the responses include "Hey papi richie i love you●💋" (Leslie ▮ 2021) and "Richard can I be yours?●" (:) [username] 2021), in addition to some complaints and objections.

The videos concerning the defense of Wuornos were, as noted, less explicitly linked to feminism than those on Tumblr. The single most well-received video in the sample features Wuornos's exclamation "Oh, you are lost, Nick!" from the Broomfield documentary (2003), over a short piece of rap music I have not been able to identify. The sound is tagged simply as "aileen wuornos—original sound," and has been re-used by ten other TikTok users, including young women mouthing the words. Users don't typically expand this to a broader feminist argument about the necessity of retaliatory violence again men, but confine their defense to Wuornos specifically. When they go beyond this, posts are less rewarded. User aileen_wuornos._.fanpage, for example, gets 87 likes on a video simply stating that Aileen deserves an apology, but only 32 on one comparing the "double standards" of Ramirez's popularity on TikTok to the relatively low appreciation of Wuornos (2021). A video by user saveaileen is captioned "T[o]m[o]r[row] is National R@pe day! PLS WOMEN AND MEN STAY INSIDE!!!!" (2021). (For an explanation of the viral "National Rape Day" hoax, see p. 133.) It plays a snippet from the song "Doubt" by twenty one pilots [*sic*] (2015) with the lyric refrain "Don't forget about me" over images of Wuornos. Killing may be justification for rape, but rape is not explicitly considered a feminist concern here: Men are warned as though they are equally at risk.

Thus the content that gathers high subcultural capital on TikTok bears some similarities to that on Tumblr, but there are also some distinct differences. Firstly, it is even more anonymous, more unfixed to user identities, than it is on Tumblr, where the blogs that turned up top in the search results tended to be quite substantial in terms of content, having built up a following over time. Many of these TikToks had just one or two videos. Capital attaches to the videos themselves and recirculates by playing into themes and tropes appreciated by the fandom. These were lighter, more playful, and with a more "trollish" edge than on Tumblr (though Tumblr could certainly be playful too): Feminism is less of a serious concern, roleplay is more approved, and information and knowledge acquisition is, notably, not rewarded. There was less evidence of translation of capital between fields; the more normative true crime content is less valued, as is the currency of feminist knowledge. Thus we *can* use cultural capital as a lens through which to view killer fandom on these rhizomatic websites, with some adaptations, but its potential is limited due to their ephemerality, particularly on TikTok. The most notable finding is probably the function of notoriety, which increases subcultural capital in a way that has not really been attended to since Thornton (2002) and to some extent Hills (2005). This is another way in which serial killer fandom fits better with older patterns of analysis.

I turn now to a different type of website. The collection of "murderabilia" is one of the most well-known aspects of serial killer fandom outside the subculture itself. Though collecting is common to most fandoms, it is only recently that fan scholars have begun to look at the practice seriously. Hills wrote that, in the early stages of fan studies, "fandom is salvaged for academic study by removing the taint of consumption and consumerism" (2002, 30). Geraghty, writing more recently, argued that "collecting has been over-looked in fan studies and [. . .] it is devalued as a fan practice because of its basis in consumption rather than production" (2014, 2). Serial killer fandom is of course devalued already, but Jack Denham (2016) has a fascinating piece on how the consumption of the killer's body after death (in the form of hair or clothes, for example) functions in the popular imagination to transfer monstrosity onto the collecting fan. The killer is no longer the consumer (of people, bodies, life) but becomes the consumed, while the collecting fan takes on the monstrous taint of consumption. Denham was actually discussing the body of Charles Manson (who was never convicted of personally killing anyone), but the broader point stands. Murderabilia collectors are aware of this taint, and for the most part—at least those who are open about their hobby—appear to revel in it.

The collection of murderabilia can be reliably dated to at least the 1700s. Ruth Penfold-Mounce (in Damon and Fiennes 2019, episode 6) describes how fingerbones of executed criminals were historically kept as good luck charms to prevent the bearer from running out of money, while hangmen themselves sold the body parts of murderers as charms against ill-health. I discussed the Victorian sale of supposed artifacts from crime scenes in chapter 1. But the online sale of murderabilia was established in the 1990s, largely due to the efforts of subcultural celebrity Erik Holler, who also goes by Erik Gein, in a distinctly fannish appropriation of a serial killer's surname. Though Gein (naturally) claims no wish to emulate said killers, his interview with Damon and Fiennes has distinctly fannish overtones. He describes Ramirez as a "rockstar," a "fucking legend"; he claims to have been "starstruck" upon receipt of letters from him (2019, episode 1). Thus I claim that he occupies a different position than professional podcasters like Morbidology, and is one of the few good examples of social capital accrual within serial killer fandom. Today, Gein is the webmaster and owner of Serial Killers Ink (http://serialkillersink.net/), one of the world's most popular murderabilia sale sites. The others, according to Google search rankings, are Cult Collectibles (https://www.cultcollectibles.org/), Murder Auction (https://www.murderauction.com/), and Supernaught (https://www.supernaught.com/).

For the collection of data, I created an account at each of the websites and joined their mailing lists, though I did not actually receive any email from them during the collection period. I then sorted the items for sale by highest to lowest value (if the site had that facility), before repeating the process for each of the killers in my sample. This was achieved either by searching for their name and manually analyzing the results, or by selecting their names from drop-down menus. I also analyzed the way the sites presented themselves—their homepages and associated media.[4]

Murderabilia sites increased in popularity and visibility when eBay banned the sale of murderabilia in 2001. Like eBay, Murder Auction brokers auction sales by third-party sellers, but the other sites both sell and host the objects at fixed prices. I noted watermarks for some of these sites on the Tumblr photographs, where cultivation and display was more a marker of subcultural capital than authenticity. On these sites, however, authenticity and the "transfer" of the aura via the killer's physical touch was undoubtedly the hallmark of value, both subcultural and economic. In fact, I would venture to say that subcultural and economic capital are interchangeable in this instance, which raises the question of whether said capital is actually "subcultural" at all. As a partial answer, recall Woo's suggestion that (sub)cultural capital in an era of convergence is not quite the same thing as economic capital—but what it does have is an exchange rate (2012), which in this case is 1:1. The authenticity of the objects on these sites, and their closeness to the killer's physical body, largely determines their value. As I

[4] All the prices quoted were correct as of September 2022.

discussed in the introduction, "authenticity" is attributed to serial killers in popular imagination: the (wo)man outside the law and of society, a law unto themselves. The other two main factors in valuation were rarity and the degree of celebrity associated with the killer. Because these factors are so intertwined, I do not separate them, but instead discuss my findings as a single narrative.

Notoriety is clearly a marker of subcultural capital within these spaces. Serial Killers Ink self-advertises:

> We have been featured on such shows as National Geographic's TABOO TV series, EXPLOSIV in Germany, The Mark Kelley Show in Canada as well as interviewed and profiled by world class news networks such as CNN, FOX News, ABC, CBS, NBC, MSNBC, The New York Times and Reuters to name just a few. (2022a)

The site's media page hosts YouTube links to said news features, which are not entirely complimentary. They are not entirely condemnatory either: Usually they serve as a quirky "weird news" segment at the end of more serious reporting slots, featuring a range of voices from reasonable-sounding collectors to the horrified mother of a victim (*Fox News Cleveland*, uploaded by serialkillersink 2012). However, Serial Killer Ink's Facebook page also links a news story in the British tabloid *The Sun*, which condemns the site in moral panic style. The post is adorned with laughing emojis, demonstrating the proprietor's amusement at their demonization. Likewise, Murder Auction self-advertises:

> In May of 2001 a popular online auction website banned the sale of items deemed offensive, including true crime memorabilia. [. . .] Despite sharp criticism from victim advocacy groups and numerous spin-off sites that spawned in its wake, Murder Auction is the world's leading true crime memorabilia auction house. (2022)

As with Thornton's subculturalists, mainstream condemnation is subcultural capital in this space.

Across all the sites, the most expensive items were associated with a killer's hands or body. These included a bathhouse membership card signed on the back by Dahmer ($125,000, Supernaught) and the windbreaker worn by Ramirez in prison, offered with a certificate of authenticity from his ex-wife ($15,000, Supernaught). Items not signed by the killers themselves tended to require some sort of certification of authenticity. A Murder Auction seller offers the copy of the *Satanic Bible* owned by Ramirez in prison for $12,500, also with a card of certification from his ex-wife: She seems to have produced quite a few of them. Other sellers offer the (non-Satanic) prison Bibles of Dahmer and Wuornos, for $10,000 and $4,500 respectively. Celebrity factor interacts with touch here to decide the specific order of value. Supernaught hosts a hair from the head of Wuornos, with a signed card by her certifying its origin ($4,200). Serial Killers Ink offers cards signed by Bundy in the low thousands.

Yet perhaps the ultimate expression of the sanctity of the body is the fact that, on Cult Collectibles, the owner claims to possess and offer the sale of Dahmer's urn. On TikTok, he explains that the ashes were scattered, but a small amount of residue remains in one of the bags inside. If true, these are the only physical remains of Dahmer's body on earth. The asking price is $250,000, but one must email for specifics: "serious enquiries ONLY" (Cult Collectibles 2022a, caps in original). This site has a specific collection devoted to Dahmer, including the glasses he wore in prison ($75,000) and miscellaneous objects from the flat where he committed his crimes. It is worth noting that the site advertises itself somewhat differently, less an appeal to notoriety than to cultural capital of a more traditional kind:

> Archiving historical true crime media, sourcing items for museums, research and consulting for documentaries, original merch, a very active YouTube channel and more.
>
> For any media inquiries or consulting work, or help finding a specific artifact please contact us. (Cult Collectibles 2022b)

The site's owner is Taylor James, who also goes by the name Robert Applewhite.[5] He positions himself very much as an expert-fan, and also as a fan-entrepreneur. He refers to his site as a "weird hobby that became a job" (Webber 2022). YouTube commenters frequently ask him how they can be assured of the authenticity of objects, to which he replies that the process is variable and too complicated to explain in a comment, but that they should contact him about specific items for details. Rather than advertising simple "certificates of authenticity," which he has criticized on TikTok as unreliable, the Cult Collectibles website tends to invite potential buyers to email

[5] This alias is a reference to Marshall Applewhite, co-leader of the Heaven's Gate cult, whose members completed mass suicide in 1997 with the aim to ascend to an evolutionary plane above human.

the administrator, implying entrance to a more private and exclusive sphere for serious collectors only.

James/Applewhite has a presence within the narrowcast media outlets common to this subculture, such as YouTube and various niche podcasts. These are not what Thornton would call restricted channels (1995, 161), because anyone can find them, but they are of special interest to collectors. His YouTube and TikTok are largely devoted to showing his wares, especially new or interesting items, and again, the expressive enthusiasm he displays towards his objects places him rather more on the fan side of the divide than the disinterested professional collector. He also appears on the videos of certain related YouTubers, who hail him with such introductions as "when it comes to the true crime community Taylor is a legend. It's an honor to be unboxing [unpacking merchandise] with you" (Webber 2022). James and Holler fill the role of those "expert fans," then—those with a high degree of social and symbolic capital who tend to function as the "spokespeople for their fandom" (Hills 2002, 69). Of course, when speaking to more mainstream media, these expert fans tend to tone down their fannish exclamations. This is from *Rolling Stone* magazine:

> According to Holler [not Gein here], "soccer moms picking up books on Charles Manson" is an indication of how mainstream the genre has become. "These items that I sell do take the books and go a little further," he says. "There are people who are proud to hang a John Wayne Gacy painting up on their wall and they're not psychos, and the dealers are not psychos. It's just a culture that interests people." (Yuko 2019)

Holler/Gein might also be one of the only fans who can claim social capital via connection to "content producers," as identified by Chin (2018). By his own testimony (Yuko 2019), he acquires much of his content by writing directly to criminals in prison. There is something ethically striking about this. Serial killers are content producers, within a broader media landscape. Murder is the content. Holler is profiting from this, but he certainly didn't start it.

Rarity can also boost the cultural and economic capital of an item. Because Ramirez wrote so many letters, they tend to be valued in the hundreds, or even less, on Serial Killers Ink, whereas Wuornos's go for thousands despite fact she is a less "popular" and "admired" killer than he is. As I descended the price ranges, I found articles *authentically associated* with the killers, but which never touched them, such as newspaper clippings and Wanted posters from their era. Contemporary reports on the Bundy trial retail for about $1,400 (Supernaught) and real courtroom sketches in the high hundreds (Serial Killers Ink). Toward the bottom of the price range, I found the cheap, mass-produced collectibles, like a Bundy "collectors card" for $35 (Supernaught), and the replicas, like a reproduction of Dahmer's seventh grade yearbook photograph for $10 (Supernaught). The difference in value between replicas and originals is neatly demonstrated by figure 7, from Cult Collectibles. This is an original and a reprint of the same Dahmer family photograph, priced $5,000 and $15, respectively:

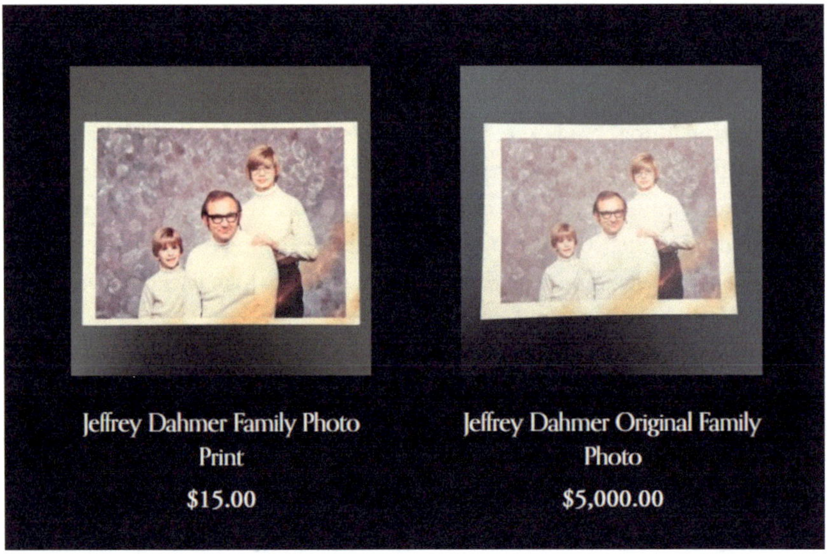

Figure 7. An original and reprint of the same Dahmer family photograph, priced $5,000 and $15 respectively (Cult Collectibles).

These are the same photograph. They look identical. But one has been touched and handled by the Dahmer family, and one has not. Thus it retains an auratic property: The touch of the celebrity-killer and his associates has given it an aura that a photograph itself would not possess. Compare Thornton's observation that the same songs became devalued within the dance subculture once they were transferred from exclusive "white label" records to a "television-advertised compilation album" (1995, 182). The nature of the thing does not confer subcultural capital; the context of production does.

However, if collectibles are rare, they can retail for a slightly higher value even with no physical connection to a killer. Serial Killers Ink offers an "18-inch plush Jeffrey Dahmer doll made by Demented Dollz" for $150, stressing that "this collectible is extremely hard to find as it has been out of production for many years" (Serial Killers Ink, 2022b). An issue of *Psycho Killers* comic book featuring Ramirez retails for $300 on Serial Killers Ink. In some unusual cases, rarity can even trump touch. For $100,000, seller Redrumautographs at Murder Auction offers the "Theodore Robert Bundy original 10 pages court document stamped and signed from August 7, 1979," claiming, "This is the most important and most significative Ted Bundy court document to ever exist" (Redrumautographs 2022). On this site, sellers and buyers can rate each other: This popular seller has 672 ratings, 99 percent of which are positive, which lends credence to the authenticity of the document. The description goes on: "The details of the crime scene is completely grotesque with more accuracy in this document than anywhere else. It's a one of kind document! [. . .] This document is for the private collector and perhaps museums." If Bundy touched the document, it isn't advertised or noted. The important factor here seems to be that there is only one, that it is original, and that it is apparently in the seller's possession. Suggesting it as a museum piece is also an appeal to a more conventional kind of cultural capital, demonstrating at least some translation between fields of cultural capital.

The cheapest items tended to be only tangentially associated with real killers: For a mere $2, one may purchase an envelope from the Washington Department of Corrections, via Supernaught. Or, not provably authentic, a knot of plastic supposedly tied by killer Richard Clary retails for $3 (Supernaught), but anyone could have made that. Trading cards, figurines, and similar mass-produced items tended to retail under $50, across these sites. One interesting finding, which demonstrates the devaluation of unrestricted information, was an offer on Serial Killers Ink for a link to Dahmer's full confession online, for $10. It offers graphic detail and a length of 243 pages, to be immediately emailed to the buyer after purchase. This looks like an attempt to monetize Thornton's observation that "subcultural capital maintains its currency [. . .] as long as it flows through channels of communication which are subject to varying degrees of restriction" (1995, 161). The problem is that the confession is not restricted, but easily discoverable online, for free. Of course, there is no law against selling things one can find for free, but the fact that the site only attempted to charge $10 for the access suggests some kind of awareness that this strategy probably wasn't going to work. Restricted knowledge is valuable within this market. Knowledge anyone can find in thirty seconds is not.

It seems, then, that the lens of subcultural capital has useful, widespread, and quite traditional application when applied to the collectible aspect of serial killer fandom. Authenticity and rarity produce both economic and subcultural value simultaneously with the celebrity of the killer concerned, and each factor influences the others. The contexts of production are paramount. This aspect of the fandom produces expert and celebrity fans, high in social and symbolic capital, in a way that TikTok and Tumblr spheres do not. Still, we should not eschew the lenses entirely when applying it to these media platforms, but note the adaptations I have drawn attention to regarding circulation, reproduction, curation over possession, and the attachment of subcultural capital to posts rather than users. As a pathologized fandom, the subcultural capital in question here has less direct relation to more mainstream cultural capital than that of bigger, more popular fandoms, but there was a still degree of translation of capital between fields, notably the capital of radical feminism as applied to Wuornos. Information and knowledge from more mainstream sources was also valued within the fannish sphere. TikTok was especially interesting with regard to the valuation of feminine sexual expression, which tends to deplete capital in most fandoms, but here plays into the strategy of appealing to notoriety within a subcultural group. Significantly, however, this lens did not fully account for the presence of humor on any site: Humor and joking can be a tactic of subcultural capital accumulation, but it is also more than that. On which note, I turn now to my final investigative chapter, through the lens of digital play.

CHAPTER 5

Serial Killer Fandom as Digital Play

The concept of fandom as playful, either as a ludic experience or a more conventional kind of play akin to gameplay, wasn't absent from early fan studies, but it wasn't particularly well developed either. For example, Henry Jenkins's concluding chapter to *Textual Poachers* described the space of the fan convention as a "weekend only world" (1992, 277). Still, early fan theorists were more concerned with justifying fandom in terms of political impetus, transformative power, and social meaning than investigating fandom as a ludic experience or experience of play. Foundational texts like *Textual Poachers* and *Enterprising Women* are ultimately concerned with resistant cultural production and ideological challenges to media narratives, without much attention to pleasure and fun. This began to change in the later 2000s, when the concept of "play" entered the discussion in earnest. By 2009, Louisa Stein and Kristina Busse were exploring fan fiction as "limit play": i.e., as explicitly playful engagement with a text, as free movement within the boundaries created by the source text by broader culture, by the technologies in use, and by the social and artistic conventions of the fan community itself (Stein and Busse 2009). Yet it was not until 2015 that a full monograph on fandom as play was published, Paul Booth's aptly titled *Playing Fans*. In this work, Booth posits that the contemporary internet has embraced a "philosophy of playfulness," which he goes on to define:

> What is a "philosophy of playfulness"? [. . .] The contemporary media scene is complex, and rapidly becoming dependent on a culture of ludism. Today's media field is fun, playful, and exuberant. More so than at any other time, the media we use in our everyday lives have been personalized, individualized, and made pleasurable to use. We play with our media; it is malleable in our hands. (2016, 8)

Though Booth is studying fandom, and finds playfulness inherent to the fan experience, he is speaking of media more broadly here; and indeed, the dividing lines between "fandom" and "media engagement," or even "media culture," are no longer as clear as they were. Booth attributes some of this convergence to the (then) popularity of Tumblr, whose technological affordances and social norms prioritize remix, transformation, replication, curation, and adaptation of media texts. These were formerly practices associated with fandom; now they are just norms of media engagement. Tumblr also upholds social norms of humor, irreverence, and emotionality over rational response and debate. Louisa Stein argues that:

> Step by step, we are moving to a millennial media landscape no longer dominated by fears of the excesses of the unruly fan, one that instead embraces personal investment, performativity, emotion, and excess, within the content of shared digital creativity. (2015, 15)

When I studied the influence of emo fandom on shaping the genre via engagement with the music industry, I thought this argument was apt. Applied to serial killer fandom, however, it is not: Fears of the unruly fan, the over-invested fan, are still very much the dominant narrative outside of the community—though, as I observed, the performance of excess can earn subcultural capital. Moreover, a great deal of the actual material of killer fandom *is* playful, at least as playful as other fandoms, if not more so. I have observed a tendency to humorous provocation at several points in this book already, from the absurdist fanfiction to the performance of excessive sexuality.

Booth notes the centrality of parody and pastiche to playful fandom. Pastiche, which is the selection, curation, and rearrangement of elements from one or more texts, does not have the social impetus or satirical bite of parody. It is a form of what Booth describes as "coloring inside the lines" (2015, 2), or pleasurable engagement with a media text that does not necessarily subvert it or its surrounding culture. It is not so easy to claim pastiche as politically or ideologically subverting the source text's narrative. As Booth puts it:

> "Media play" has many meanings, as the term "play" itself is in inherently ambiguous. I use the term "media play" as a characteristic of contemporary media culture to focus on those instances in which individuals create meaning from activities that articulate a connection between their own creativity and mainstream media, all the while working within the boundaries of the media text. (2015, 15)

Fans are not "resisting" the text; they are playing with it and in it. One example might be what Booth calls "identity roleplay," in which "fans both act as if they were [a] character and 'play' with the characteristics that define that character" (2016, 116). Online communities which enable fans to create fictional profiles for themselves are an obvious resource for this play. Another example might be media properties actually licensed by rights holders, such as the "collaborative storytelling system" Storium or the licensed game *Star Wars Rebellion* (Booth 2017). Both of these franchises set authorized lines within which fans may move freely, shifting elements of the game or the narrative around, but only within a set of rules set by the rights holders. This is the sort of fandom that theorists invested in a resistance model have, understandably, paid less attention to.

My aim in this chapter is to make a somewhat bold argument: that much of the fandom I observe from serial killer fans is, counter-intuitively, "coloring inside the lines." Those lines are already drawn by the mainstream fascination with serial killers—the endless stream of content. It might operate at the edges of the discourse formation—*just* inside the lines—but I don't think serial killer fan-play is beyond them. I have already observed that the sexualization and lionization of serial killers in the fanwork analyzed in chapter 1 takes precedent from the mainstream media. So does the primacy of straight men as the most "impressive" killers, as opposed to the pathetic abjection of the monstrous queer. At the time I was researching this chapter in late 2022, Netflix launched its new top-ranking drama *Dahmer—Monster: The Jeffrey Dahmer Story*. Though my focus is not on fans who engage specifically with fictionalized dramas, the series generated a vast wave of playful content across the sites where I've collected data. The posts and comments, I found, were more reflective of mainstream culture's fascination with serial killers than subversive of it.

When Booth discusses parody, much of his focus is on the way that media industries strategically parody fan engagement, though he also introduces the concept of "sociocultural parody." He offers pornographic parodies of major franchises as an example, arguing that "in this mode of parody, parodic discourse has an effect of unsettling 'established normative systems' in order to subvert traditional structures and create alternative cultural meanings" (2015, 123). Pornographic parody highlights "what is always pornographic about mainstream culture" (128), exposing the "undercurrent of sexuality within all mainstream texts by providing negotiated readings of mainstream media" (128). As I read it, many of the fan texts generated around serial killers are doing the same thing. They are exposing our already-extant fascination with serial killing, the media's endless profit from it, and the circular relationship between the public and the media industry in valorizing serial killers. Indeed, Jacqueline Vickery (2020) has made a similar point about the "memeification" of school shootings. Short, humorous, and ironic videos on the subject have been circulating on youth-dominant social media for years. Vickery writes:

> While these videos may be read as inappropriate, dark, or crass, it is the very absurdity of the memes that sheds light on the equally—and arguably exponentially more—absurd responses by adults and policymakers that have failed to safeguard children's protection and well-being. (2020)

Memes about school shooting are absurd and insulting—but not as absurd and insulting as the absolute lack of action that the US legal system is taking to prevent them. Memes are a key example of where fannish play and online play more generally overlap.

Limor Shifman defines an internet meme as "(a) a group of digital items sharing common characteristics of content, form, and/or stance; (b) that were created with awareness of each other; and (c) were circulated, imitated, and/or transformed via the internet by many users" (2014, 7–8). This is a good working definition, but it may be a little rigid for the way the term "meme" is now used. In searching TikTok and Tumblr for serial killer memes (see below), I found that the term could be used for almost any text that referentially hails another text, or group of texts, via imitation and adaptation. Playful engagement with school shooter media was also noted by Whitney Phillips and Ryan Milner in their significant and insightful book *The Am-*

bivalent Internet (2017). As Ashley Hedrick et al. have noted in their review of Phillips and Milner, too many studies of online cultures and movements

> have at their foundation a model of what we call an "earnest Internet." By this, we mean that communication scholarship generally posits that people act rationally and in good faith; care about facts, truth, and authenticity; pursue ends in line with their political and social values and aspirations. (2018)

This is a mistake. Online cultures are not necessarily "earnest," and fan cultures certainly are not. On the contrary, they usually exhibit a high degree of ambivalence, which, as Phillips and Miller point out themselves, is not the same as indifference. The prefix ambi- "refers to 'both,' on both sides, both at the same time" (2017, 9). Serious and not serious, simultaneously. Meaningful and nonsensical. Art and trash. Significant and mundane. Their book is "full of cases that could go either way, in fact could go any way simultaneously, immediately complicating any easy assessment of authorial intent, social consequence, and cultural worth" (9). In their introduction, titled "Some Initial Oddities to Set the Scene," they present

> an image posted to microblogging platform Tumblr, the yearbook pictures of [Columbine school shooter] Eric Harris and second gunman Dylan Klebold are decorated with hearts and captions. Dylan's images are captioned with the inscriptions "cute but psycho" and "3000 %," while Harris's images are captioned with "now real life has no appeal" and another "psycho" (this one inscribed in cartoon hearts). Harris and Klebold are both wearing photoshopped princess flower crowns. (2017, 5)

What do these posts mean? Nothing? Something? Compare the anarchic proliferation of signs at Ted Bundy's execution (chapter 1). If Phillips and Milner are right regarding the fundamental ambivalence of online cultures, this sort of post means several contradictory things all at once:

> Playful fawning over mass shooters could be seen from several co-occurring vantage points, from excessive attachment to excessive dissociation to a pointed satire [or Booth's sociocultural parody?] of the idolatrous 24-hour news coverage that invariably follows American mass shootings. Maybe the people who post Columbine sweetheart photos are just assholes. Maybe all of the above. (11)

In my opinion, ambivalence and digital play are very useful lenses with which to view serial killer fandom, especially with regard to Tumblr and TikTok. The two sites are built on architectures, and host cultures, which are fruitful grounds for ambivalent digital play. I have argued previously that the phenomenon of the Tumblr "hateblog," a blog supposedly devoted to hatred of a text or media person, is actually a form of ambiguous pastiche:

> Far from a straightforward display of antifandom, what we find here is a comic pastiche of fragments enabled by the postmodern flatness of the medium. [. . .] I suggest we can read these pastiches as critique without authority—as a polyphonic surface that undermines both claims to discursive dominance and the dominance of mass media cultural icons. [. . .] [The surfaces of] Tumblr produce a distinct mode of critique, one which rebuffs depth hermeneutics in a comic display of postmodern pastiche that both invokes and satires fandom discourses across its depthless surface. (Fathallah 2018b)

The pastiche, copy-and-paste, always-juxtaposed effects of Tumblr mean that all statements are automatically critiqued and self-critiqued, and the authority of any voice is deconstructed. It is a playful platform, and an ambivalent one. Hedrick et al. independently reached similar conclusions to the ones I have been making; in their review of Phillips and Milner, they write that "much of the fan fiction literature fails to acknowledge any sort of ambivalence in fandom" (2018). This is "understandable given the subfield's origins in the attempt to reclaim popular culture as an important object of study"—but it isn't accurate, and it is past time to move on.

Further, Phillips and Milner argue that the understanding of ambivalence functions as a social bond within certain online communities. If you understand the ambivalent way in which a text is meant to be received, you are part of the group. If you misunderstand, and take it earnestly, you are not. This aligns with Yuval Katz and Limor Shifman's position on "the structure and meanings of digital memetic nonsense" (2017). They write that "digital nonsense may potentially serve as a social glue that bonds members of phatic, image-oriented, communities" (825). Contemporary memes can be polyvocal to the point of incoherence, enabled by the digital technologies that mean "elements that could not previously be imagined appearing together are now juxtaposed in seconds" (834). The authors claim that such memes carry affective meaning, rather than referential meaning: They serve to tie together the community of those who "know"—those who understand ambivalence,

I would argue—rather than outsiders who attempt to decode the meme in an earnest fashion, as though there were a stable referent underneath it.

In a similar vein, Clinton Lanier et al. have offered a conceptualization of fans in digital culture as "tricksters, or those crafty entities that call an established order into question by disrupting conventional behavior" (2022, 384). Digital technology has increased both the amount of information available to fans, and "the tools and spaces for fans' trickster activities" (384). There is both a resistant and a ludic element to this conception of fandom. Lanier et al. contend that "elements of the trickster underlie much of fan creativity," in drawing "(critical) attention to the established meanings of the text, which, in turn, often leads to new meanings and cultural forms" (387). Digital fandom practices frequently "lend themselves to fans' tricksterish activities" such as roleplay, including "screen name, avatar, and profile, created by fans to express their desired connection to a cultural text," even as they undermine and unsettle it (388–89). Deliberately calling back to early fan culture scholarship, the authors argue that fans' activities "often lie outside the accepted social order" (392). They do not, however, really give any concrete examples, and their assertions are too generic to simply apply in broad brushstrokes to "fans." What about those fans Booth described, who create stories firmly within the bounds of licensed official material provided by copyright holders? Or forms of roleplay which don't challenge accepted narratives and definitions? Even so, it is true that Lanier et al.'s observations can often be applied to serial killer fandom, specifically when viewing it through the lens of ambivalence. They write: "The trickster is fundamentally an ambiguous and anomalous figure who does not fit well in any category and who always operates on the edge" (392). As suggested above, much of the material I will examine in this chapter is very much "on the edge": on the edge of acceptable discourse around serial killers, not fundamentally different from or opposed to the serial killer discourse provided by mainstream media, but operating at its outer boundaries. Play at the outer limits of the rigid structure (discursive or otherwise) may be most likely to alter those limits, but such play is not a direct confrontation or opposition.

Lanier et al. do acknowledge that not all fans are tricksters, that indeed:

> There are pressures within all fandoms toward order, control, and predictability. This is exacerbated by the more recent push within digital fandom for activism and advocacy. [. . .] Community naturally engenders constraints that can blunt the creativity of the trickster. [. . .] Given that the trickster is inherently a boundary

> breaker, role disrupter, and mischievous deceiver, community and tricksterism are seemingly at odds. (2022, 394–95)

It seems that the authors feel fandom is becoming too domesticated, perhaps deliberately domesticated by the corporations which would seek to monetize it. There is an echo here of critics like Mark Andrejevic (2008), who argued that Jenkins's poaching model neglected the real monetary value of the labor fans performed on behalf of media corporations, offering up a wealth of free data. They suggest:

> Perhaps in their push to move fandom from the deviant margins of society and remove the stigmatization of fans as fanatics, both fans and aca-fans may have cut themselves off from the very source of their fannish practices. If digital fandom is going to retain its vitality, it must figure out how to transgress and subvert itself. What digital fandom may really need is the resurrection of the crafty, unconstrained, and irreverent trickster. (Lanier et al. 2022, 395)

If we as scholars are going to follow this suggestion, I would argue, we need to start considering forms of fandom that we are not entirely comfortable with, which do not align so neatly with our more mainstream and acceptable political impulses. The present study is one example.

When Booth wrote *Playing Fans,* Tumblr was very much a center of fannish activity. Thus he paid particular attention to Tumblr's affordances. More recent research has explored TikTok as an "inherently playful social media platform" (Duval et al. 2021, 2), though not necessarily with regard to fannish play in particular. Jared Duval et al.'s quantitative study found that performance and dramatization are key to TikTok culture: "TikTok is generally more outward-facing [than interior focused]. [. . .] content on TikTok is generally performative, exaggerated, and dramatized, indicating that [some of its] design concepts are more likely to elicit these types of experiences" (2021). At the level of architecture, Ethan Bresnick argues for TikTok as a "virtual play structure: a recreational space manifested in electronic media" (2019, 1). In his formulation, "virtual play structures (i.e., virtual playgrounds) are digital experiences that correspond to physical playground experiences" (1). Some of the comparisons that Bresnick makes between editing functions and physical playground equipment might be a little stretched, but I agree that, overall, the affordances of TikTok encourage playful engagement. It is perhaps too broad and diverse a platform to strictly comprise the "magic circle" that early fan studies borrowed from play theory: that is, a circumscribed arena within which all participants understand the rules of play and their separation from the rest of life. But it certainly lends itself easily and readily towards playful forms of production. These include rapid video creation and sharing, the ability to enhance videos with cartoon-style effects, augmented reality features, and the "back and forth motion between creators" enabled by the common use of hashtags and the ability to "duet" one's response to an earlier video, so that original and response play side-by-side (2019, 56). Bresnick also recognizes the popularity of a "rise-and-fall" format on TikTok (7), analogous to a playground swing. Traditional narratives have a beginning, a middle, and an end, but TikTok culture favors the jump-cut between two clips, which one popular TikTok creator described as typically "going from seriousness to humour" (quoted in Bresnick 2019, 7). All these elements contribute to the expression of play as free movement within (an admittedly broad) structure, one defined by both technology and platform social norms.

Further, Diana Zulli and David Zulli have helpfully extended the "theoretical and methodological utility" of the meme "by conceptualizing the TikTok platform as a memetic text in and of itself" (2022, 1872). We typically think of memes as individual units of media, but TikTok is mimetic at the level of platform architecture. Zulli and Zulli argue that the "principles of mimesis—imitation and replication—are encouraged by the platform's logic and design" (1872). I have already indicated the ability of TikTok users to respond to each other's videos via "dueting" their response into a split screen. Further, the "use this sound" affordance allows many videos to be created to the same music or sound effect, linking them together and inflecting their meaning with the meaning of all the other videos using that sound. Imitation and replication are also fundamental TikTok social norms. Zulli and Zulli write:

> On any given day, we observed users replicating the same type of video or similar video concepts using a sound or effect over and over again. These videos primarily took the form of "challenge" videos, whether that be dancing or "check" videos were users described and projected identities in a roll-call fashion (e.g., "Texas check"). (2022, 1881)

In a video hashtagged "Texas check," a user would rapidly perform a series of poses or showcase a series of images associating themselves with the state of

Texas. TikTok "checks" typically use the same sound and can refer to almost any facet of one's identity, even a tangential one. I have recently observed a "famous relative check" wherein users display family photographs or home media of a famous person to whom they happen to be related. Another memetic trend I have observed is the use of captions starting "POV: You [. . .]" These videos purport to present the viewer's perspective as he or she fulfills whatever position the video is assigning them. Zulli and Zulli persuasively argue that TikTok "extends the Internet meme to the level of platform infrastructure" (2022, 1873), which helps constitute it as a site for digital play.

Given this previous research, then, I focused the data collection for this chapter on Tumblr and TikTok. I also drew upon some of the data gathered during earlier collection periods—examples particularly appropriate to analyze through the lens of digital play, including data on Tumblr roleplay accounts. However, for this data collection cycle, I did create a new Tumblr account from which to search and follow blogs, in order that the sample not be overwhelmed by posts that were less relevant to the concept of play. Rather than focusing on individual blogs, I searched and followed the hashtags "serial killer meme," "serial killer joke," and "serial killer humour," as well as the alternative spellings, appropriate plurals, and hashtags written as single words, e.g., "serialkillermeme(s)." I then repeated those searches, replacing "serial killer" with each of the names of the serial killers in the sample, and inductively coded the collected posts for common themes. The process on TikTok was the same. The data for this chapter was gathered between September and December 2022.

The Tumblr data fell into the following primary categories:

A. Roleplay as serial killers, often self-consciously humorous

B. The adaptation of memes from broader pop culture

C. Visual humor through juxtaposition

D. Linguistic humor/puns

E. Nonsense

I am using the term "nonsense" here in a slightly technical way. I am referring to posts that deliberately rebuff coherent referential meaning, "absurdities" of the same sort recognized by Phillips and Milner. Often, these recalled the "flat parody" I identified in work on Tumblr as pastiche, undercutting all claims to authoritative discourse, including their own. Across all the data categories, but perhaps most acutely in the last, I also detect an element of Booth's sociocultural parody—i.e., parody that highlights the mainstream media's obsession with serial killers and the profitability of the serial killer industry. Parody may or may not be the intention of the creator, but the effect stands. As noted above, Netflix's *Dahmer—Monster: The Jeffrey Dahmer Story* aired during this data collection cycle. As a result, a good deal more of this material was focused on Dahmer and humor relating to cannibalism.

Roleplaying blogs on Tumblr often utilize the title "the-real-[name of person or character]," sometimes addending "blog." Others simply use the name in question. I located roleplay blogs of this sort for Bundy, Dahmer, Richard Ramirez, Aileen Wuornos, and other serial killers such as Gary Ridgeway, who was convicted of murdering forty-nine women and girls in the state of Washington, mostly sex workers. These blogs interacted with each other in the killer's "voice," as well as with roleplay blogs for other infamous criminals, such as "the-real-squeaky."[1] Some of the roleplay involves "shipping" killers with each other—i.e., imagining them in romantic relationships as though they were fictional characters. Here is a good example of play "at the edges" of mainstream discourse. The media already treats serial killers like fictional characters, imagining their private and romantic lives. Shipping them together is probably the outer limit of this discursive construction, but not beyond it.

One Bundy roleplay blog invites viewers to "ask the professional lawyer (me)" (the-real-ted-bundy-blog 2022), then displays these anonymous "asks" with responses as though from Bundy himself. There is a slight satirical edge to this: Bundy was not a professional lawyer, though he seemed to believe he was, and the insertion of the pronoun in parentheses as though to clarify "me" draws attention to this claim. I previously observed other users appealing to the creator of this blog to join a Discord server, a private chat channel where people are apparently continuing the roleplay. "We talk about you all the time," wrote one anonymous commenter (Anon. 10 2018). Other roleplayers assume the killer personas more explicitly: "You're the only (former) prostitute I'd never kill, Aileen . . . if that makes you feel any better" (garyleonridgway 2012). "Uhh, it sorta does," replies user aileenwuornos-blog, "cause at least I know I won't be dead" (2012). She, in turn, promises that she would "*never*" (italics in original) kill garyleonridgway with a gun, and the commenters exchange expressions of humor. This play seems very

[1] "Squeaky" is the nickname of Lynette Fromme, a member of the Manson Family cult.

Figure 8. "Is this a total stranger?"

much like the sort of roleplay fans engage in for fictional murderers, mixing properties of the self with properties of the character one is performing. The practice was nowhere near as common on Tumblr as on TikTok (see below). I would describe these practices as simple "identity roleplay," the assumption of a media-created mask for a form of online play that combines known characteristics of the killer with the fan's own personality (cf. Booth 2016, 116). In this way, the roleplay is a key example of Phillips and Milner's ambivalence, tied to a (terrible) reality, one within living memory for some people alive today, yet self-consciously "not real," as the references to one's "dash[board]" illustrate. The real killers would not be making reference to the affordance of their Tumblr account. Besides which, most of them are dead.

The second category of Tumblr posts adapted memes from pop culture to serial killers. Below is an example, based on the meme "Is this a pigeon?" from the 1990s anime *The Brave of Sun Fighbird* [*sic*], wherein an android mistakenly identifies a butterfly as a pigeon. The meme has been developed to comment on misconceptions, with the android labeled as the subject misperceiving something, the butterfly labeled as the object, and the caption "Is this . . . ?" expressing the misconception. For example, it has been used to satirize out-of-touch media corporations who cast obviously adult actors as high school students, with the android labeled "High School TV dramas," the butterfly labeled "sexy 28-year-old actor" and the caption reading "Is this a teen?" (See: https://knowyourmeme.com/photos/1370553-is-this-a-pigeon). In the instance pictured in figure 8, which appeared several times on my dashboard from the searches above, the meme draws attention to Bundy's supposed facility with disguise and his chameleon-like ability to change appearance, implying that this myth is born of police incompetence rather than any mysterious ability.

In most memes of this sort, including this one, the humor is no more and no less offensive than a great deal of mainstream comedy. It is humor about murder, certainly. But so are comedy true crime podcasts. In fact, I think these sorts of memes are a clear example of sociocultural parody, pointing up the media and law enforcement's collaboration in portraying serial killers as more intelligent, more cunning, indeed more special than the average person, sliding neatly over the errors and oversights in investigations that allowed them to continue with their crimes.

Sociocultural parody is not always this pointed. In another example, a very popular meme—featuring the rapper Drake appearing to disapprove of something in one frame and approve of an alternative in the next (see: https://knowyourmeme.com/memes/drakeposting)—was adapted to feature the face of Dennis Rader, known as BTK, or the Bind Torture Kill killer. In one frame, he disapproves of a "Live Laugh Love" placard; in the second, he approves of a placard reading "Bind Torture Kill." While not directly satirizing the FBI, the image remains a pointed comment on mainstream serial killer obsession. Why do we still refer to Rader by a catchy three-part nickname—one he gave *himself*—catering directly to the desire for fame and notoriety he expressed in his taunting letters to police? We consume his life and crimes as easily as we consume a mass-produced piece of home décor.

We saw above that Shifman has drawn attention to how digital play is facilitated by the ability to juxtapose "elements that could not previously be imagined appearing together" (2017, 834). In serial killer fandom, this facility creates humor through incongruity. I also observed, in common with Bresnick, that a "rise and fall," or serious-to-humor format, is popular on TikTok. It was also popular on Tumblr. A common type of Tumblr post juxtaposed one image, which seemed to set an earnest tone, with a second image to overturn it (see figure 9). These posts effect an argument in microcosm against the naïve model of an "earnest internet" that Phillips and Milner (2017) and Hedrick et al. (2018) were critiquing. In the meme (figure 9), which appeared on my dashboard multiple times when I searched "Ted Bundy humo[u]r," a black and white image of a young woman gazing romantically into the distance is captioned, "Ever daydream about going somewhere and never coming back?" Edited below it, like the second frame of a comic strip, is an image of Bundy entering his Volkswagen, with the caption ". . . Hi. I'm Ted." The object of this rather biting satire is (small-r) romanticism, sentiment, and naivety: Imagining one is about to run off with a charming handsome stranger, for example, certainly might lead to "never coming back," though not in the way the first image intimates. Recall Laura Browder's observation that true crime as literary genre may be critical of the patriarchal family, given how often women are killed by their partners (2006, 938).

There were several images of this type, and the object of parody wasn't always so clear. For example, a meme that featured an image of a knife captioned "regular serial killers" above a picture of a pizza cutter captioned "Italian serial killers" appeared once, posted by user slayersbookofdeathblog (2017). Still, we can read these images through Booth's lens of sociocultural parody, as a flat comment on our collective ease with violence. The intentions of the creator are not so important. Like the costumes and props at Bundy's execution, such images are not really "saying" anything in a referential sense. They just are, the way violence just "is," without comment, part of the fabric of our mediated existence. We scroll on.

That said, I also found that linguistic humor and puns, which *do* turn on referential meanings, were also a popular category. Given the timing of the data collection, it is not surprising that most of them referenced Dahmer and cannibalism. The posts are not insults, precisely, neither to Dahmer nor to his victims. They simply use cannibalism as a source of humor. The posts use visual and verbal puns that turn on incongruity—specifically, the incongruity of cannibalism with dating, daily life, and Dahmer's rather geekish, dispassionate, nonthreatening appearance. Most were tagged with "meme," and although it is questionable whether or not they are high circulation enough to be memes strictly speaking, the same puns did appear multiple times within the searches, sometimes with slightly different images. For example, I have already noted the image of Dahmer's face superimposed

Figure 9. "Hi. I'm Ted."

over that of a man in a fast-food restaurant, with the caption "I don't think there's actually Five Guys in this" (moonlitnitely 2021). There were several very similar images making the same joke. Dahmer's face superimposed onto that of a man sitting on a toilet is captioned "Jeffrey Dahmer dumping his last boyfriend," the deliberately disgusting pun capturing the slide of meaning between dating and digestion (memes4ya 2021). The coincidence of the terms is not entirely random; plenty of words elide sexual and gustatory appetite: to devour with one's eyes, to eat someone up, to look good enough to eat. The sociocultural parody here highlights the aggression inherent in so much sexual content, via its physical and semantic links to consumption and/or rejection.

In a topical reference to the threat of the COVID-19 virus, an image of Dahmer's face is pasted below the caption "TV: The CDC says to refrain from handshakes. Jeffrey Dahmer: *stops blender*" (immaturegrammy 2021). The pun turns on the double meaning of "shake," but humor is also created by the incongruity between Dahmer's characteristically flat, expressionless face and the extremity of his actions. Not all the puns referenced cannibalism, though most of them did. Some referred to Bundy's necrophilia (utilizing the double-meanings of "stiff," for example, referring to both a penis and a corpse). More randomly, one pictured Ramirez's face superimposed onto that of a supermarket worker, describing him as a "night stocker" (vodkancheese 2021), homophonically punning on his nickname. This sort of humor is not qualitatively different to the bad-taste jokes that appear in the wake of any highly mediated tragedy. Some Tumblr posts drew attention to the widespread nature of this sort of humor, such as a screencap from Facebook wherein a user has asked a community page for "an air fryer that can handle a family of 8." In addition to being completely mainstream, Facebook has a reputation as a rather stolid, older social media site populated by middle-aged and elderly people. Nonetheless, the first response is "take it easy Jeffrey Dahmer." To the outraged objections of another commenter that "MURDER IS NOT FUNNY," a user replies, "First day on the [ambivalent] internet?" (robotsvsdinosaurs 2017). Even on Facebook, cannibalism is funny.

The final group of posts I categorized as "nonsense." By this, I mean posts that seem deliberately constructed to be nonsensical, to rebuff referential and/or logocentric meaning. As Katz and Shifman (2017) noted, this sort of post can carry "affective meaning," which is to say the post functions as a signal of recognition between those in the know: those who understand that the posts are not to be read in earnest, that there is no referential meaning underneath to be sought. Bracketing these sorts of posts as their own category is slightly artificial, for as I noted above, there is overlap with some of the other categories, such as visual humor. However, I have selected here some examples that seem to push the tendency to the extreme, in order to better illustrate the theme. Some of these were tagged "shitpost," which functions as a signal for the way in which they are (not) to be interpreted. I can merely offer some examples of their content with my own understandings of their referents in popular culture:

A. In 2022, popular singer and reality TV judge Adam Levine was subject to a minor scandal when leaked text messages demonstrated his infidelity. These included such comments as "Holy fucking fuck" and "that body of yours is absurd." They have been photoshopped to look as though they are sent to Dahmer, fully clothed, in prison attire (zodiacgirl666 2022).

B. Dahmer in green is placed next to Kermit the Frog (oh-that's-good-ta-hear 2022).

C. An audio meme created using the app Songify designates Bundy and Dahmer as "one thick bih" (slang for a generously proportioned woman). The lanky Ramirez is designated by variation on the sound, as "one sticc bih." The "singer" requests to see their handcuffs, fridge, and dick respectively (truecrimedittys 2022).

D. A long description of "Serial Killers as People You Regret Swiping Right on Dating Apps":

> Richard Ramirez aka the Night Stalker:
>
> -fake woke
>
> -has taken one (1) philosophy class and thinks he knows everything about the human condition
>
> -doesn't know what a toothbrush is
>
> Jeffrey Dahmer:
>
> -always drunk
>
> -REALLY wants to photograph you naked
>
> -profile says "no fatties"
>
> -won't shut up about his pet fish
>
> [...]
>
> Aileen Wuornos:
>
> -basically the personification of that "Florida Man" meme except female

> [. . .]
>
> Ted Bundy:
>
> -profile is basically a resume
>
> -treats your date like a job interview
>
> -Republican
>
> [There are several more killers included in the post.] (orevet 2018)

This last example has a little more referential meaning than the preceding: The statements could "make sense" to a person well-versed in serial killer history. For example, Ramirez's "one (1) philosophy class" probably refers to his over-estimation of how deep, interesting, and original his insights on the supposed evil of humanity are. It thus serves to puncture the "special" and "charismatic" status attributed to Ramirez by mainstream media like the *Night Stalker* docuseries (2021), which in turn raises the question of why such an unimpressive person evaded the police so long. But what are these statements doing here? Why would the serial killers have dating site profiles? No particular reason—except for fannish play. A similar template sometimes appears to be describing killers as personalities one might meet on social media, but also randomly insults them in the same format: "You look like a big ol poof," is directed at cannibal Dennis Nilsen, who is named as "British Jeffrey" (a-top-hat 2021).

The reader has probably noticed the relative lack of playful data on Wuornos. There were a few posts of her face caught in expressions of extremis, whose purpose seems to mock her appearance, and a few brief references to her as in the dating post above. Also filed under the category of nonsense was the following text:

> lesbians forced aileen wuornos to murder 7 people and then we snuck into the death chamber and swapped out the lethal injection for an electric chair. And that is why lesbians can not use the electric chair meme because it is offensive and rubs in the faces of others the [*sic*] we committed against feminist icon aileen. People using the electric chair meme is a reclaimation of the abuse from lesbians and our murder of innocent aileen wuornos. Know ur herstory.
>
> #death (kiluwa 2019)

The object of parody is indiscernible. The text mocks and undercuts feminist interpretations of Wuornos's death, but equally disavows any claim to a voice of authority via deliberate absurdity and self-parody. Via the personal pronoun, the "author" positions herself as a "lesbian," even while apparently rejecting this position as one from which to make any serious social critique.

On the rare occasions that posts objected to using serial killers and killing as humor, however, they tended to point out another double standard in the media treatment of Wuornos: "I love how people joke about male serial killers like theres no tomorrow but you like say the name aileen wuornos and everyones like ooh dont joke about that shes scary O_o" (jackpotcomicsno5 2022). Admittedly, I did not actually find any data to back up this assertion of "everyone's" objection to Wuornos jokes—but I did not find many jokes, either. It seems that serial killer fandom on Tumblr is, by and large, fruitfully analyzed through the lens of ambivalent play, especially with regard to sociocultural parody. Most of this play takes place inside the lines drawn by mainstream media, however: It might be just inside the lines, but such is the nature of parody. Even Facebook users joke about cannibalism. Moreover, Tumblr play quite often overturns the conservative impulse of some true crime texts, pointing up the inefficiency of law enforcement. Sociocultural parody also functions at the level of form, as the flat surfaces of Tumblr offer mediated violence as just one more scrollable product that we casually consume in our media-saturated day. But again, it seems that Wuornos might be qualitatively different, more serious, and better viewed through the other lenses. Playful manifestations do appear, but they are quite rare.

Turning to TikTok, I performed the same searches by hashtag as outlined above. I also created a new account, so that the data not be overwhelmed by non-humorous or non-play content. The primary themes were as follows:

A. Performance and roleplay (most dominant)

B. Puns in visual form, often the same puns as were circulating on Tumblr

C. Adaptation of popular culture memes

D. Nonsense (rare)

There were also several instances of professional comedians and standups using serial killer material for humor, especially Dahmer. After some consideration, I elected not to include these in the analysis, as they are not really "fannish" or professionalized fan material. Unlike the professionalized fans who collect and sell murderabilia, these comedians have not built their careers around serial killer material; they are simply using a topical subject for professional benefit, riffing on contemporary media trends as part of a larger set. This does, however, lend credence to my perception that most of this material is play "inside the lines" of more mainstream media.

The dominance of performance and roleplay in the TikTok sample gives weight to both Duval et al.'s (2021) observation that TikTok is a performance-based, outward facing platform and to Zulli and Zulli's (2022) insights on TikTok as exemplifying mimesis at the level of platform. Many of the search results followed a common memetic template, captioned either "POV: You [. . .]" (wherein the creator assumes the perspective of the viewer in some interaction with a serial killer) or "If [serial killer] was [. . .]" (wherein the creator performs a scenario that might take place if a serial killer had some particular characteristic, such as a stereotyped nationality). Serial killer roleplay is popular enough that user sotrueiris444 draws attention to it in a video criticizing fellow users for joking about Dahmer's crimes (2022). Again, given the timing of the data collection, it is not surprising that Dahmer dominated.

Many users created videos in which they roleplay a potential victim of Dahmer, with captions like "POV: Jeffrey Dahmer invited you to hang at his place" (eggplantsworldd 2020). Often the joke is on oneself, as in eggplantsworldd's example, wherein he is saved by virtue of being too heavy for Dahmer to carry. Some played on national stereotypes, roleplaying for example what a Mexican or an Australian would experience in Dahmer's flat. The Australian is so tolerant of intoxicants that he cannot be drugged, as empty drink cups pile up around him to Dahmer's increasing despair (itsjulianwoods 2022). Other roleplays included that of an unsuspecting guest finding body parts in the fridge, being offered a suspect sandwich by the killer (as was one character in the drama), or in one absurdist instance, "POV: You're a fish in Dahmer's tank watching him take his next victim" (landtron 2022). This video utilizes a filter to impose human eyes and speaking mouth onto an image of a tropical fish, in line with Bresnick's (2019) observations on the playful editing affordances of the platform.

There were also some roleplays which did not seem designed for humor. Quite strikingly, these seemed to genuinely roleplay a death at Dahmer's hands, using techniques such cutting to black when the "victim" is to be murdered. Some users seriously imitated Dahmer's mannerisms and posture, using their own kitchens as "sets." It would be a mistake to conflate "play" with "funny":

These roleplays are identity play, free movement within the structure set by the accepted narrative, but they are not designed to be humorous. It is a question beyond the scope of this book as to whether we ought to address the two kinds of fannish play as qualitatively different, but my inclination is to think not. Humor is subjective anyway: The common playful factors are identity roleplay and mimesis at the level of the site.

Bundy-related roleplays were also fairly popular. User get_raccd_24 edits a section of the 2002 Eminem track "Without Me" over a short video captioned "God noticing the world overpopulated with women." In response, God sprinkles "razzle dazzle" to create Ted Bundy, whom the user roleplays turning to face the camera in time with the lyric "This looks like a job for me" (get_raccd_24 2022). Juxtaposing audio clips from various discrete sources to a performance was a standard form of creativity on TikTok. User nuhchez roleplays Bundy disposing of a body while an audio clip of two commentators praising a person's skill is attributed to "Death" and "Satan" (2020). User ted_bundy_epic roleplays Ramirez entering court to an approximation of an old comedy soundtrack, exaggerating his mannerisms. An announcer hails him: "Ladies and gentlemen, Richard Ramirez," with applause and a canned laugh track timed to position him as a celebrity (which, of course, he was). Other types of roleplay utilized computer games such as *Grand Theft Auto* and *The Sims,* in which characters and their behavior may be customized, to create digital avatars of killers.

Roleplays of Wuornos were qualitatively different, and all the examples except for one fell under the rubric of what I would call "serious (identity) play." One memetic pattern was for women to assume an iconic pose of Wuornos holding her cuffed hands to her throat, before cutting to the image of her, as a response and reaction to expressions of male violence. Often these were cut to the lyric "Don't forget about me" from the song "Doubt" by twenty one pilots (2015), invoking Wuornos as a sort of vengeful spirit and recalling her parting assertion that she would return after death. Sometimes the duet feature is used in these responses: User korimari_locx utilizes images of Wuornos as a duetted response to the "God creating Ted Bundy" meme just referenced (2022). Similarly, user thehighpriestess assumes the handcuff pose and then replaces herself with an image of Wuornos, in a duet response to a user who supposedly morphs into Brian Laundrie, who murdered his girlfriend Gaby Petitio, "when [his] girl laughs at little too hard at another dude's jokes" (2021). The message is that if you men can turn into murderers, well, so can women.

These exchanges are an example of how the duet response is used creatively and memetically as a form of serious play. Continuity is also achieved by the persistent use of present-tense "When x" statements as captions and overlays. This particular video is overlaid with the text "When I keep seeing men's posts about unaliving women." (The verb "unalive" is used in several online spaces to avoid automatic censorship of terms like kill, suicide, and murder.) A final memetic pattern drew on audio from Wuornos's interviews, as an "acting challenge" by user stormiej222, who lip syncs to Wuornos's assertion that it is men, not her, who are "out of control," with their assumptions that women's bodies are theirs to take and use (2021). (One of these audio clips is actually a misattribution: Though often captioned "Aileen Wuornos interview," the audio is actually killer Angela Simpson explaining how she murdered a man. Their voices do sound quite similar.) This sort of play is also at the edges of the lines established by mainstream media and culture. Many women are extremely angry about our collective treatment by men, but positing that violent men deserve to die is a fringe (though recognizable) response. Nonetheless, several of the videos are positioned as an exactly proportional response to the frequency with which men really do kill women, *and* continue to joke about it.

The only deliberately humorous Wuornos roleplay was a "day in the life" video by user lucypopmama, in which Wuornos enacts a series of exaggerated "redneck" stereotypes, such as brushing her teeth with beer, and "hoot[ing] and holler[ing] till dusk" (2020). This recalls the single "joke" I found about her in the Tumblr sample, comparing her to the chaotic "Florida man" meme. ("Florida man" refers to a hypothetical man derived from miscellaneous absurd and outrageous headlines originating in Florida. The joke implies that every bizarre incident is the work of one individual person.)

Most of the visual puns in the sample were cannibalism jokes based on Dahmer. Often they were the very same puns circulated on Tumblr, simply adapted to be told as two-frame visual stories for the setup and response ("What did they find in Jeffrey Dahmer's freezer? Ben and Jerry's. What did they find in Jeffrey Dahmer's shower? Head and Shoulders. What did Jeffrey Dahmer call the guy who ran from him? Fast food.") These videos generally adhered to the structure recognized by Bresnick (2019) as common to TikTok: a truncated rise and fall, setup and surprise format, rather than a beginning, middle, and end. The first frame would pose the question, and the second give the answer over related and easily sourced images (a freezer, a carton of Ben and Jerry's ice cream). However, some of them were more elaborate: The "Five Guys" pun is extended by user ftwinzgottalent to a short skit wherein Dahmer goes for a job interview at the franchise, expressing how enthusiastic and passionate he is about eating "five guys" (2022). This skit was quite elaborate, involving a wig, set, and secondary actor.

Recall Andrew Rico's (2015) observation that some "Columbiners" might perform their supposed "fandom" of school shooters simply to provoke a reaction. Some of these TikTok performances could be viewed in the same way, as utilizing sensational and attention-grabbing material to draw attention to oneself and one's social media profile. Other puns-in-skits played on the contemporary slang equating an attractive person to a "snack" or "full course meal," humorously implying that, in the present climate, Dahmer could simply state his intentions to his victims and be taken for flirting. I noted above that the linguistic conflation of eating and sex could be read as a form of sociocultural parody highlighting sexual aggression, and here it is more explicit: Calling someone a "full course meal," after all, implies that one intends to consume them with relish. Similarly, one user animates Dahmer's face (in his mugshot) to pronounce the line, "Your honor, I'm slaying," before "performing" a dance with camp and effeminate expressions (mr_oh_sangwoo 2022). "Slaying" is queer-originating slang for performing exceptionally well, particularly with regard to style and dance. The extension of the puns to skit format demonstrates again the importance of performance and roleplay to TikTok culture. But aside from that factor, this finding was not qualitatively different to the Tumblr case. The even greater dominance of Dahmer on TikTok indicates that the app is even more heavily influenced by trends in contemporary media than Tumblr, probably because it is a newer platform. There was, however, a much smaller set of static images using Bundy's image as the background for a verbal pun ("What's the difference between women and onions? I cry when I cut up onions") that only related to the image by virtue of its subject.

Considering the prevalence of edited media on TikTok, adaptations from pop culture texts were surprisingly rare. It should be noted, however, that given the rule of excluding fantexts of fictionalized representations of serial killers, I was not counting videos wherein fans directly edited images and audio from Netflix's *Monster,* of which there were several. There were, however, a handful of videos adapting other texts. User rainy.msx takes a short sequence from the Amazon Prime (anti) superhero series *The Boys* (2019–), in which the cryogenically defrosted hero "Soldier Boy" informs now-adult son "Homelander" that, perhaps if he had raised him, he would not have turned out to be a "weak and snivelling pussy," or such a "fucking disappointment." The video is captioned "Ted Bundy when he meets Jeffrey Dahmer on doomsday" (rainy.msx 2022).

In some way, all the play analyzed in this chapter is what Booth would call "within the lines" set by mainstream media. It is all reflective of our collective fascination with serial killers, our cultural inclination to create humor out of tragedy, and our focus on particularly grotesque aspects of certain crimes such as cannibalism and necrophilia. I also found examples of non-transformative play concerning the differing media treatment of Bundy and Dahmer: Bundy, the virulent, successful, charismatic psychopath; Dahmer, the pathetic, monstrous queer. Other pop culture adaptations include a (quite technically impressive) digital animation of an image of Bundy's face, so that he appears to sing the chorus of the 1999 song "Mambo no. 5" by Lou Vega (lameadults 2020). The chorus lists "a little bit of" various women, and the video is superimposed with the caption "IYKYK" (if you know you know). Presumably this refers to Bundy's penchant for decapitating his victims and keeping their heads as trophies. Another TikTok edits Bo Burnham's 2021 comedy song "Bezos I" in ironic praise of Amazon CEO Jeff Bezos, over images of Dahmer (nem.tudom._.xd 2022). Several lines of the song make no particular sense in this context, but it does contain general encouragement to someone named "Jeff," as well as the injunctions "drink their blood" and "Come on Jeff, get em!" This sociocultural parody conflates one rapacious form of consumption and exploitation, Bezos's brand of neoliberal turbocapitalism, with the literal consumption of humans. In a third example, Bundy is "interviewed" in hell to the audio of a quotation from the Will Ferrell film *Talladega Nights: The Ballad of Ricky Bobby.* In the clipped audio, the lead character (a NASCAR driver), is congratulating himself on his success:

> Well, Dick, here's the deal: I'm the best there is, plain and simple. I mean, I wake up in the morning and I piss excellence. You know, nobody can hang with my stuff. I'm just a—just a big, hairy, American winning machine. (McKay 2006)

Putting these words in Bundy's mouth (ted_bund_epic 2022b) illuminates the way that, far from an exception, he was from a feminist perspective the pinnacle of male entitlement and misogyny that runs through American society. Relatedly, I found an interestingly self-referential video which could be described as sociocultural parody of this type. The user intercuts images and sequences from TikTok into a TikTok video to suggest what would happen if Bundy became a TikTok user: In short, he would become extremely popular very fast. The video makes rapid visual reference to pop-news stories on the popularity of serial killers, especially those considered attractive (dictatorxtc 2022). All of this content seems like a twenty-first century echo of the impetus behind works like Bret Easton Ellis's novel *American Psycho* (1991), a slightly hysterical, hyperreal reflection on the cultural appropriateness of serial killing.

The final category, which I coded as "nonsense," referred to content that was deliberately difficult to parse for referential meaning. This type was significantly rarer on TikTok than Tumblr. The posts in this category don't appear to "say" anything, unlike, for example, a roleplay or a pun. In one, for example, a Sim character approximating Dahmer dances to a hard rap song. That's it: He just dances. The video is captioned: "Jeffrey is vibing" (lsxy2 2022). Where nonsense did occur, it was of this type: an image or short video related to a serial killer, in which they perform a random action or with a random annotation. This was not common—and dancing is not an entirely random action for a Dahmer Sim to perform, given that he did frequent gay clubs. But again, it doesn't *mean* anything, beyond the caption: "Jeffrey is vibing." (Or perhaps, at a stretch, vibing queerly, though the Sim is pictured in a living room, not a club.) There is also a video editing the faces of Dahmer and Ramirez onto crudely animated figures in police uniforms, on a stage, dancing to the 1986 song "You Can Leave Your Hat On" by Joe Cocker (trebkatrebka 2022). Ramirez was certainly not gay; indeed, he was obsessively and sadistically fixated on the female body. This video means even less than the last. I attribute the rarity of this category on TikTok to two factors: Firstly, it is harder to create "nonsense" in video form. A video is always sequential, so in some ways, it is always "sensical," whereas an image can just "be." One frame leads into the next frame, creating some kind of narrative logic. Secondly, as Duval et al. (2021) write, TikTok is an outward-facing platform. Katz and Shifman (2017) write that nonsense functions to signal affiliation with an in-group, and TikTok is more dominated by public performance than intergroup bonding. The roleplayers do not interact with each other as they do on Tumblr; they are playing to "the public," not each other.

Overall, then, it seems that ambiguous play and sociocultural parody are extremely useful lenses through which to view serial killer fandom, highlighting especially the degree to which such fannish expressions are *not* opposed to mainstream culture, merely operating at the edges of it.

The fandom's very existence satirizes our collective fascination with the serial killer industry, and the ease with which a neoliberal, turbocapitalist, endlessly mediated society facilitates the consumption of serial killing. Some examples are more specifically parodic, whether of institutions like the police, romantic notions about charming strangers, or the necessarily aggressive undertone in the popular metaphoric conflation of sex and eating. The specifically playful and ambiguous affordances of sites like Tumblr and TikTok provide the architecture that shapes and enables this fannish play, as do their cultures. Again, I found that fandom concerning Wuornos was qualitatively different, more serious and (fringe) feminist focused; its analysis needs to be supplemented with other theoretical frameworks. Playful does not necessarily mean funny: I found that the performative norms of TikTok enabled a serious kind of identity play, wherein users invoked iconic poses and/or used editing tools to "morph" themselves into a female killer in response to male violence. I did not find convincing evidence that serial killer fandom comprises a "magic circle" within which the rules of play are recognized. If the circle exists at all, it probably comprises something much bigger like "the media landscape." Overall, however, the concept of a magic circle relatively circumscribed from the rest of life did not seem a good fit with the expansive qualities of this play, or indeed, with our media-saturated environment.

One of the primary arguments of Booth's *Playing Fans* was that fandom is no longer a restricted category. Many of the practices that used to be perceived as strictly fannish, such as intense engagement with a media text, knowledge acquisition and curation, and the creation of user generated content, are now common markers of a converged multimedia landscape. Engagement with a favored text takes less effort and less commitment: One does not have to locate a physical zine or a fan convention but can simply open a Tumblr and start reblogging posts. Throughout this study, which applied some of the classic frames from fan studies to the fandom of serial killers, I have discovered that not only is serial killer fandom understandable in terms of frames common to all mediated fandom, but that, to a large extent, it is understandable in terms of the broader media culture. The fandom may be deliberately provocative or purposefully edgy—and the term "edge" is instructive here, because it does, by and large, operate at the "edge" of a discourse already predefined by the mainstream media without clearly opposing, contradicting, or subverting it. The serial killer industry is alive and well and streaming now on Netflix, probably starring the latest teenage heartthrob hoping to break into "serious" acting.

Like the fans studied in the 1990s, serial killer fans are a relatively marginalized and maligned group that converges around favored texts. Serial killer fans poach the storylines and multimediated material made available to them through a variety of channels. Fanfiction, fanart, and fanvids are just as likely to pastiche and illustrate pre-received narratives as they are to overturn them, whether this be the valorization of the genius killer who thwarts the blameless system of law enforcement at every turn, or sympathy for the queer monster with a damaged past. Fans also create their own narratives, "cuteifying" killers that have personal appeal to them with aesthetics borrowed from illustration and anime, or arranging extant material for a radical feminist justification of retaliatory violence. This last practice was the most explicitly political form of textual poaching I found, and probably the most distinct "counter" narrative. Yet much of the fan material, particularly the visual sort, created the pastiche, non-political effect Booth considers a form of coloring inside the lines, such as setting clips of serial killers to horror film aesthetics. Notably, as a pathologized fandom, serial killer fan material often fits better into a textual poaching model than the more modern concept of media convergence, due to the fact it is less recuperable by the media industries.

The reservations I now have regarding theories of community could equally well apply to any other fandom. Initially, I had thought that the relative instability of identity on contemporary platforms would inhibit communal gifting, but this wasn't borne out by the data. Gifting still takes place, whether that be in the form of specially created videos and edits or appreciative comments. It is true that contemporary platforms used by fans may lend themselves more to networked individualism than community in the sense I used to apply to it fannish circles, but that would be the case for any contemporary fandom. The relative dispersion, instability, and impermanence of platforms like Twitter and Tumblr do not really support community in the same way as platforms like LiveJournal once did, but community persists in at least a weak sense through the exchange of supportive and affectionate comments, empathy, and affective bonding over shared material. Moreover, fans referred to themselves and each other as being part of a community, often embracing a pathologized identity as a point of distinction, against outsiders. There are still platforms such as Reddit which can support community in a more traditional sense, though the most fannish subreddit devoted to serial killers was deleted by the platform shortly after I finished collecting the data.

Moreover, despite the relative lack of stable online personas, the collection and performance of subcultural capital proved a useful lens to understand serial killer fandom. Some of the strategies, such as the display of knowledge, were recognizable, and others were more platform-dependent: The scrapbook-like affordances of Tumblr, for example, meant that the curation and display of fannish objects was valued even when they were not in the fans' possession. The more traditional values of touch and authenticity certainly did apply in the sphere of murderabilia—the branch of killer fandom with the most obvious economic interchange. The murderabilia domain also produced fans with high social capital, the closest thing to celebrity-fans I observed in this study. These figures are the brokers of high-value objects, which granted an auratic quality by their physical association with serial killers. They also served as intermediaries with mainstream media. Unlike most fandoms, however, I found that in many cases the performance of excess, associated with feminine sexuality, actually functioned as a method of gaining capital rather than depleting it. This may have something to do with the revaluation of emotion and affect we see across the media landscape, but I think it more likely relates to the value of notoriety. Sarah Thornton (1995) observed in her classic study how subculturalists valued being demonized by the mainstream media: Serial killer fans know they are demonized, and relish in the scandal. Many of these performances had a distinctly humorous or slightly trollish tone, which led directly into the final and most important theoretical lens, that of playing fans.

Phillips and Milner (2017) are correct in their claims for the ambivalence of online culture. Some of the most useful insights in studying killer fandom have been from quite traditional, even old-fashioned models, which are stimulating but insufficient. Hedrick et al. (2018) are likewise correct that too many fan theorists have proceeded from an assumption of earnestness: that people believe what they say, say what they mean, and engage in fannish activity from a straightforward position of good faith. This is not true of any fan culture, and it certainly isn't true of this one. Serial killer fans are playing online. Trollishly, provocatively, ironically, they are playing at the boundaries of a contemporary discourse that makes celebrities of serial killers. Their creations, deliberately or not, function frequently as sociocultural parody which highlights our cultural obsession with serial killers, the endless stream of media we consume on the topic (which makes up a fraction of a percentage of all crime), and the ease with which we consume mediated violence. Serial killer fans are constructed, and even self-construct, as the Bad Other of true crime aficionados. This notoriety serves to reinforce communal identity. But in truth, fans operate not on one side of a binary, but rather at the end of a continuum which we all occupy in our media-saturated, twenty-four-hour news culture.

There is a broader question here, beyond the scope of this book, with which I will close this exploration of a neglected fandom. What does it mean, in this media environment, to be a fan? Are we all fans now, and if we are all fans, does the identity have any distinction left, enough to define a subfield? The secondary question relates to the division between fandoms concerned with killing and violence and other kind of fans. So much of the media we consume concerns tragedy—fictional and real. At what point do we stop being disinterested, reasonable consumers, and start to enter that "Other" realm to which serial killer fandom and other pathologized fandoms have artificially been confined? I hope this book will serve as a provocation, as scholars begin to venture into the sorts of fandom we have so far passed over in silence, posing a question mark over both the term "fan," and the separation of pathologized fandoms from broader media culture.

References

._tedbundy. 2021. TikTok video. Accessed September 9, 2022. Content no longer online.

りムノ丂リ ♥ [username]. 2022. Comment on TikTok. Accessed May 7, 2022. Content no longer online.

acidburns. 2021. Comment on Reddit. Accessed May 8, 2022. Content no longer online.

:) [username]. 2021. Comment on TikTok. https://www.tiktok.com/@real.ramirez/video/6996533200432450821?is_copy_url=1&is_from_webapp=v1.

● [username]. 2022. Comment on TikTok. Accessed May 7, 2022. Content no longer online.

🔪🔪 [username]. 2021. Comment on TikTok. Accessed May 7, 2022. Content no longer online.

✪[username]. 2021. Comment on TikTok. Accessed May 7, 2022. Content no longer online.

🕊 [username]. 2022. Comment on TikTok. Accessed June 6, 2022. Content no longer online.

. [username]. 2021. Comment on TikTok. Accessed June 6, 2022. Content no longer online.

.213 [username]. 2022a. Comment on TikTok. Accessed May 7, 2022. Content no longer online.

.213 [username]. Comment on TikTok. Accessed May 7, 2022. Content no longer online.

Daddy🐱💕 [username]. 2020. Comment on TikTok. Accessed May 7, 2022. Content no longer online.

Белый Русский [username]. 2020. “Ted Bundy Footage | Lana Del Rey—Summertime Sadness.” YouTube video. Accessed March 24, 2022. https://www.youtube.com/watch?v=-28Um7h64_I.

2Lady4Mental6Hospital8. 2020. “A Collection of Poems about Jeffrey Dahmer and the Original Female Character . . .” Archive of Own Own (website). Accessed May 8, 2022. https://archiveofourown.org/works/26879557/chapters/65585596.

a-top-hat. 2021. Tumblr post. Accessed December 22, 2022. https://at.tumblr.com/a-top-hat/huge-meme/zi1meax252j7.

A B. 2021. Comment on “Jeffrey Dahmer | Edit | Maneater (lyrics).” YouTube. Accessed March 24, 2022. https://www.youtube.com/watch?v=jUZvzgiJ3BY.

afacewithouteyes. 2021. Comment on Tumblr. Accessed May 6, 2022. https://nightst4lkerxx.tumblr.com/post/663755473888198656/chibi-stalker-ricky-treats-himself-to-dinner.

Aggravating-Bag6986. 2021. Comment on Reddit. Accessed May 8, 2022. Content no longer online.

aileen_wuornos._.fanpage. 2021. TikTok video. Accessed September 20, 2022. Content no longer online.

Aileenslvr. 2022. Comment on TikTok. Accessed June 6, 2022. Content no longer online.

aileenwuornos-blog. 2011. Tumblr post. Accessed March 24, 2022. https://aileenwuornos-blog.tumblr.com/post/15055362079/i-really-dont-think-i-deserved-it-either.

aileenwuornos-blog. 2018. Tumblr post. Accessed December 22, 2022. https://aileenwuornos-blog.tumblr.com/post/15341130311/garyleonridgway-aileenwuornos.

aleks_toddy. 2021. Comment on TikTok. Accessed May 7, 2022. https://www.tiktok.com/@richardsleatherjacket/video/6967233340088798470?is_from_webapp=1&sender_device=pc&web_id=6930854616536172037.

Amber Bell. 2018. Comment on “Aileen Wuornos: Sweet Dreams (Are Made of This).” YouTube. Accessed May 08, 2022. https://www.youtube.com/watch?v=MriWNndljQ0.

Amyna_summer. 2021. Comment on TikTok. Accessed May 8, 2022. Content no longer online.

ang3l-bitch. 2021. Comment on Tumblr. Accessed May 30, 2022. https://the-real-ricardo-ramirez.tumblr.com/post/643760468041908224/kys-fat-cunt#notes.

Anonymous. 2021. Tumblr post. Accessed September 16, 2022. Content no longer online.

Anderson, Benedict. 1983. *Imagined Communities.* London: Verso.

Andrejevic, Mark. 2008. "Watching Television without Pity: The Productivity of Online Fans." *Television & New Media* 9, no. 1: 24–46.

Anon 1. 2022. Comment on Tumblr. Accessed May 30, 2022. Content no longer online.

Anon 2. 2021. Comment on Tumblr. Accessed May 30, 2022. https://the-real-ricardo-ramirez.tumblr.com/post/643760468041908224/kys-fat-cunt#notes.

Anon 3. 2021. Comment on Tumblr. Accessed May 30, 2022. https://the-real-ricardo-ramirez.tumblr.com/post/642309182206377984/his-nasty-ass-raped-children-you-and-this-sick#notes.

Anon 4. 2018. Comment on Tumblr. Accessed May 30, 2022. https://the-real-ricardo-ramirez.tumblr.com/post/172543828183/i-want-you-in-these-guts#notes.

Anon 5. 2018. Comment on Tumblr. Accessed May 30, 2022. https://the-real-ricardo-ramirez.tumblr.com/post/172499963168/are-you-the-real-richard#notes.

Anon 6. 2018. Comment on Tumblr. Accessed May 1, 2022. https://the-real-ted--bundy-blog.tumblr.com/post/172540630998/omg-r-u-the-real-ted-bundy-shook-omg#notes.

Anon 7. 2018. Comment on Tumblr. Accessed May 1, 2022. https://the-real-ted--bundy-blog.tumblr.com/post/172661108873/join-the-discord-chat-teddy-boi-all-the-killers#notes.

Anon 8. 2018. Comment on Tumblr. Accessed May 1, 2022. https://the-real-ted--bundy-blog.tumblr.com/post/172662803438/theres-no-drama-whats-been-said-about-us-is.

Anon 9. 2018. Comment on Tumblr. Accessed December 22, 2022. https://at.tumblr.com/the-real-ted--bundy-blog/we-talk-about-you-all-the-time/fdduxoy2bzrt.

Applebaum, Stephen. 2018. "'There Was Always a Darkness about Him': My Friend Dahmer Author John Backderf on Growing up with a Serial Killer." *The Independent,* May 30, 2018. https://www.independent.co.uk/arts-entertainment/films/features/my-friend-dahmer-john-backderf-film-jeffrey-comic-book-interview-serial-killer-a8375866.html.

Avdeeff, Melissa K. 2021. "TikTok, Twitter, and Platform-Specific Technocultural Discourse in Response to Taylor Swift's LGBTQ+ Allyship in 'You Need to Calm Down.'" *Contemporary Music Review* 40, no. 1: 78–98. https://doi.org/10.1080/07494467.2021.1945225.

axolotlcore. 2021. "Friendship Goes a Long Way." Wattpad. Accessed February 2, 2022. Content no longer online.

Bacon-Smith, Camille. 1992. *Enterprising Women: Television Fandom and the Creation of Popular Myth*. Philadelphia: University of Pennsylvania Press.

Backderf, John. 2012. *My Friend Dahmer.* New York: Abrams ComicArts.

Balanzategui, Jessica, and Andrew Lynch. 2022. "'Shudder' and the Aesthetics and Platform Logics of Genre-Specific SVOD Services." *Television & New Media* 24, no. 2: 156–72. https://doi.org/10.1177/15274764221093602.

Barnes, Naomi. 2019. "Killer Folklore: Identity Issues in the True Crime Community." *Ethnologies* 41, no 1: 153–72. https://doi.org/10.7202/1069850ar.

Barrett-Ibarria, Sofia. 2019. "How Serial Killer Aileen Wuornos Became a Cult Hero." *Vice,* September 19, 2019. https://www.vice.com/en/article/mbm3j4/how-serial-killer-aileen-wuornos-became-a-cult-hero.

Baym, Nancy. 1998. "The Emergence of an On-Line Community." In *Cybersociety 2.0: Revisiting Computer-Mediated Communication and Community,* edited by Steve Jones, 35–68. London: Sage.

Baym, Nancy. 2000. *Tune In, Log on: Soaps, Fandom, and Online Community.* Thousand Oaks, CA: Sage.

Baym, Nancy. 2007. "The New Shape of Online Community: The Example of Swedish Independent Music Fandom." *First Monday* 12, no. 8. https://firstmonday.org/ojs/index.php/fm/article/view/1978/1853.

Baym, Nancy . 2010. *Personal Connections in the Digital Age.* Malden, MA: Polity.

Benjamin, Walter. (1936) 2005. "The Work of Art in the Age of Mechanical Reproduction." Translated by Harry Zohn. Marxists.org. https://www.marxists.org/reference/subject/philosophy/works/ge/benjamin.htm.

Belli, Willam. 2018. "Aileen: Now That's What I Call Drag Music Vol. 1." YouTube video. Accessed March 23, 2022. https://www.youtube.com/watch?v=dC193lIaGEc.

Bennett, Lucy. 2012. "Music Fandom Online: R.E.M. Fans in Pursuit of the Ultimate First Listen." *New Media & Society* 14, no. 5: 748–63.

Bennett, Lucy. 2014. "Tracing Textual Poachers: Reflections on the Development of Fan Studies and Digital Fandom." *Journal of Fandom Studies* 2, no. 1: 5–20. https://doi.org 10.1386/jfs.2.1.5_1.

Benetto, Jason. 2006. "Notes in Margin of Book 'Solve Ripper's Identity.'" *Independent,* July 14, 2006. https://web.archive.org/web/20090912214406/http://www.independent.co.uk/news/uk/crime/notes-in-margin-of-book-solve-rippers-identity-407881.html.

Bergstrom, Kelly, and Nathaniel Poor. 2021. "Reddit Gaming Communities During Times of Transition." *Social Media and Society* 7, no. 2. https://doi.org/10.1177/20563051211010167.

Berlinger, Joe, dir. 2019a. *Conversations with a Killer: The Ted Bundy Tapes.* Elastic, Gigantic Studios, Outpost Digital, and RadicalMedia. Netflix.

Berlinger, Joe, dir. 2019b. *Extremely Wicked, Shockingly Evil and Vile.* Screenplay by Michael Werwie. COTA films, Voltage Pictures, and Third Eye Motion Picture Company. Netflix.

blee. 2021. Comment on TikTok. Accessed May 7, 2022. https://www.tiktok.com/@richardsleatherjacket/video/6967233340088798470?is_from_webapp=1&sender_device=pc&web_id=6930854616536172037.

Bloom, Clive. 2007. "The Ripper Writing: A Cream of a Nightmare Dream." In *Jack the Ripper: Media, Culture, History,* edited by Alexandra Warwick and Martin Willis, 91–109. Manchester: Manchester University Press.

bluudstainbarbie. 2021. Tumblr post. Accessed September 9, 2022. https://bluudstainbarbie.tumblr.com/post/644445518642216960/jeffreysdahmer-as-befits-a-man-who-himself.

Boffone, Trevor. 2022. "Introduction: The Rise of TikTok in US Culture." In *TikTok Cultures in the United States,* edited by Trever Boffone, 1–13. London: Routledge.

Bonn, Scott A. 2014. *Why We Love Serial Killers: The Curious Appeal of the World's Most Savage Murderers.* New York: Skyhorse. EBSCO.

Boling, Kelli S., and Kevin Hull. 2018. "Undisclosed Information—Serial Is My Favorite Murder: Examining Motivations in the True Crime Podcast Audience." *Journal of Radio & Audio Media* 25, no. 1: 92–108. https://doi.org/10.1080/19376529.2017.1370714.

Booth, Paul. 2015. *Playing Fans: Negotiating Fandom and Media in the Digital Age*. Iowa City: University of Iowa Press. Kindle.

Booth, Paul. 2016. *Digital Fandom* 2.0. New York: Peter Lang.

Booth, Paul. 2017. "Playing by the Rules: Storium, Star Wars and Ludic Fandom." *Journal of Fandom Studies* 5, no. 3: 267–84.

Bourdieu, Pierre. 1984. *Distinction: A Social Critique of the Judgment of Taste.* Translated by Richard Nice. London: Routledge.

Bourdieu, Pierre. 1991. *Language and Symbolic Power.* Cambridge, UK: Polity.

Bourdieu, Pierre. 1993. *The Field of Cultural Production*. New York: Columbia University Press.

Bourdieu, Pierre. 1996. *The Rules of Art: Genesis and Structure of the Literary Field.* Translated by Susan Emanuel. Cambridge, UK: Polity.

Boswell, Charles, and Lewis Thompson. 1955. *The Girls in Nightmare House.* New York: Fawcett.

Braudy, Leo. 1986. *The Frenzy of Renown: Fame and its History*. New York: OUP.

Bresnick, Ethan. 2019. "Intensified Play: Cinematic Study of TikTok Mobile App." Unpublished manuscript, University of Southern California. https://www.researchgate.net/publication/335570557_Intensified_Play_Cinematic_study_of_TikTok_mobile_app.

Broll, Ryan. 2020. "Dark Fandoms: An Introduction and Case Study." *Deviant Behavior* 41, no. 6: 792–804. https://doi.org/10.1080/01639625.2019.1596453.

Broomfield, Nick, dir. 1992. *Aileen Wuornos: The Selling of a Serial Killer.* Netflix.

Broomfield, Nick, dir. 2003. *Aileen: Life and Death of a Serial Killer*. Netflix.

Browder, Laura. 2006. "Dystopian Romance: True Crime and the Female Reader." *Journal of Popular Culture* 39, no. 6: 928–53.

Bumi. 2021. Comment on "Jeffrey Dahmer | Edit | Maneater (lyrics)." YouTube. Accessed September 9, 2022. https://www.youtube.com/watch?v=jUZvzgiJ3BY.

bundysimp 2022. Reddit post. Accessed May 25, 2022. Content no longer online.

Bury, Rhiannon. 2001. "X Marks the G-Spot: Femininity and Desire in a Women-Only Cyberspace." *Michigan Feminist Studies* 15. http://hdl.handle.net/2027/spo.ark5583.0015.005.

Bury, Rhiannon. 2005. *Cyberspaces of Their Own: Female Fandoms Online.* New York: Peter Lang.

Bury, Rhiannon. 2017. "Technology, Fandom and Community in the Second Media Age." *Convergence* 23, no. 6: 627–42.

Bury, Rhiannon, Ruth A. Deller, Adam Greenwood, and Bethan Jones. 2013. "From Usenet to Tumblr: The Changing Role of Social Media." *Participations* 10, no. 1: 299–318.

Busse, Kristina. 2006. "Podcasts and the Fan Experience of Disseminated Media Commentary." Flow Conference, 2006. http://kbusse.wordpress.com/2007/05/01/my-presentation-for-flow-2006.

Busse, Kristina. 2013. "Geek Hierarchies, Boundary Policing, and the Gendering of the Good Fan." *Participations: A Journal of Audience and Reception Studies* 10, no. 1: 73–91.

Busse, Kristina. 2015. "Fan Labor and Feminism: Capitalizing on the Fannish Labor of Love." *Cinema Journal* 54, no. 3: 110–15. https://doi.org/10.1353/cj.2015.0034.

C. M. B. 2021. Comment on "Ted Bundy: Sweet Serial Killer." YouTube. Accessed March 24, 2022. https://www.youtube.com/watch?v=XBw7m9Z_iRs.

Cameron, Deborah. 1994. "St-i-i-i-ll going . . . The Quest for Jack the Ripper." *Social Text* 40:147–54.

Capote, Truman. 1966. *In Cold Blood*. New York: Random House.

Caputi, Jane. 1989. "The Sexual Politics of Murder." *Gender & Society* 3, no. 4: 437–56.

Cavicchi, Daniel. 1998. *Tramps Like Us: Music & Meaning Among Springsteen Fans*. New York: OUP.

CBC Radio. 2015. "Inside the Online Subculture of Columbiners." February 20, 2015. https://www.cbc.ca/radio/day6/episode-221-inside-the-world-of-columbiners-kidults-radical-homemakers-and-more-1.2961895/inside-the-online-subculture-of-columbiners-1.2961908.

cheeto_twat. 2021a. "Book One: Jefferey Lionel Dahmer—The History." Archive of Our Own. Accessed March 24, 2022. https://archiveofourown.org/works/30750548.

cheeto_twat. 2021b. "Book Two: Theodore Robert Cowell [Ted Bundy]." Archive of Our Own. Accessed March 24, 2022. https://archiveofourown.org/works/30885131.

Chen, Adrian. 2012. "Why James Holmes Has Fans On the Internet." Gawker, July 31, 2012. https://www.gawker.com/5930565/why-james-holmes-has-fans-on-the-internet.

Chesler, Phyllis. 1993. "A Woman's Right to Self-Defense: The Case of Aileen Carol Wuornos." *Off Our Backs* 23, no. 6: 6–15. http://www.jstor.org/stable/20834468.

Chin, Bertha. 2018. "It's About Who You Know: Social Capital, Hierarchies, and Fandom." In *A Companion to Media Fandom and Fan Studies*, edited by Paul Booth, 243–55. Hoboken, NJ: John Wiley & Sons.

Chloe <3. 2022. Comment on TikTok. Accessed May 7, 2022. Content no longer online.

Clausen, Line S., and Stine. A Sikjær. 2021. "When Podcast Met True Crime: A Genre-Medium Coevolutionary Love Story." *Leviathan: Interdisciplinary Journal in English* 7:139–214. https://doi.org/10.7146/lev.v0i7.125213.

Clerc, Susan J. 1996. "Estrogen Brigades and 'Big Tits' Threads: Media Fandom Online and Off." In *Wired Women: Gender and New Realities in Cyberspace,* edited by Lynn Cherny and Elizabeth Reba-Wise, 73–97. Seattle: Seal Press.

Connie. 2017. Comment on "Aileen Wuornos: Sweet Dreams (Are Made of This)." YouTube. Accessed March 24, 2022. https://www.youtube.com/watch?v=MriWNndljQ0.

Coppa, Francesca. 2006. "Writing Bodies in Space: Media Fanfiction as Theatrical Performance." In *Fan Fiction and Fan Communities in the Age of the Internet: New Essays,* edited by Karen Hellekson and Kristina Busse, 225–44. Jefferson, NC: McFarland.

crowbar_p1per. 2021. Comment on "Safe and Sound." Archive of Our Own. Accessed March 30, 2022. https://archiveofourown.org/works/30313527?view_full_work=true.

cr0w-is-dummy. 2022. Tumblr post. Accessed May 30, 2022. https://cr0w-is-dummy.tumblr.com/post/648289486971846656.

Cult Collectibles. 2022a. "Jeffrey Dahmer's Urn." CultCollectibles.org. Accessed September 22, 2022. https://www.cultcollectibles.org/shop/p/klij9jantf0psfdin1lq1ne3mgc0vq.

Cult Collectibles. 2022b. "About Us." CultCollectibles.org. Accessed September 20, 2022. Content no longer online.

Curtis, L. Perry, Jr. 2001. *Jack the Ripper and the London Press.* London: Yale University Press.

Cuthberson, Anthony. 2019. "TikTok Secretly Loaded with Chinese Surveillance Software, Lawsuit Claims." *Independent,* December 3, 2019. https://www.independent.co.uk/tech/tiktok-china-data-privacy-lawsuit-bytedance-a9230426.html.

Daggett, Chelsea. 2015. "Eric Harris and Dylan Klebold: Antiheroes for Outcasts." *Participations* 12, no. 2: 45–77.

dahmerfordayz-blog. 2018. Tumblr post. Accessed September 16, 2022. https://dahmerfordayz-blog.tumblr.com/post/178639604736/as-a-high-school-student-future-serial-killer.

Dan●. 2022. Comment on TikTok. Accessed September 16, 2022. Content no longer online.

Damon, Poppy, and Alice Fiennes. 2019. *Murderabilia* podcast. Audible. Accessed December 09, 2021.

darknight8200. 2022. Reddit post. Accessed May 6, 2022. Content no longer online.

datingdahmer-blog. 2017a. Tumblr post. Accessed March 2, 2022. https://datingdahmer-blog.tumblr.com/post/167928350256.

datingdahmer-blog. 2017b. Tumblr post. Accessed March 2, 2022. https://datingdahmer-blog.tumblr.com/post/167928868421/do-you-not-think-that-dahmer didnt-actually-want.

datingdahmer-blog. 2017c. Tumblr post. Accessed March 2, 2022. https://datingdahmer-blog.tumblr.com/post/167928231761.

dead-desert-star. 2021. Comment on Tumblr. Accessed May 6, 2022. https://nightst4lkerxx.tumblr.com/post/663755473888198656/Chibi-stalker-ri“ky-treats-himself-to-dinner.

deadmayo. 2022. “Clifford’s Big Red Cumshot.” Wattpad. Accessed February 15, 2022. https://www.wattpad.com/story/291685203-clifford%27s-big-red-cumshot.

deathrowrorry. 2020. Tumblr post. Accessed May 6, 2022. https://deathrowrorry.tumblr.com/post/638377466608615424/crime-scene-photos-are-the-most-fascinating-types.

deathrowrorry. 2021. Tumblr post. Accessed September 9, 2022. https://deathrowrorry.tumblr.com/post/641332758577332224/richardramirez-thenightstalker-eva-o-the-diva#notes.

Deleted user 1. 2021. Comment on TikTok. Accessed March 18, 2022. Content no longer online.

Deleted user 2. 2022. Reddit post. Accessed May 25, 2022. Content no longer online.

Deleted user 3. 2022. Comment on Reddit. Accessed May 25, 2022. Content no longer online.

Deleted user 4. 2022. Reddit post. Accessed May 25, 2022. Content no longer online.

Deleted user 5. 2022. Comment on Reddit. Accessed May 25, 2022. Content no longer online.

Deleted user 6. 2022. Comment on Reddit. Accessed May 25, 2022. Content no longer online.

Deleted user 7. 2021. Reddit post. Accessed May 25, 2022. Content no longer online.

Deleted user 8. 2021. Comment on Reddit. Accessed May 25, 2022. Content no longer online.

Deleted user 9. 2022. Comment on Reddit. Accessed May 30, 2022. Content no longer online.

Deleted user 10. 2022. Comment on Reddit. Accessed May 30, 2022. Content no longer online.

Deller, Ruth. 2014. "A Decade in the Lives of Online Fan Communities." In *The Ashgate Research Companion to Fan Cultures*, edited by Linda Duits, Stijn Reijnders, and Koon Zwaan, 237–48. Farnham: Ashgate.

Denham, Jack. 2016. "The Commodification of the Criminal Corpse: 'Selective Memory' in Posthumous Representations of Criminal." *Mortality* 21:229–45.

dictatorxtc. 2022. TikTok video. Accessed December 22, 2022. Content no longer online.

Divon, Tom, and Tobias Ebbrecht-Hartmann. 2022. "#JewishTikTok: The JewToks' Fight against Antisemitism." In *TikTok Cultures in the United States*, edited by Trevor Boffone, 47–58. London: Routledge.

Duncan, Sophie. 2019. "Personating the Ripper: Civilian Performance and the Melodramatic Mode." *Nineteenth Century Theatre and Film* 46, no. 2: 190–209.

Duval, Jared, Ferran Altarriba Bertran, Siying Chen, Melissa Chu, Divya Subramonian, Austin Wang, Geoffrey Xiang, Sri Kurniawan, and Katherine

Isbister. 2021. "Chasing Play on TikTok from Populations with Disabilities to Inspire Playful and Inclusive Technology Design." In *Proceedings of the 2021 CHI Conference on Human Factors in Computing Systems*. Association for Computing Machinery, New York, Article 492. https://doi.org/10.1145/3411764.3445303.

Eggplantsworldd. 2020. TikTok video. Accessed December 15, 2022. https://www.tiktok.com/@eggplantsworldd/video/7155621419748150574?is_copy_url=1&is_from_webapp=v1&item_id=7155621419748150574&q=jeffrey%20dahmer%20meme&t=1668762438235.

eliasblas. 2017. Tumblr post. Accessed September 16, 2022. https://eliasblas.tumblr.com/post/156144636709/i-wasnt-gonna-share-this-on-here-but-i-knew.

FandomVulture333. 2022a. Reddit comment. Accessed May 30, 2022. Content no longer online.

FandomVulture333. 2022b. Reddit comment. Accessed May 30, 2022. Content no longer online.

Farmaki, Anna. 2013."Dark Tourism Revisited: A Supply/Demand Conceptualisation." *International Journal of Culture, Tourism and Hospitality Research* 7, no. 3: 281–92. https://doi.org/10.1108/IJCTHR-05-2012-0030.

Fathallah, Judith. 2017. *Fanfiction and the Author: How Fanfic Changes Popular Cultural Texts*. Amsterdam: Amsterdam University Press.

Fathallah, Judith. 2018a. "Reading Real Person Fiction as Digital Fiction: An Argument for New Perspectives." *Convergence* 24, no. 6: 568–86. https://doi.org/10.1177/1354856516688624.

Fathallah, Judith. 2018b. "Polyphony on Tumblr: Reading the Hateblog as Pastiche." In *Tumblr and Fandom*, ed. Lori Morimoto and Louisa Ellen Stein, special issue, *Transformative Works and Cultures* 27. https://dx.doi.org/10.3983/twc.2018.1210.

Fathallah, Judith. 2020. *Emo: How Fans Defined a Subculture.* Iowa City: Iowa University Press.

Fathallah, Judith. 2021. "'Getting by' on 4chan: Feminine Self-Presentation and Capital-Claiming in Antifeminist Webspace." *First Monday* 26, no. 6: https://firstmonday.org/ojs/index.php/fm/article/view/10449/10149.

Fathallah, Judith. 2022. "'Being a Fangirl of a Serial Killer Is Not Okay': Gatekeeping Reddit's True Crime Community." *New Media & Society*. OnlineFirst. https://journals.sagepub.com/doi/10.1177/14614448221138768.

Felicino. 2021. Comment on Reddit. Accessed May 8, 2022. Content no longer online.

Fiske, John. 1989. *Understanding Popular Culture.* London: Routledge.

Fiske, John. 1992. "The Cultural Economy of Fandom." In *The Adoring Audience: Fan Culture and Popular Media,* edited by Lisa A. Lewis, 30–49. London: Routledge.

Fisher, Joseph C. 1997. *Killer Among Us: Public Reactions to Serial Murder.* Westport, CT: Praeger.

FlaerZz. 2022. Comment on Reddit. Accessed May 8, 2022. Content no longer online.

Foley, Malcolm, and John J. Lennon. 1996. "JFK and Dark Tourism: A Fascination With Assassination." *International Journal of Heritage Studies* 2, no. 4: 198–211. https://doi.org/10.1080/13527259608722175.

Fox, James Allen, and Jack Levin. 2005. *Extreme Killing: Understanding Serial and Mass Murder.* Thousand Oaks, CA: Sage.

Frayling, Christopher. 2007. "The House that Jack Built." In *Jack the Ripper: Media, Culture, History,* edited by Alexandra Warwick and Martin Willis, 13–28. Manchester: Manchester University Press.

Freund, Katie. 2006. "Convention of Fools: The Bakhtinian Carnival and the Anime Fan Community." *Fanthropology* (blog). Accessed March 23, 2022. https://fanthropology.wordpress.com/2006/03/30/convention-of-fools-the-bakhtinian-carnival-and-the-anime-fan-community/.

Ftwinzgottalent. 2020. TikTok video. Accessed December 22, 2022. https://www.tiktok.com/@ftwinzgottalent/video/7154100633459543338?is_copy_url=1&is_from_webapp=v1&q=%23jeffrey%20dahmer%20humour&t=1669042506129.

Fuckyou. 2021. Comment on "The Most Beautiful Happiness for Lizzie and Ted." Archive of Our Own. https://archiveofourown.org/works/*25486579*.

gabi mejia. 2022. Comment on "Ted Bundy Footage | Lana Del Rey—Summertime Sadness." YouTube. Accessed March 24, 2022. https://www.youtube.com/watch?v=-28Um7h64_I.

Garden Dormouse. 2019. Comment on "Ted Bundy—The Unknown." YouTube. Accessed September 16, 2022. https://www.youtube.com/watch?v=ixzZcdLNZXg.

garyleonridgway. 2012. Tumblr post. Accessed December 22, 2022. https://aileenwuornos-blog.tumblr.com/post/15341130311/garyleonridgway-aileenwuornos.

Geraghty, Lincoln. 2014. *Cult Collectors: Nostalgia, Fandom and Collecting Popular Culture*. New York: Routledge.

Geraghty, Lincoln. 2018. "Passing Through: Popular Media Tourism, Pilgrimage, and Narratives of Being a Fan." In *The Routledge Handbook of Popular Culture and Tourism,* edited by Christine Lundberg and Vassilios Ziakas. London: Routledge. Kindle.

get_raccd_24. 2022. TikTok video. Accessed December 22, 2022. Content no longer online.

Gibson, Dirk C. 2006. *Serial Murder and Media Circuses*. Westport, CT: Praeger.

Gn, Joel. 2011. "Queer Simulation: The Practice, Performance and Pleasure of Cosplay." *Continuum* 25, no. 4: 583–93. https://doi.org/10.1080/10304312.2011.582937.

Grenier, Keith. 2021. Comment on "Richard Ramirez (Devil Eyes—Hippie Sabotage)." YouTube. Accessed May 8, 2022. https://www.youtube.com/watch?v=A0_zeUynvKI.

Haggerty, Kevin D. 2009. "Modern Serial Killers." *Crime, Media, Culture: An International Journal* 5, no. 2: 168–87. https://doi.org/10.1177/1741659009335714.

Hammond, Michael. 2017. "What is an Online Community? A New Definition Based Around Commitment; Connection; Reciprocity; Interaction; Agency; and Consequences." *International Journal of Web Based Communities.* Author's archived version. http://wrap.warwick.ac.uk/78922/.

Hannell, Briony. 2017. "*Game of Thrones'* 'War on Women': Fandom and Feminist Discourse on Tumblr." Fan Studies Network Conference, University of Huddersfield, June 25, 2017.

Harris, Bill, dir. 1996. "Jeffrey Dahmer: The Monster Within." *Biography.* Originally broadcast on June 3, 1996. Tower Productions. YouTube. https://www.youtube.com/watch?v=RzSxU1GoL6I.

Hautsch, Jessica. 2018. "The Rhetorical Affordance of GIFs by Tumblr's *Supernatural* Fandom." In "Tumblr and Fandom," ed. Lori Morimoto and Louisa Ellen Stein, special issue, *Transformative Works and Cultures* 27. http://dx.doi.org/10.3983/twc.2018.1165.

Haze Dante. 2021. Comment on "Ted Bundy Edit—Criminal." YouTube. Accessed September 16, 2022.

Hedrick, Ashley, Dave Karpf, and Daniel Kreiss. 2018. "The Earnest Internet vs. the Ambivalent Internet." *International Journal of Communication* 12. https://ijoc.org/index.php/ijoc/article/view/8736.

Hellekson, Karen. 2009. "A Fannish Field of Value: Online Fan Gift Culture." *Cinema Journal* 48, no. 4: 113–18. https://doi.org/10.1353/cj.0.0140.

Hiebert, Alexa, and Kathy Kortes-Miller. 2021."Finding Home in Online Community: Exploring TikTok as a Support for Gender and Sexual Minority Youth throughout COVID-19." *Journal of LGBT Youth* 20, no. 4: 800–17. https://doi.org/10.1080/19361653.2021.2009953.

Hillman, Serena, Jason Procyk, and Carman Neustaedter. 2014a. "alksjdf;lksfd: Tumblr and the Fandom User Experience." *Proceedings of the Conference on Designing Interactive Systems*, ACM Press, 775–84.

Hillman, Serena, Jason Procyk, and Carman Neustaedter. 2014b. "Tumblr Fandoms, Community & Culture." *Proceedings of the CSCW Conference on Computer Supported Cooperative Work and Social Computing* (CSCW), ACM Press, 285–88.

Hartmann, Rudi, John Lennon, Daniel P. Reynolds, Alan Rice, Ada T. Rosenbaum, and Phillip R. Stone. 2018. "The History of Dark Tourism." *Journal of Tourism History* 10, no. 3: 269–95. https://doi.org/10.1080/1755182X.2018.1545394.

Hills, Matt. 2002. *Fan Cultures.* London: Routledge.

Hills, Matt. 2005. *The Pleasures of Horror.* London: Continuum.

Hills, Matt. 2015. "Cult Cinema and the 'Mainstreaming' Discourse of Technological Change: Revisiting Subcultural Capital in Liquid Modernity." *New Review of Film and Television Studies* 13, no. 1: 100–21. https://doi.org/10.1080/17400309.2014.982928.

Hilton, Jeff. 2021. Comment on "Makayla Singleton—Ted Bundy (Audio)." YouTube. Accessed December 8, 2022. https://www.youtube.com/watch?v=NOh8ZoDwdlU.

Hobbs, Thomas. 2018. "From Ted Bundy to Jeffrey Dahmer: What It's Like To Be Part of a Serial Killer Fandom." *New Statesman,* October 16, 2018. https://www.newstatesman.com/2018/10/ted-bundy-jeffrey-dahmer-what-it-s-be-part-serial-killer-fandom.

Hoebink, Dorus, Stijn Reijnders, and Abby Waysdorf. 2014. "Exhibiting Fandom: A Museological Perspective." In "Materiality and Object-Oriented Fandom," ed. Bob Rehak, special issue, *Transformative Works and Cultures* 16. https://doi.org/10.3983/twc.2014.0529.

Horeck, Tanya. 2019. *Justice on Demand: True Crime in the Digital Streaming Era*. Detroit: Wayne State University Press.

hyejooloveclub. 2021a. Reddit post. Accessed May 8, 2022. Content no longer online.

hyejooloveclub. 2021b. Comment on Reddit. Accessed May 8, 2022. Content no longer online.

immaturegrammy. 2021. Tumblr post. Accessed December 22, 2022. https://at.tumblr.com/immaturegrammy/660365115209760768/pf5r5uoihmw4.

İnceoglu, İrem, and Kaya Yiğit Bahadır. "TikTokivism: Grouping of LGBTI+ Youth on TikTok's Semi-Discrete Environments." TikTok and Social Movements (online symposium), TikTok Cultures Research Network, September 20, 2021. Accessed December 12, 2022. https://tiktokcultures.com/tiktok-and-social-movements-recordings/.

Irwin, Hannah. 2014. "Not of This Earth: Jack the Ripper and the Development of Gothic Whitechapel." *M/C Journal* 17, no. 4. https://doi.org/10.5204/mcj.845.

Its-jilleus. 2021. Tumblr post. Content no longer online.

Izzy. 2021. Comment on TikTok. Accessed December 22, 2022. Content no longer online.

Jackpotscomicno5. 2022. Tumblr post. Accessed December 22, 2022. https://at.tumblr.com/jackpotcomicsno5/i-love-how-people-joke-about-male-serial-killers/dg5xtkjuvdbu.

James, Roxie J., and Katherine E. Lane. 2020. "'I Need a Hero:' Representation and Reinvention of the Criminal Hero in Mass Media." In *Criminals As Heroes in Popular Culture,* edited by Roxie J. James and Katherine E. Lane, 1–15. Cham: Palgrave Pivot.

Jameson, Frederic. 1991. *Postmodernism or The Cultural Logic of Late Capitalism*. Durham: Duke University Press.

Jarvis, Brian. 2007. "Monsters Inc.: Serial killers and Consumer Culture." *Crime, Media, Culture* 3, no. 3: 326–44. https://doi.org/10.1177/1741659007082469.

JaŻ. 2022. Comment on TikTok. Accessed December 22, 2022. Content no longer online.

jdimh7. 2022a. "In This Together." Archive of Our Own. https://archiveofourown.org/works/30342417?view_full_work=true.

Jeffery_dahmer17. 2020. TikTok video. Accessed December 22, 2022. Content no longer online.

Jeffreydahmereditzz. 2022a. Comment on TikTok. Accessed May 7, 2022. Content no longer online.

Jeffreydahmereditzz. 2022b. TikTok. Accessed May 7, 2022. Content no longer online.

Jeffreydahmereditzz. 2022c. Comment on TikTok. Accessed May 7, 2022. Content no longer online.

Jeffreydahmereditzz. 2022d. Comment on TikTok. Accessed May 7, 2022. Content no longer online.

jeffreydahmerlover. 2017. TikTok video. Accessed September 9, 2022. https://www.tiktok.com/@jeffreydahmerlover/video/195502678238679040?is_copy_url=1&is_from_webapp=v1.

jeffreydrunk. 2018. Comment on Tumblr. Accessed September 16, 2022. https://dahmerfordayz-blog.tumblr.com/post/178639604736/as-a-high-school-student-future-serial-killer.

Jelicaalynn. 2021. Comment on Tumblr. Accessed May 30, 2022. https://the-real-ricardo-ramirez.tumblr.com/post/643760468041908224/kys-fat-cunt#notes.

Jenkins, Henry. 1992. *Textual Poachers: Television Fans and Participatory Culture*. London: Routledge.

Jenkins, Henry. 2006. *Convergence Culture: Where Old and New Media Collide*. New York: New York University Press.

Jenkins, Henry. 2013. *Textual Poachers: Television Fans and Participatory Culture*. 20th anniversary ed. New York: Routledge. https://doi.org/10.4324/9780203114339.

Jenkins, Henry, Sam Ford, and Joshua Green. 2013. *Spreadable Media: Creating Value and Meaning in a Networked Culture*. New York: New York University Press.

Jensen, Joli. 1992. "Fandom as Pathology: The Consequences of Characterization." In *The Adoring Audience: Fan Culture and Popular Media,* edited by Lisa A. Lewis, 9–26. London: Routledge.

Jessica Pazo. 2021. Comment on "Ted Bundy Footage | Lana Del Rey—Summertime Sadness." YouTube. Accessed March 24, 2022. https://www.youtube.com/watch?v=-28Um7h64_I.

JiKook_Namjin_taegiseok. 2019. Comment on "Life's Too Short to Match Your Socks." Archive of Our Own. Accessed December 22, 2022. https://archiveofourown.org/works/17175839?view_full_work=true.

JoeLedeen. 2022. Comment on TikTok. Accessed May 7, 2022. Content no longer online.

Jones, Bethan. 2021. "'Do Your Part Spreading My Message, Making Memes and Shitposting:' Dark Fandom and/as Sites of Resistance." *Society for Cinema and Media Studies Conference* (online), March 17–21, 2021.

Jude_The_Dude. 2021. Comment on TikTok. Accessed December 22, 2022. Content no longer online.

Katz, Yuval, and Limor Shifman. 2017. "Making Sense? The Structure and Meanings of Digital Memetic Nonsense." *Information, Communication & Society* 20, no. 6: 825–42. https://doi.org/10.1080/1369118X.2017.1291702.

Kaye, D. Bondy Valdovinos, Aleesha Rodriguez, Katrin Langton, and Patrik Wikstrom. 2021. "You Made This? I Made This: Practices of Authorship and (Mis)Attribution on TikTok." *International Journal of Communication* 15:3195–215.

Kaye, D. Bondy Valdovinos, Jing Zeng, and Patrik Wikström. 2022. *TikTok: Creativity and Culture in Short Video*. Cambridge, UK: Polity.

Ken. 2021. Comment on TikTok. Accessed December 22, 2022. Content no longer online.

Kesling, Ben, and Georgia Wells. 2020. "U.S. Military Bans TikTok Over Ties to China." *The Wall Street Journal,* January 3, 2020. https://www.wsj.com/articles/u-s-military-bans-tiktok-over-ties-tochina-11578090613.

kiluwa. 2019. Tumblr post. Accessed December 22, 2022. https://at.tumblr.com/killuwa/lesbians-convinces-aileen-wuornos-to-murder-7/4lqpo4y4srl6.

Kirkpatrick, Ellen. 2015. "Toward New Horizons: Cosplay (Re)imagined through the Superhero Genre, Authenticity, and Transformation." *Transformative Works and Cultures* 18. https://doi.org/10.3983/twc.2015.0613.

kkg108. 2019. Comment on "Ted Bundy—The Unknown." YouTube. Accessed December 22, 2022. https://www.youtube.com/watch?v=ixzZcdLNZXg.

korimari_locx. 2022. TikTok video. Accessed December 22, 2022. https://www.tiktok.com/@korimari_locx/video/7055092746423438638?is_copy_url=1&is_from_webapp=v1&item_id=7055092746423438638&q=aileen%20wuornos%20joke&t=1669124145963.

Krishna, Manoj. 2021. Comment on "Ted Bundy Edit—Criminal." YouTube. Accessed December 22, 2022.

KRON 4. 2014 (1990). "The Night Stalker's Groupies." Originally broadcast January 9, 1990. YouTube video. https://www.youtube.com/watch?v=-Rlm-n3vfVM.

Kulinicheva, Ekaterina. 2021. “Sneakerheads as Fans and Sneaker Fandom as Participatory Culture.” *Transformative Works and Cultures* 36. https://doi.org/10.3983/twc.2021.1991.

Kumar, Sneha. 2021. “*Carmilla* Fandom as a Lesbian Community of Feeling.” *Transformative Works and Cultures* 36. https://doi.org/10.3983/twc.2021.2007.

Kunert, Jessica. 2021. “The Footy Girls of Tumblr: How Women Found Their Niche in the Online Football Fandom.” *Communication & Sport* 9, no. 2: 243–63.

Laclau, Ernesto, and Chantal Mouffe. 1985. *Hegemony and Socialist Strategy: Towards a Radical Democratic Politics*. London: Verso.

Lambert, Kelly. 2016. “Richard Ramirez—Dirty Mind.” YouTube. Accessed December 22, 2022. https://www.youtube.com/watch?v=JGwuK3NAdIg.

lameadults. 2020. TikTok video. Accessed December 22, 2022. https://www.tiktok.com/@lameadults/video/7055095186057088302?is_copy_url=1&is_from_webapp=v1&item_id=7055095186057088302&q=ted%20bundy%20jokes&t=1668508814946.

Lamerichs, Nicolle. 2011. “Stranger than Fiction: Fan Identity in Cosplay.” *Transformative Works and Cultures* 7. https://doi.org/10.3983/twc.2011.0246.

landtron. 2022. TikTok video. Accessed December 22, 2022. https://www.tiktok.com/@_landtron_/video/7148521049314053422?is_copy_url=1&is_from_webapp=v1&item_id=7148521049314053422&q=jeffreydahmermeme&t=1668763074453.

Lanier, Clinton D. Jr., C. Scott Rader, and Aubrey R. Fowler III. 2022. “Digital Fandom (Revisted): Exploring the Role of the Hypermediated Fan as Trickster.” In *The Routledge Handbook of Digital Consumption,* edited by Rosa Llamas and Russell Belk. 2nd ed. 384–98, Taylor and Francis e-book.

Larsen, Kathy, ed. 2014a. *The Journal of Fandom Studies* 2, no. 1. https://www.ingentaconnect.com/content/intellect/jfs/2014/00000002/00000001.

Larsen, Kathy, ed. 2014b. “Moving Forward, Looking Back.” *The Journal of Fandom Studies* 2, no. 1: 3–4. https://doi.org/10.1386/jfs.2.1.3_2.

Lennon, John, and Malcom Foley. 2000. *Dark Tourism: The Attraction of Death and Disaster.* New York: Continuum.

Leppänen, Sirpa. 2009. "Playing with and Policing Language Use and Textuality in Fan Fiction." In *Internet Fictions*, edited by Ingrid Hotz-Davies, Anton Kirchofer, and Sirpa Leppänen, 62–83. Newcastle upon Tyne: Cambridge Scholars.

Leslie [redacted] [username]. 2021. Comment on TikTok. Accessed September 9, 2022. https://www.tiktok.com/@real.ramirez/video/6996533200432450821?is_copy_url=1&is_from_webapp=v1.

Levin Russo, Julie. 2013. "Textual Orientation: Queer Female Fandom Online." In *The Routledge Companion to Media and Gender*, edited by Cindy Carter, Linda Steiner, and Lisa McLaughlin, 450–60. Oxon: Routledge.

Löbert, Anya. 2012. "Fandom as a Religious Form: On the Reception of Pop Music by Cliff Richard Fans in Liverpool." *Popular Music* 31, no. 1: 125–41. http://www.jstor.org/stable/23325835.

Lokisnotdead. 2018. Comment on *The One Where True Crime Meets High School.* Archive of Our Own. Accessed December 22, 2022. https://archiveofourown.org/works/14352558?view_full_work=true.

Lothian, Alexis. 2009. "Living in a Den of Thieves: Fan Video and Digital Challenges to Ownership." *Cinema Journal* 48, no. 4: 130–36.

Lothian, Alexis, Kristina Busse, and Robin Anne Reid. 2007. "'Yearning Void and Infinite Potential': Online Slash Fandom as Queer Female Space." *English Language Notes* 45, no. 2: 103–11.

lovemusicmusa. 2021. Comment on "Richard Ramirez 'Fell with the Devil.'" YouTube. Accessed December 22, 2022. Content no longer online.

lucypopmama. 2020. TikTok video. Accessed December 22, 2022. https://www.tiktok.com/@lucypopmama/video/6900283994525404421?is_copy_url=1&is_from_webapp=v1&item_id=6900283994525404421&q=aileen%20wuornos%20humor&t=1669209249658.

Lynch, Kimery S. 2022. "Fans as Transcultural Gatekeepers: The Hierarchy of BTS' Anglophone Reddit Fandom and the Digital East-West Media Flow." *New Media & Society* 24, no. 1: 105–21.

Lyons, Tom, and Lisa Trei. 1989. "Celebration Sets Up Near Execution." *Gainesville Sun*, January 25, 1989.

lsxy2. 2022. TikTok video. Accessed December 22, 2022. https://www.tiktok.com/@lxsy2/video/7157473378117438726?is_from_webapp=v1&item_id=7157473378117438726.

McKay, Adam, dir. 2006. *Talladega Nights: The Ballad of Ricky Bobby*. Written by Will Ferrell. Columbia Pictures, Relativity Media, The Apatow Company, and Mosaic Media Group.

Makayla Singleton. 2021a. "Makayla Singleton—Ted Bundy (Audio)." YouTube. Accessed March 24, 2022. https://www.youtube.com/watch?v=NOh8ZoDwdlU.

Makayla Singleton. 2021b. Comment on "Makayla Singleton—Ted Bundy (Audio)." YouTube. Accessed March 24, 2022. https://www.youtube.com/watch?v=NOh8ZoDwdlU.

male-to-catgirl. 2021. Tumblr post. Accessed March 3, 2022. https://male-to-catgirl.tumblr.com/post/666664747985453056/too-many-women-called-evil-for-what-is-honestly-a.

malscat. 2019. Comment on "Carl Azuz x Ted Bundy." Wattpad. Accessed February 17, 2022. Content no longer online.

Mandy Monroe. 2021. Comment on "Richard Ramirez 'Fell with the Devil.'" YouTube. Accessed May 7, 2022. Content no longer online.

marimbasolo4. 2022. Comment on TikTok. Accessed May 7, 2022. Content no longer online.

mark quish. 2021. Comment on "Ted Bundy—In the End—Music Tribute." YouTube. Accessed May 8, 2022. https://www.youtube.com/watch?v=SRZy3DoFFqE.

Matt. 2020. Comment on "The Most Beautiful Happiness for Lizzie and Ted." Archive of Our Own. Accessed May 7, 2022. https://archiveofourown.org/works/25486579.

Matthews, Jolie C. 2018. "A Past That Never Was: Historical Poaching in *Game of Thrones* Fans' Tumblr Practices." *Popular Communication* 16, no. 3: 225–42. https://doi.org/10.1080/15405702.2018.1453070

medeakid. 2021. Comment on Reddit. Accessed May 8, 2022. Content no longer online.

michaelsmistress. 2019a. "Comment on Life's Too Short to Match Your Socks." Archive of Our Own. Accessed May 7, 2022. https://archiveofourown.org/works/17175839?view_full_work=true.

michaelsmistress. 2019b. "Life's Too Short to Match Your Socks." Archive of Our Own. Accessed May 7, 2022. https://archiveofourown.org/works/17175839?view_full_work=true.

memes4ya. 2021. Tumblr post. Accessed December 22, 2022. https://at.tumblr.com/memes4ya/640403951573942272/1ch7u1gnxj37.

Meyers, Marc, dir. 2017. *My Friend Dahmer*. Ibid Filmworks, Aperture Entertainment, and Attic Light Films.

Milner, R. M. 2011. "Discourses on Text Integrity: Information and Interpretation in the Contested Fallout Knowledge Community." *Convergence: The International Journal of Research into New Media Technologies* 17, no. 2: 159–75.

Miss Noir in the shadow. 2020. Comment on "Aileen Wuornos—Edit." YouTube. Accessed May 7, 2022. https://www.youtube.com/watch?v=1V86bHyN_Cw.

MKManiac. 2019. Comment on "Ted Bundy—The Unknown." YouTube. Accessed May 7, 2022. https://www.youtube.com/watch?v=ixzZcdLNZXg.

Moonlitnitely. 2021. Tumblr post. Accessed December 22, 2022. https://www.tumblr.com/slayersbookofdeath-blog/164319149291.

MozzUpDown. 2022. Comment on Reddit. Accessed September 5, 2022. Content no longer online.

mr_oh_sangwoo. 2022. TikTok video. Accessed December 22, 2022. Content no longer online.

muan muan. 2021. Comment on "Richard Ramirez 'Fell with the Devil.'" YouTube. Accessed May 7, 2022. Content no longer online.

Murder Auction. 2022. "About Us." MurderAuction.com. Accessed September 20, 2022. https://www.murderauction.com/auction/about-us.

murder-mystery-theatre. 2022a. Tumblr post. Accessed September 16, 2022. https://www.tumblr.com/murder-mystery-theatre/690903030670999552.

murder-mystery-theatre. 2022b. Tumblr post. Accessed September 16, 2022. https://murder-mystery-theatre.tumblr.com/post/694608166789513216.

Murley, Jean. 2008. *The Rise of True Crime: 20th-Century Murder and American Popular Culture.* Santa Barbara, CA: ABC-CLIO.

Nathan. 2021. Comment on "Richard Ramirez 'Fell with the Devil.'" YouTube. Accessed May 7, 2022. Content no longer online.

nem.tudom._.xd. 2021. TikTok video. Accessed December 22, 2022. Content no longer online.

nevermoreflesh. 2018. "A Handsome Face with a Monster Inside." Archive of Our Own. Accessed December 22, 2022. https://archiveofourown.org/works/15067349.

nights4lkerxx. 2014. Tumblr post. Accessed March 1, 2022. https://nightst4lkerxx.tumblr.com/post/645303803356266496/im-sorry-for-this.

nights4lkerxx. 2021a. Tumblr post. Accessed March 1, 2022. https://nightst4lkerxx.tumblr.com/post/663755473888198656/chibi-stalker-ricky-treats-himself-to-dinner.

nights4lkerxx. 2021b. Tumblr post. Accessed March 1, 2022. https://nightst4lkerxx.tumblr.com/post/645714418913755136/this-is-actually-so-sad.

Nini, Andrea. 2018. "An Authorship Analysis of the Jack the Ripper Letters." *Digital Scholarship in the Humanities* 33, no. 3: 621–36. https://doi.org/10.1093/llc/fqx065.

Nguyen, Josef. 2016. "Performing as Video Game Players in Let's Plays." *Transformative Works and Cultures* 22. http://dx.doi.org/10.3983/twc.2016.0698.

Nuhchez. 2020. TikTok video. Accessed December 22, 2022. https://www.tiktok.com/@nuhchez/video/6855018593311132933?is_copy_url=1&is_from_webapp=v1&item_id=6855018593311132933&q=tedbundymemes&t=166850801353.

obsession_inc. 2009. "Affirmational Fandom vs. Transformative Fandom." Dreamwidth. Accessed March 24, 2022. https://obsession-inc.dreamwidth.org/82589.html.

oh-thats-good-ta-hear. 2022. Tumblr post. Accessed December 22, 2022. Content no longer online.

orevet. 2018. Tumblr post. Accessed December 22, 2022. https://at.tumblr.com/orevet/serial-killers-as-people-you-regret-swiping-right/nbwxg-pviudgs.

orphan_account 1. 2020. "Spinning Wheel." Archive of Our Own. Accessed December 22, 2022. https://archiveofourown.org/works/23078827?view_full_work=true.

orphan_account 2. 2020. "Baby, I'm an Animal (But You Can Have a Taste)." Archive of Our Own. Accessed December 22, 2022. https://archiveofourown.org/works/27548836.

orphan_account 3. 2019. Comment on "The One Where True Crime Meets High School." Archive of Our Own. Accessed December 22, 2022. https://archiveofourown.org/works/14352558?view_full_work=true.

Palmer, Zachary D. 2021. "'I'm Going to Love and Tolerate the Shit Out of You:' Hybrid Masculinities in the Brony Community." *Men and Masculinities* 5, no. 1: 87–105. https://doi.org/10.1177/1097184X211031969

Pande, Rukmini. 2018. *Squee from the Margins: Fandom and Race.* Iowa City: University of Iowa Press.

Paredes, Anthony J., and Elizabeth D. Purdum. 1990. "'Bye-bye Ted . . .' Community Response in Florida to the Execution of Theodore Bundy." *Anthropology Today* 6, no. 2: 9–11.

partyhardcake. 2022. Comment on Reddit. Accessed May 25, 2022. Content no longer online.

Paula Moyano. 2022. Comment on "Aileen Wuornos Edit—I Was Made for Lovin You." YouTube. Accessed May 7, 2022. https://www.youtube.com/watch?v=Ps3j8HqpkTM.

Pearson, Kyra. 2007. "The Trouble with Aileen Wuornos, Feminism's 'First Serial Killer.'" *Communication and Critical/Cultural Studies* 4, no. 3: 256–75.

Pearson, Roberta. 2010. "Fandom in the Digital Era." *Popular Communication* 8, no. 1: 84–95. https://doi.org/10.1080/15405700903502346.

PEEK-A-BOO. 2021. "Richard Ramirez—Animal (Glitch Remix)." YouTube. Accessed December 22, 2022. https://www.youtube.com/watch?v=xtmQpkDKPyU.

Penley, Constance. 1997. *Nasa/Trek: Popular Science and Sex in America*. London: Verso.

Phan, Michelle. 2020. "Biopower, Police Accountability, and Emotional Labour in the Age of Social Media." *The iJournal: Student Journal of the Faculty of Information* 5, no. 2. https://doi.org/10.33137/ijournal.v5i2.34466.

Phillips, Whitney, and Ryan M. Milner. 2017. *The Ambivalent Internet: Mischief, Oddity, and Antagonism Online*. Cambridge, UK: Polity. Kindle.

Poems of Plupp. 2021. "Summertime Sadness [Jeffrey Dahmer]." YouTube. Accessed May 8, 2022. Content no longer online.

Princesss7. 2021. Comment on Reddit. Accessed May 8, 2022. Content no longer online.

Queen Bee. 2017. "Richard Ramirez (Devil Eyes—Hippie Sabotage). " Accessed May 8, 2022. YouTube. https://www.youtube.com/watch?v=A0_zeUynvKI.

Queertcc. 2018. Comment on Tumblr. Accessed September 16, 2022. https://dahmerfordayz-blog.tumblr.com/post/178639604736/as-a-high-school-student-future-serial-killer.

Radykalny-feminizm. 2022. Tumblr post. Accessed September 18, 2022. https://radykalny-feminizm.tumblr.com/post/689561073833197568.

rainy.msx. 2022. TikTok video. Accessed December 22, 2022. Content no longer online.

Ramsland, Katherine. 2012. "Women Who Love Serial Killers." *Psychology Today,* April 20, 2012. https://www.psychologytoday.com/gb/blog/shadow-boxing/201204/women-who-love-serial-killers.

real.ramirez. 2021. TikTok video. Accessed September 9, 2022. https://www.tiktok.com/@real.ramirez/video/6996533200432450821?is_copy_url=1&is_from_webapp=v1.

PotatoMuffinMafia. 2021. "Unpopular opinion: Comedy true crime podcasts are disrespectful and inappropriate." Reddit post. R/TrueCrime. Accessed March 24, 2022. https://www.reddit.com/r/TrueCrime/comments/qeo0pg/unpopular_opinion_comedy_true_crime_podcasts_are/.

Redrumautographs. 2022. “Theodore Robert Bundy original 10 pages court document stamped and signed from August 7, 1979.” Murder Auction lot. MurderAuction.com. Accessed September 22, 2022.

Reijnders, Stijn L. 2011. “Stalking the Count: Dracula, Fandom and Tourism.” *Annals of Tourism Research: A Social Sciences Journal* 38, no. 1: 231–48. https://doi.org/10.1016/j.annals.2010.08.006.

Repent to kidzbopism. 2021. Comment on TikTok. Accessed May 7, 2022. https://www.tiktok.com/@richardsleatherjacket/video/6967233340088798470?is_from_webapp=1&sender_device=pc&web_id=6930854616536172037.

Rheingold, Howard. 1993. *The Virtual Community: Homesteading on the Electronic Frontier*. Boston: Addison-Wesley.

Richard Ramirez♥. 2021. TikTok video. Accessed May 7, 2022. Content no longer online.

RichardLittleDevil. 2021. Comment on TikTok. Accessed May 7, 2022. https://www.tiktok.com/@richardsleatherjacket/video/6967233340088798470?is_from_webapp=1&sender_device=pc&web_id=6930854616536172037.

richardsleatherjacket. 2021. TikTok video. Accessed May 7, 2022. https://www.tiktok.com/@richardsleatherjacket/video/6967233340088798470?is_from_webapp=1&sender_device=pc&web_id=6930854616536172037.

richardramirez9996. 2021. Comment on TikTok. Accessed May 7, 2022. Content no longer online.

RICHIES_ANGEL. 2021a. “Richard Ramirez Imagines.” Wattpad. Accessed February 17, 2022. Content no longer online.

RICHIES_ANGEL. 2021b. “Richard Ramirez Imagines.” Wattpad. Accessed February 2, 2022. Content no longer online.

richiessshadesofgrey. 2022. “Richard Ramirez: One Shots.” Wattpad. Accessed February 2, 2022. Content no longer online.

Rico, Andrew Ryan. 2015. “Fans of Columbine Shooters Eric Harris and Dylan Klebold.” *Transformative Works and Cultures* 20. https://doi.org/10.3983/twc.2015.0671.

richardramirezsbadbreath. 2021. Comment on TikTok. Accessed May 30, 2022. Content no longer online.

Rochford, Elle, and Zachary D. Palmer. 2022. "Trans TikTok: Sharing Information and Forming Community." In *TikTok Cultures in the United States,* edited by Trevor Boffone, 84–94. London: Routledge.

Rogers, Christine. 2010. "Aileen Wuornos: Sympathy for the Devil." In *Illuminating the Dark Side: Evil, Women & the Feminine,* edited by Andrea Ruthven and Gabriela Mádlo, 53–64, Brill e-book.

Robinson, Mary. 2014. "Hell's Belles: The Adaptive Treatment of Lizzie Borden, Ruth Snyder, and Aileen Wuornos as a Process of Female Demonization." MA diss., Tufts University.

robotsvsdinosaurs. 2017. Tumblr post. Accessed December 22, 2022. https://robotsvsdinosaurs.tumblr.com/post/187020094537.

Romano, Aja. 2014. "Inside Tumblr's Obsession with Mass Murderers." *The Daily Dot,* September 13, 2014. https://www.dailydot.com/irl/tj-lane-dylan-klebold-fandom-tumblr/.

rrebelyell. 2022. "Just Another Lost Angel." Wattpad. Accessed May 30, 2022. Content no longer online.

rrmyloverr. 2022b. TikTok video. Accessed May 7, 2022. Content no longer online.

Ruby is eating my heart? [username]. Comment on TikTok. Accessed May 7, 2022. Content no longer online.

Russell, Tiller, and James Carroll, dirs. 2021. *Night Stalker: The Hunt For a Serial Killer.* Netflix.

rxbbitl0ser. 2019. "Carl Azuz x Ted Bundy." Wattpad. Accessed February 20, 2022. Content no longer online.

S [username]. 2021. Comment on TikTok. Accessed September 9, 2022. https://www.tiktok.com/@thenightstalker1960s/video/7047932141031771398?is_copy_url=1&is_from_webapp=v1&item_id=7047932141031771398.

Sacks, Sarah. 2017. "'Let's Get Comfy and Cozy and Cuddle Up and Talk About Murder:' My Favorite Murder and the New True Crime." MA diss., University of Oregon. https://scholarsbank.uoregon.edu/xmlui/handle/1794/22686.

Salen, Katie, and Eric Zimmerman. 2004. *Rules of Play: Game Design Fundamentals.* Cambridge, MA: MIT Press.

Saltzman, Rachelle H. 1995. "'This Buzz Is for You:' Popular Responses to the Ted Bundy Execution." *Journal of Folklore Research* 32, no. 2: 101–19. http://www.jstor.org/stable/3814368.

Salviano, Antonio. 2021. "Comment on Richard Ramirez—Dirty Mind." YouTube. Accessed September 9, 2022. https://www.youtube.com/watch?v=JGwuK3NAdIg.

Sandvoss, Cornel. 2005. *Fans: The Mirror of Consumption*. Cambridge, UK: Polity.

Scott, Suzanne. 2011. "Revenge of the Fanboy: Convergence Culture and the Politics of Incorporation." PhD diss., University of Southern California.

Scott, Suzanne. 2019. *Fake Geek Girls: Fandom, Gender, and the Convergence Culture Industry.* New York: NYU Press.

saveaileen. 2021. TikTok video. Accessed September 20, 2022. https://www.tiktok.com/@saveaileen/video/6954545304066624773?is_copy_url=1&is_from_webapp=v1.

Schilt, Paige. 2000. "Media Whores and Perverse Media: Documentary Film Meets Tabloid TV in Nick Broomfield's *Aileen Wuornos: The Selling of a Serial Killer.*" *Velvet Light Trap*, Spring 2000: 50–61. https://go.gale.com/ps/i.do?p=AONE&u=googlescholar&id=GALE|A90190351&v=2.1&it=r&sid=AONE&asid=ca714458.

Schmid, David. 2005. *Natural Born Celebrities: Serial Killers in American Culture*. Chicago: University of Chicago Press.

Schmidt, Martha A. 1994. "Dahmer Discourse and Gay Identity: The Paradox of Queer Politics." *Critical Sociology* 20, no. 3: 81–105.

Schulenberg, Kelsea S. 2021. "'You're in a Cult, Call Your Dad:' An Investigation into the True Crime Podcast *My Favorite Murder* and Its Online Fan Communities." MA diss., Clemson University.

Seltzer, Mark. 2013. *Serial Killers: Death and Life in America's Wound Culture.* New York: Routledge.

serialkillersink. 2012. "Murderabilia—Serial Killers Ink on Fox News Cleveland November 2012." YouTube. Accessed September 20, 2022. https://www.youtube.com/watch?v=ug8k8nXabUM.

Serial Killers Ink. 2022a. "About Us." SerialKillersInk.net. Accessed September 20, 2022. https://serialkillersink.net/about-us.html.

Serial Killers Ink. 2022b. "Jeffrey Dahmer—18-inch Demented Dollz Dahmer Plush Doll (out of package)." Accessed September 22, 2022.

serial killer edits. 2021. "Jeffrey Dahmer | Edit | Maneater (lyrics)." YouTube. Accessed September 9, 2022. https://www.youtube.com/watch?v=jUZvzgiJ3BY

Serial Productions. 2014–. Serial podcast. Accessed December 12, 2023. https://serialpodcast.org/.

Shifman, Limor. 2014. *Memes in Digital Culture.* Cambridge, MA: MIT Press.

Shefrin, Elana. 2004. "Lord of the Rings, Star Wars, and Participatory Fandom: Mapping New Congruencies Between the Internet and Media Entertainment Culture." *Critical Studies in Media Communication* 21, no. 3: 261–81.

Sherminator. 2021. Comment on "Richard Ramirez 'Fell with the Devil.'" YouTube. Accessed May 7, 2022.

sick-girl-666. 2021a. Tumblr post. Accessed March 24, 2022. https://sick-girl-666.tumblr.com/post/647653233060397056.

sick-girl-666. 2021b. Tumblr post. Accessed March 24, 2022. https://sick-girl-666.tumblr.com/post/647653004950011904.

sick-girl-666. 2021c. Tumblr post. Accessed March 24, 2022. https://sick-girl-666.tumblr.com/post/647652608176226304.

sick-girl-666. 2022. Tumblr post. Accessed May 6, 2022. https://sick-girl-666.tumblr.com/post/647650277484298240/im-back#notes.

Simpson, Ellen, and Semaan, Bryan. 2021. "For You, or For 'You'? Everyday LGBTQ+ Encounters with TikTok." *Proceedings of the Association for Computing Machinery on Human-Computer Interaction* 4, no. CSCW3: 1–34. https://doi.org/10.1145/3432951.

Skinner, Claudia. 2022. "'Do You Want to Form an Alliance with Me?' Glimpses of Utopia in the Works of Queer Women and NonBinary Creators on TikTok." In *TikTok Cultures in the United States,* edited by Trevor Boffone, 72–83. London: Routledge.

Slayersbookofdeath-blog. 2017. Tumblr post. Accessed December 22, 2022. https://www.tumblr.com/slayersbookofdeath-blog/164319149291.

somebody-help-meee. 2020. Comment on Tumblr. Accessed May 6, 2022. https://deathrowrorry.tumblr.com/post/638377466608615424/crime-scene-photos-are-the-most-fascinating-types.

Soo Soo. 2021. Comment on "Richard Ramirez (Devil Eyes—Hippie Sabotage)." YouTube. Accessed September 16, 2022. https://www.youtube.com/watch?v=A0_zeUynvKI.

Sotrueiris444. 2022. TikTok video. Accessed January 11, 2023. https://www.tiktok.com/@sotrueiris444/video/7147828437766409515?is_copy_url=1&is_from_webapp=v1&q=%40sotrueiris44&t=1673438489104.

stalkersdisneyland. 2022. Tumblr post. Accessed May 6, 2022. https://stalkersdisneyland.tumblr.com/post/676787789608747008/friendly-reminder-in-case-you-need-someone-to.

Steenberg, Lindsay. 2017. "Crime and Celebrity." *Oxford Research Encyclopedia of Criminology.* https://doi.org/10.1093/acrefore/9780190264079.013.26

Stein, Louisa. 2015. *Millennial Fandom: Television Audiences in the Transmedia Age.* Iowa City: University of Iowa Press.

Stein, Louisa, and Kristina Busse. 2009. "Limit Play: Fan Authorship Between Source Text, Intertext, and Context." *Popular Communication* 7, no. 4: 192–207. https://doi.org/10.1080/15405700903177545.

Stjerneby, Luna. 2018. "Fuck Politeness: Resistive Discourse in the My Favorite Murder Fan Community." MA diss., Roskilde University. https://rucforsk.ruc.dk/ws/portalfiles/portal/63519709/Thesis_done__1_.pdf.

stormiej222. 2022. TikTok video. Accessed December 22, 2022. https://www.tiktok.com/@stormiej222/video/7093246008347446534?is_copy_url=1&is_from_webapp=v1&item_id=7093246008347446534&q=aileen%20wuornos%20memes&t=1669121316648.

Stratton, Jon. 2021. "Parodies For a Pandemic: Coronavirus Songs, Creativity and Lockdown." *Cultural Studies* 35, no. 2–3: 412–31. https://doi.org/10.1080/07494467.2021.1945225.

sunhealer24. 2021. "Safe and Sound." Archive of Our Own. Accessed March 23, 2022. https://archiveofourown.org/works/30313527?view_full_work=true.

Surtees, Joshua. 2016. "Inside the World of Feminist Teen Girls Obsessed with Serial Killers." *Vice*, May 20, 2016. https://www.vice.com/en/article/ppvewv/serial-killer-twitter-teenage-girl-fans.

szarvasoks. 2022. Tumblr post. Content no longer online.

symphony-of-damage. 2021. Comment on Tumblr. Accessed May 6, 2022. Content no longer online.

tedbundy_2. 2022. TikTok video. Content no longer online.

Ted_bundy_epic. 2022a. TikTok video. Accessed December 22, 2022. https://www.tiktok.com/@ted_bundy_epic/video/7098975548654882050?is_copy_url=1&is_from_webapp=v1&item_id=7098975548654882050&q=richardramirezmeme&t=166868973362

Ted_bundy_epic. 2022b. TikTok video. Accessed December 22, 2022. Content no longer online.

the-real-jazzy-richardson-blog. 2018. Comment on Tumblr. Accessed May 6, 2022. https://the-real-ricardo-ramirez.tumblr.com/post/172502201483/u-disappoint-me-sometimes-but-i-still-love-u-in-a.

the-real-ricardo-ramirez. 2018a. Comment on Tumblr. Accessed May 30, 2022. https://the-real-ricardo-ramirez.tumblr.com/post/172543828183/i-want-you-in-these-guts#notes.

the-real-ricardo-ramirez. 2018b. Comment on Tumblr. Accessed May 30, 2022. https://the-real-ricardo-ramirez.tumblr.com/post/172499963168/are-you-the-real-richard#notes.

the-real-ricardo-ramirez. 2018c. Comment on Tumblr. Accessed May 30, 2022. https://the-real-ricardo-ramirez.tumblr.com/post/172502201483/u-disappoint-me-sometimes-but-i-still-love-u-in-a.

the-real-ricardo-ramirez. 2021a. Comment on Tumblr. Accessed May 30, 2022. https://the-real-ricardo-ramirez.tumblr.com/post/643760468041908224/kys-fat-cunt#notes.

the-real-ricardo-ramirez. 2021b. Comment on Tumblr. Accessed May 30, 2022. https://the-real-ricardo-ramirez.tumblr.com/post/642309182206377984/his-nasty-ass-raped-children-you-and-this-sick#notes.

the-real-ricardo-ramirez. 2021c. Comment on Tumblr. Accessed May 30, 2022. https://the-real-ricardo-ramirez.tumblr.com/post/172504669203/your-gf-is-super-offensive-like-wtf#notes.

The-real-ted-bundy--blog. 2018a. Comment on Tumblr. Accessed May 1, 2022. https://the-real-ted--bundy-blog.tumblr.com/post/172540630998/omg-r-u-the-real-ted-bundy-shook-omg#notes.

The-real-ted-bundy--blog. 2018b. Comment on Tumblr. Accessed May 1, 2022. https://the-real-ted--bundy-blog.tumblr.com/post/172661108873/join-the-discord-chat-teddy-boi-all-the-killers#notes.

The-real-ted-bundy--blog. 2022. Tumblr header. Accessed December 22, 2022. https://the-real-ted--bundy-blog.tumblr.com/ask.

Thechildkiller. 2022. Comment on Reddit. Accessed May 25, 2022. Content no longer online.

Thehighpriestess. 2021. TikTok video. Accessed December 22, 2022. https://www.tiktok.com/@thehighpriestess1322/video/7029681148460797230?is_copy_url=1&is_from_webapp=v1&item_id=7029681148460797230&q=aileenwuornosmeme&t=1669122211987.

thenightstalker1960s. 2021. Comment on TikTok. Accessed September 9, 2022. https://www.tiktok.com/@thenightstalker1960s/video/7047932141031771398?is_copy_url=1&is_from_webapp=v1&item_id=7047932141031771398.

The Uncombed One. 2017. "A Current Affair: 'Death Row Romeo'—Richard Ramirez Groupies." YouTube. Accessed March 23, 2022. https://www.youtube.com/watch?v=cYbIdHKksnw&t=2s.

theuncombedone. 2021. "Richard Ramirez—Heaven." YouTube. Accessed March 23, 2022. https://www.youtube.com/watch?v=zQJRDkaPZ0E.

Thomas, Lynn. 2002. *Fans, Feminisms and "Quality" Media*. London: Routledge.

Thornton, Sarah. 1995. *Club Cultures: Music, Media, and Subcultural Capital.* Cambridge, UK: Polity.

Throwaway-num1. 2021. Comment on Reddit. Accessed May 8, 2022. https://www.reddit.com/r/RichardRamirezFans/comments/o09oj4/i_did_some_practice_with_my_drawing_tablet_and_i/hkxm7og/?utm_source=reddit&utm_medium=web2x&context=3.

Throwaway-num1. 2022. Comment on Reddit. Accessed May 8, 2022. Content no longer online.

TikTok. 2020. "How TikTok Recommends Videos #ForYou." TikTok newsroom, June 18, 2020. https://newsroom.tiktok.com/en-us/how-tiktok-recommends-videos-for-you.

Timnick, Lois, and John H. Lee. 1989. "Ramirez Must Die, 'Stalker' Judge Decides: Crime—'I Will be Avenged,' Slayer Declares at Sentencing; Victims Tell Court of Continuing Psychological Pain." *Los Angeles Times,* November 8, 1989. https://www.latimes.com/archives/la-xpm-1989-11-08-me-891-story.html.

Tiny_Cryptographer25. 2021. Comment on Reddit. Accessed May 8, 2022. Content no longer online.

Tithecott, Richard Frank. 1995. "Making Monsters: Jeffrey Dahmer and the Social Construction of the Serial Killer." PhD diss., University of Southern California.

Tortellini. 2019. Comment on "The One Where True Crime Meets High School." Archive of Our Own. Accessed July 25, 2022. https://archiveofourown.org/works/14352558?view_full_work=true.

trebkatrebka. 2022. TikTok video. Accessed December 22, 2022. https://www.tiktok.com/@trebkatrebka/video/7158393558800600326?is_copy_url=1&is_from_webapp=v1&item_id=7158393558800600326&q=%23richardramirezhumour&t=1668691967323.

true-crime-fiend. 2022. Comment on Tumblr. Accessed May 6, 2022. https://yourickie-x.tumblr.com/post/680444540255158272/im-in-here-but-my-heart-is-with-you-love#notes.

Truecrimedittys. 2022. Tumblr post. Accessed December 22, 2022. Content no longer online.

Turk, Tisha. 2014. "Fan Work: Labor, Worth, and Participation in Fandom's Gift Economy." In "Fandom and/as Labor," ed. Mel Stanfill and Megan Condis, special issue, *Transformative Works and Cultures* 15. https://doi.org/10.3983/twc.2014.0518.

Trilling, Lionel. 1972. *Sincerity and Authenticity*. Cambridge, MA: Harvard University Press.

Unipan, Gabby. 2021. "Placemaking and Community-Building among Lesbian, Bisexual, and Queer (LBQ) Women and Non-Binary People during the Covid-19 Pandemic." Honors project, Bowdoin College. https://digitalcommons.bowdoin.edu/honorsprojects/240.

Upset. 2020. "A Second Chance." Archive of Our Own. Accessed July 25, 2022. https://archiveofourown.org/works/18653371?view_full_work=true.

user9361478211356. 2020. Comment on TikTok. Accessed July 25, 2022. Content no longer online.

V [username]. 2022a. Comment on TikTok. Accessed July 25, 2022. Content no longer online.

V [username]. 2022b. Comment on TikTok. Accessed July 25, 2022. Content no longer online.

v1ntage-p3ps1. 2020. "What is Okay: Being Interested in True Crime." Tumblr. Accessed December 3, 2021. https://v1ntage-p3ps1.tumblr.com/post/624446137668157440/what-is-okay-being-interested-in-true-crime. Accessed 03/12/2021.

Valentina Flores. 2021. Comment on "Richard Ramirez (Devil Eyes—Hippie Sabotage)." YouTube. Accessed September 16, 2022. https://www.youtube.com/watch?v=A0_zeUynvKI.

Vicary, Amanda M., and Chris R. Fraley. 2010. "Captured by True Crime: Why Are Women Drawn to Tales of Rape, Murder, and Serial Killers?" *Social Psychological and Personality* Science 1, no. 1: 81–86. https://doi.org/10.1177/1948550609355486.

Vickery, Jacqueline R. 2020. "The Memeification of #Schoolshootings in the U.S.: Youth, TikTok, and Playful Mediated Bodies." *AOIR Selected Papers of Internet Research, 2020.* https://spir.aoir.org/ojs/index.php/spir/article/view/11357.

Victoria♥. 2021. Comment on TikTok. Accessed May 7, 2022. https://www.tiktok.com/@richardsleatherjacket/video/6967233340088798470?is_from_webapp=1&sender_device=pc&web_id=6930854616536172037.

vodkancheese. 2021. Tumblr post. Accessed December 22, 2022. https://at.tumblr.com/vodkancheese/lol/rll4yxonovrl.

Vronsky, Peter. 2004. *Serial Killers: The Method and Madness of Monsters.* New York: Berkley.

Walliss, John. 2010. "Fan Filmmaking and Copyright in a Global World: 'Warhammer 40,000' Fan Films and the Case of 'Damnatus.'" *Transformative Works and Cultures* 5. https://doi.org/10.3983/twc.2010.0178.

Wang, Jufang. 2020. "From Banning to Regulating TikTok: Addressing Concerns of National Security, Privacy, and Online Harms." *Foundation for Law, Justice and Society,* November 6, 2020. https://www.fljs.org/banning-regulating-tiktok-addressing-concerns-national-security-privacy-and-online-harms.

Warwick, Alexandra. 2007. "Blood and Ink: Narrative and the Whitechapel Murders." In *Jack the Ripper: Media, Culture, History,* edited by Alexandra Warwick and Martin Willis, 71–87. Manchester: Manchester University Press.

Webber, Jake. 2022. "Revealing Jeffrey Dahmer's Personal Items." YouTube video. Accessed September 20, 2022. https://www.youtube.com/watch?v=0KJAMZgQ6nw&t=135s.

Whoneedsanameforthissite. 2020. Comment on "A Collection of Poems about Jeffrey Dahmer and the Original Female Character." Archive of Our Own. Accessed September 20, 2022. https://archiveofourown.org/works/26879557/chapters/65585596.

Wiest, Julie B. 2011. *Creating Cultural Monsters: Serial Murder in America.* Boca Raton, FL: CRC Press.

Wiest, Julie B. 2016. "Casting Cultural Monsters: Representations of Serial Killers in U.S. and U.K. News Media." *Howard Journal of Communications* 27, no. 4: 327–46. https://doi.org/10.1080/10646175.2016.1202876.

Wilcox, Dennis. 2006. Foreword to *Serial Murder and Media Circuses,* by Dirk C. Gibson, ix–x. Westport, CT Praeger.

Wilkinson, Alissa. 2019. "The Ted Bundy Movie Starring Zac Efron Sure Does Love Ted Bundy." *Vox*, May 3, 2019. https://www.vox.com/culture/2019/2/5/18210945/ted-bundy-extremely-wicked-shockingly-evil-vile-review-netflix.

Williams, Rebecca. 2010. "Good Neighbours? Fan/Producer Relationships and the Broadcasting Field." *Continuum: Journal of Media & Cultural Studies* 24, no. 2: 279–89.

Williams, Rebeccca. 2017. "Fan Tourism and Pilgrimage." In *The Routledge Companion to Media Fandom,* edited by Melissa A Click and Suzanne Scott, 98–106. New York: Routledge.

Williamson, Milly. 2005. *The Lure of the Vampire: Gender, Fiction and Fandom from Bram Stoker to Buffy*. London: Wallflower Press.

Willoughby, Vanessa. 2017. "Killer Crush: Inside Tumblr's Serial Killer Fandom Problem." *Bitch Media*, October 9, 2017. https://www.bitchmedia.org/article/serial-killer-fandom-on-tumblr/.

Wilson, Jacqueline Z. 2008. *Prison: Cultural Memory and Dark Tourism*. New York: Peter Lang.

Woo, Benjamin. 2012. "Alpha Nerds: Cultural Intermediaries in a Subcultural Scene." *European Journal of Cultural Studies* 15, no. 5: 659–76.

Wu, Xianwei. 2019. "Hierarchy Within Female ACG Fandom in China." *Transformative Works and Cultures* 30. https://dx.doi.org/10.3983/twc.2019.1456.

X_Paranormal_X. 2021. *The Viper in the Glass.* Wattpad. Accessed February 26, 2022. Content no longer online.

XianTan99. 2021. *Jack.* Wattpad. Accessed February 26, 2022. https://www.wattpad.com/story/288347681-jack.

xiigauge. 2021. Comment on Tumblr. Accessed May 6, 2022. https://the-real-ricardo-ramirez.tumblr.com/post/643854910895636480/your-blog-makes-for-free-birth-control#notes.

xkx09977. 2021. Reddit post. Accessed May 8, 2022. Content no longer online.

xscumfucx. 2022. Reddit comment. Accessed May 30, 2022. Content no longer online.

Yatabe, Katsuyoshi, dir. 1991. *The Brave of Sun Fighbird.* Tokyo: Sunrise studio. ANN (Nagoya TV).

Yolandi. 2019. *Candy Necklace.* Archive of Our Own. Accessed September 20, 2022. https://archiveofourown.org/works/18773080.

Young, Robert J. C. 2001. *Postcolonialism: An Historical Introduction.* Oxford, UK: Blackwell.

your-little-edit-witch. 2021. Comment on "Jeffrey Dahmer | Edit | Maneater (lyrics)." YouTube. Accessed September 20, 2022. https://www.youtube.com/watch?v=jUZvzgiJ3BY.

yourboyfriendsbimbo2. 2021. Comment on "Richard Ramirez Imagines." Wattpad. Accessed February 18, 2022. Content no longer online.

your-rickie-x. 2022. Tumblr post. Accessed May 6, 2022. https://yourickie-x.tumblr.com/post/680444540255158272/im-in-here-but-my-heart-is-with-you-love#notes.

Yuko, Elizabeth. 2019. "Inside the Murderabilia Machine: How Macabre Artifacts Became a Booming Industry." *Rolling Stone,* August 9, 2019. https://www.rollingstone.com/culture/culture-features/manson-murder-murderabelia-true-crime-collectibles-869058/.

Zappavigna, Michele. 2011. "Ambient Affiliation: A Linguistic Perspective on Twitter." *New Media & Society* 13, no 5: 788–806.

zClosurez. 2019. Comment on "Aileen Wuornos: Sweet Dreams (Are Made of This)." YouTube. Accessed September 20, 2022. https://www.youtube.com/watch?v=MriWNndljQ0.

Zeng, Jing, Crystal Abidin, and Mike S. Schäfer. 2021. "Research Perspectives on TikTok and Its Legacy Apps—Introduction." *International Journal of Communication* 15: 3161–72.

Zhao, Shan Mu. 2019. "How the Green Hornet Became Chinese: Cross-Racial Mimicry and Superhero Localization in Hong Kong." In "Fans of Color, Fandoms of Color," ed. Abigail De Kosnik and André Carrington, special issue, *Transformative Works and Cultures* 29. https://doi.org/10.3983/twc.2019.1531.

Zodiacgirl666. 2022. Tumblr post. Accessed December 22, 2022. Content no longer online.

Zubernis, Lynn, and Katherine Larsen. 2018. "Make Space for Us! Fandom in the Real World." In *A Companion to Media Fandom and Fan Studies,* edited by Paul Booth, 145–59. Hoboken, NJ: Wiley Blackwell.

Zulli, Diana, and David J. Zulli. 2022. "Extending the Internet Meme: Conceptualizing Technological Mimesis and Imitation Publics on the TikTok Platform." *New Media & Society* 24, no. 8: 1872–90. https://doi.org/10.1177/1461444820983603.

ACKNOWLEDGMENTS

I sincerely thank Jeff Pooley for his enthusiasm and support for this project, as well as my line managers Joe Deville and Janneke Adema for their encouragement and support in all aspects of my work. I also thank Lancaster University for its support of this project.

Made in the USA
Monee, IL
23 January 2026

42231302R00142